The Brightest Lights of the Silver Age

NIKOLAI BERDYAEV

THE BRIGHTEST LIGHTS OF THE SILVER AGE

Essays on Russian Religious Thinkers

Compiled & Translated by
BORIS JAKIM

First published in the USA
by Semantron Press
an imprint of Angelico Press 2015
© Boris Jakim 2015

All rights reserved

No part of this book may be reproduced or transmitted,
in any form or by any means, without permission.

For information, address:
Angelico Press, Ltd.
4709 Briar Knoll Dr. Kettering, OH 45429
www.angelicopress.com

978-1-62138-152-5
978-1-62138-153-2

Cover illustration and design: Michael Schrauzer

Dedicated to the Memory
of
George L. Kline

CONTENTS

Translator's Introduction 1
1. The New Religious Consciousness 7
2. Tolstoy 47
3. The Old and New Testaments in Tolstoy's Religious Consciousness 53
4. Vladimir Solovyov's Fundamental Idea 77
5. The Problem of East and West in the Religious Consciousness of Vladimir Solovyov 85
6. Christ and the World: In Response to Vasily Rozanov 109
7. The Fundamental Idea of Lev Shestov's Philosophy 127
8. Lev Shestov and Kierkegaard 133
9. Theosophy and Anthroposophy in Russia 141
10. Darkened Countenances: *Remembrances of A. A. Blok by Andrey Bely* 163
11. Stylized Orthodoxy: On Father Pavel Florensky 175
12. The Rebirth of Orthodoxy: On Father Sergius Bulgakov 197

Translator's Introduction

I

Nikolai Berdyaev (1874–1948) was one of the greatest religious thinkers of the 20th century. His adult life, led in Russia and in western European exile, spanned such cataclysmic events as the Great War, the rise of Bolshevism and the Russian Revolution, the upsurge of Nazism, and the Second World War. He produced profound commentaries on many of these events, and had many acute things to say about the role of Russia in the evolution of world history. There was sometimes almost no separation between him and these events: for example, he wrote the book on Dostoevsky while revolutionary gunfire was rattling outside his window.

Berdyaev's thought is primarily a religious metaphysics, influenced not only by philosophers like Kant, Hegel, Schopenhauer, Solovyov, and Nietzsche, but also by religious thinkers and mystics such as Meister Eckhart, Jacob Boehme, and Dostoevsky. He showed an interest in philosophy early on, at the age of 14 reading the works of Kant, Hegel, and Schopenhauer. While a student at St. Vladimir's University in Kiev, he began to participate in the revolutionary Social-Democratic movement and to study Marxism. In 1898, he was sentenced to one month in a Kiev prison for his participation in an anti-government student demonstration, and was later exiled for two years (1901–02) to Vologda, in the north of Russia.

His first book, *Subjectivism and Individualism in Social Philosophy* (1901), represented the climax of his infatuation with Marxism as a methodology of social analysis, which he attempted to combine with a neo-Kantian ethics. However, as early as 1903, he took the path from "Marxism to idealism," which had already been followed by such former Marxists as Peter Struve, Sergey Bulgakov, and S.L. Frank. In 1904 Berdyaev became a contributor to the philosophical magazine *Novyi Put'* (The New Path). The influence exerted upon him by the writers and philosophers Dmitry Merezhkovsy and Zinaida Gippius in 1907–08 led him to embrace the Russian Orthodox faith. He joined the circle of Moscow Orthodox philosophers united around the *Put'* (*The Path*) publishing house (notably Bulgakov and Pavel Florensky) and took an active part in organizing the religious-philosophical Association in Memory of V. Solovyov. Around this time, Berdyaev published a work which inaugurated his life-long exploration of the concept of freedom in its many varieties and ramifications. In *The Philosophy of Freedom* (1911), a critique of the "pan-gnoseologism" of recent German and Russian philosophy led Berdyaev to a search for an authentically Christian ontology. The end result of this search was a philosophy of freedom, according to which human beings are rooted in a sobornost of being and thus possess true knowledge. In 1916, Berdyaev published the most important work of his early period: *The Meaning of the Creative Act*. The originality of this work is rooted in the refusal to accept the view that creation and revelation have come to an end and are complete. The central element of the "meaning of the creative act" is the idea that man reveals his true essence in the course of a continuing creation realized jointly with God (a theurgy). Berdyaev's notion of "theurgy" is distinguished by the inclusion of the element of freedom: the creative act is a means for the positive self-definition of freedom not as the choice and self-definition of persons in the world but as a "foundationless foundation of being" over which God the creator has no power.

Berdyaev's work from 1914 to 1924 can be viewed as being largely influenced by his inner experience of the Great War and the Russian Revolution. His main themes during this period are the "cosmic collapse of humanity" and the effort to preserve the hierarchical order of being (what he called "hierarchical personalism"). Revolutionary violence and nihilism were seen to be directly opposed to the creatively spiritual transformation of "this world" into a divine "cosmos." In opposing the chaotic nihilism of the first year of the Revolution, Berdyaev looked for support in the holy ontology of the world, i.e., in the divine cosmic order. The principle of hierarchical inequality, which is rooted in this ontology, allowed him to nullify the main argument of the leveling ideology and praxis of Communism—the demand for "social justice." His attacks against the Bolshevik regime became increasingly intense: he called the Bolsheviks nihilists and annihilators of all spiritual values and culture in Russia. His activities and statements, which made him a noticeable figure in post-revolutionary Moscow, began to attract the attention of the Soviet authorities. In 1922 he was arrested and expelled from Russia on the so-called "philosopher's ship" with other ideological opponents of the regime such as Bulgakov, Frank, and Struve.

Having ended up in Berlin, Berdyaev gradually entered the sphere of post-War European philosophy. In 1924, he moved to Paris, where he became a founder and professor of the Russian Religious-Philosophical Academy. In 1925, he helped to found and became the editor of the Russian religious-philosophical journal *Put'* (*The Path*), arguably the most important Russian religious journal ever published. He organized inter-confessional meetings of representatives of Catholic, Protestant, and Orthodox religious-philosophical thought, with the participation of such figures as Maritain, Mounier, Marcel, and Barth. In the émigré period, his thought was primarily directed toward what can be called a liberation from ontologism. Emigration became for him an existential experience of "rootless" extra-hierarchical existence, which can find a foundation solely in "the kingdom of the Spirit," i.e., in the person or personality. The primacy of "freedom" over "being" became the determining principle of his philosophy, a principle which found profound expression in his book *On the Destiny of Man: An Essay on Paradoxical Ethics* (1931), which he considered his "most perfect" book.

At around the same time, Berdyaev formulated a key principle of his personalism: the doctrine of "objectification," which he first systematically developed in *The World of Objects: An Essay on the Philosophy of Solitude and Social Intercourse* (1934). Berdyaev viewed objectification as an epistemological interpretation of the fallenness of the world, of the state of enslavement, necessity, and disunitedness in which the world finds itself. Using man's creative powers, it is possible to pierce this layer of objectification, and to see the deeper reality. Man's "ego" (which knows only the objectified world) then regains its status of "person," which lives in the non-objectified, or real, world. After the Second World War, Berdyaev 's reflections turned again to the role of Russia in the world. His first post-war book was *The Russian Idea: The*

Fundamental Problems of Russian Thought of the 19th Century and the Beginning of the 20th Century (1946), in which he tried to discover the profound meaning of Russian thought and culture. Himself being one of the greatest representatives of this thought and culture, he saw that the meaning of his own activity was to reveal to the western world the distinctive elements of Russian philosophy, such as its existential nature, its eschatalogism, its religious anarchism, and its preoccupation with the idea of "Divine humanity."

Berdyaev is one of the greatest religious existentialists. His philosophy goes beyond mere thinking, mere rational conceptualization, and tries to attain authentic life itself: the profound layers of existence that touch upon God's world. He directed all of his efforts, philosophical as well as in his personal and public life, at replacing the kingdom of this world with the kingdom of God. According to him, we can all attempt to do this by tapping into the divine creative powers which constitute our true nature. Our mission is to be collaborators with God in His continuing creation of the world.

II

Berdyaev published many essays in Russia before the Revolution and later in European exile. The present collection is the first volume of his essays ever to appear in English translation.

The first essay in the present volume is justly famous, providing us as it does with the fullest definition of "the new religious consciousness" as it emerged in Russia in the first decade of the 20th century. In fact, almost all the essays in this collection refer, in one way or another, to "the new consciousness." Berdyaev, like Merezhkovsky and Blok among others, believed that the dawn of the new century would bring an end to the old atheistic and positivistic world-view and the beginning of a new era of the spirit. The other essays treat such figures as Tolstoy, Solovyov, Rozanov, Blok, Bely, Florensky, and Bulgakov, all of whom were instrumental in creating the new era. The essay on Rozanov, one of Berdyaev's best, criticizes Rozanov's essay "Sweetest Jesus and the Bitter Fruits of this world," perhaps the harshest critique of Christianity in the Russian literature. The essay "Theosophy and Anthroposophy in Russia" does not appear, at first glance, to be about

Translator's Introduction

Russian thinkers (though at least two important theosophists—Blavatsky and Ouspensky—were Russian), but Berdyaev emphasizes the importance of this movement for contemporary Russian thought. In his essay on Blok and Bely, "Darkened Countenances," Berdyaev unleashes a powerful attack on what he considers Gnostic sophiology. Shestov stands outside of "the new religious consciousness," though in his existentialism he is perhaps more kindred to Berdyaev than any other Russian philosopher.

Except for Solovyov and Tolstoy, Berdyaev was acquainted with and even had close personal ties with the other writers he discusses in these essays. He pulls no punches: he harshly criticizes what he regards as their deficiencies, though one sometimes has the feeling that he criticizes them chiefly for not being Berdyaev—with his existential exaltation of freedom and denunciation of objectification. They are castigated for not measuring up to the "new religious consciousness." It should be noted that Berdyaev criticizes Florensky for only having a "theodicy," for not posing the problem of man. Unbeknownst to Berdyaev, Florensky treated this problem in his masterly "anthropodicy," *At the Watersheds of Thought*. As for Bulgakov, Berdyaev considers the doctrines he developed in Russia prior to the Revolution; he does not deal with Bulgakov's émigré period, thus ignoring his two great trilogies.[1]

BORIS JAKIM
August 2015

---

1. The first trilogy written in the 1920s comprises *The Burning Bush* (on the Mother of God), *The Friend of the Bridegroom* (on John the Baptist), and *Jacob's Ladder* (on angels); the second trilogy, written in the 1930s, comprises *The Lamb of God*, *The Comforter*, and *The Bride of the Lamb*.

1

The New Religious Consciousness[1]

Heaven is above and heaven is below.
The stars are above and the stars are below.
All that is above is also below.
To understand is to be happy.[2]

"I and my Father are one."
(John 10:30)

V.V. Rozanov has written an article about D.S. Merezhkovsky with the very characteristic title "Among Speakers of a Foreign Tongue." In this article which touches on the sad fate of this remarkable writer, Rozanov senses something remote and non-Russian in Merezhkovsky, the spirit of the "eternal companions,"[3] the spirit of the great European and antique traditions. Rozanov is saddened by the fate of his literary friend, but he is not surprised that this writer of European significance is so little appreciated and understood among us, that our uncultured intelligentsia does not wish to listen to him, that in his homeland it is as if he dwells "among speakers of a foreign tongue." At one time Merezhkovsky was close to the Slavophile belief that Russian has a religious mission, and he has more deeply than anyone else understood

---

1. First published in the magazine *Voprosy zhizni*, September 1905.—Trans.

2. These verses, taken from the Tabula Smaragdina, are quoted by D.S. Merezhkovsy in his novel *The Resurrected Gods (Leonardo da Vinci)*.—Trans.

3. *The Eternal Companions* (1897) is a collection of Merezhkovsky's essays on great European writers, including Pushkin, Homer, Dante, and Cervantes.—Trans.

Pushkin and Dostoevsky,[4] yet he still remains a foreign "westerner" for the Russian intelligentsia. Though he is read and recognized as one of the leading writers of our contemporary Russian literature, people do not hear what he calls us to, and his themes have been assimilated by very few. There must be some secret here. What is it?

Rozanov has a remarkable aphorism: "I may be talentless, but my theme is a talented one." The author of this aphorism is extraordinarily talented, and Merezhkovsky is highly talented too, but their themes are more talented than they are. The fact is that people with untalented themes cannot forgive Merezhkovsky his talent, his genius. Meanwhile, the majority of our intelligentsia, professing the positivistic faith, lives by untalented themes, labors over the most banal and boring themes, and is extremely proud of this. Not only do they not understand talented themes, new and large ones, but they cannot forgive those who pose such themes and call us to assimilate them. We get a kind of slaves' malice against noble themes of genius which stir the depths of our being. And there is no doubt that *Merezhkovsky has been attacked because of the talent and universality of his themes.* The Russian democratic intelligentsia, though western in its superficial beliefs, reminds one of poorly dressed people of the provinces: it lacks great *universal* traditions and a universal spirit; it has trouble assimilating anything that is too cultured or too complex. But this is not the fault of the unfortunate Russian intelligentsia alone, this intelligentsia which is still superior to the cultured European bourgeoisie; it is the fault of our entire historical epoch—of the dilution of culture, of the betrayal of truly universal traditions, of the spirit of positivism, of the petty demon of the earth, of the mediocrity and vulgarity of our bourgeois era. In western Europe too, Merezhkovsky would feel as if he were "among speakers of a foreign tongue," even though he is known and appreciated there, his books having been translated into many languages. There too, in cultured Europe which is filled with great monuments of the past, Merezhkovsky's themes offend the spirit of the epoch, which has betrayed the

---

4. Merezhkovsky has written the best essay on Pushkin in the Russian literature if one does not count Dostoevsky's brilliant speech. In general, Merezhkovsky is our most remarkable literary critic.

great universal traditions. In western Europe, he would not even have the few friends he has here in his homeland, the land of Dostoevsky—friends who are tormented by the same thirst as he.

The unfortunate thing is not that Merezhkovsky is insufficiently Russian and too cultured (in a certain sense he is even very Russian), but that his themes are too enormous and that he has been alienated from the epoch and from the people of the epoch by that universal spiritual homeland from which he has brought these themes. Merezhkovsky's spiritual growth has taken place in an utterly special atmosphere; far from the interests of the moment, far from the petty disputes of the decades, his attention has been intensely focused on problems of the millennia, and perhaps he has insufficiently seen what has been happening around him and his words have been heard as too literary.[5] The disputes of the Marxists and the populists, factional fights, current politics, the rapid change of sociological orientations, all the things that constitute "life" for the enormous majority of the Russian intelligentsia and over which it fusses so much—all this is alien to a man who is tormented by the millennial universal theme of the relation of Christianity and paganism, a man for whom "life" and its meaning consist in Greek tragedy, in the death of the pagan gods and the birth of the Christian God, in the epoch of the Renaissance with its great art, in the resurrection of the ancient gods, in the mysterious personalities of Julian the Apostate and Leonardo da Vinci, in Peter the Great,[6] in Pushkin, in Tolstoy and Dostoevsky. This is a romantic trait of Merezhkovsky, this aversion to the small scales of our contemporary epoch and veneration of the large scales of the universal past. Merezhkovsky vividly experienced the great epochs of the past, wishing to decipher some mystery and to cast a glance into the souls of such enormous personalities as Julian, Leonardo, and Peter, since their mystery seemed universal to him. In godless and bourgeois European culture, which had forgotten universal ideas and lived by petty, provincial interests, he was struck only by Nietzsche, who was driven mad by religious torment. Only the

---

5. He is too much the *littérateur* and what he writes does not sound like living religious speech.

6. Merezhkovsky's trilogy of novels, *Christ and Antichrist* (1895–1904), is devoted to Julian, Leonardo, and Peter.—Trans.

"decadents,"[7] precursors of future rebirth, seemed kindred to Merezhkovsky.

After all, it is impossible to deny the obvious truth that our contemporary culture is paltry and inconsequential compared, say, to the culture of the Renaissance or of ancient Greece. It is impossible to deny that the prevailing spiritual life is no longer concerned with solving problems of universal importance, or that geniuses and heroes are dying out, or that the meaning of life has gotten lost among the successes of life. We must have the courage to say that the kingdom of democracy, while in one of its aspects indisputably affirming justice, in other aspects infringes on noble values, turns mountains into flatlands, and does not act in the name of anything higher than itself. Social democracy, this axis of history of our time, can be regarded as a good and just endeavor, a useful and necessary one, but it lacks a truly universal spirit and displays a provincialism in the disputes among its factions. One feels that it has forgotten the most important question: In the name of what God is it worth living? All of us are Marthas, "troubled about many things," and there is no sign of Mary.[8] Godless epochs, living without God, organizing their life independently of its meaning, are the most boring, colorless, tedious, and shallow epochs; even their atheism is insipid and vulgar instead of being profound or frightening. In epochs such as ours, all large things are devalued and diminished.

So disdained by our bourgeois society, the "decadents"—distant descendants of a great universal culture—are alienated from what in our epoch people have agreed to call "life," and they long for a new, mighty culture. The strata of various great epochs intersect in the soul of the *new* man: paganism and Christianity; the ancient god Pan and the new God who died on the cross; Greek beauty and Medieval romanticism; Dionysus, in whom the image of the pagan god merged with the image of the Christian God; the rebirth and birth of the man of the new history and the yearning for a new, future rebirth. The new soul becomes divided and complex to the final extreme; it proceeds towards some crisis, both desirable and terrifying. The decadents are trans-

---

7. Russian poets and artists of the 1890s who rebelled against the reigning drab realism in art and positivism in philosophy.—Trans.

8. See Luke 10:41.—Trans.

formed into symbolists and mystics. Gods and God are resurrected in us;[9] the universal themes, becoming the most important themes, regain their eternal rights. And now we live not only in an epoch of cultural decline and diminution, not only in a godless epoch of small deeds on a flat land, but also in an epoch of the beginning of a new religious rebirth which captivates us with its universal significance and interest—the epoch of *the new religious consciousness*.

A characteristic and essential feature of *our* new rebirth is that it is dual in nature: the Christian God is reborn and resurrected but the pagan gods, too, are reborn and resurrected. We are experiencing not only a Christian renaissance, but also a pagan renaissance. The appearance of Nietzsche in the West and of Rozanov in Russia, the rebirth of Dionysus in our contemporary art, our tormented interest in the problem of sex, our striving to sanctify the flesh—all this indicates the duality of our renaissance. We are enchanted not only by Golgotha, but also by Olympus; we are summoned and drawn not only by the suffering God who died on the cross, but also by the god Pan, the god of the earthly element, of sensual gratification, and by ancient Aphrodite, the goddess of plastic beauty and earthly love. In our golden dreams we see not only heaven, filled with immaterial spirits; we also see the transfigured earth, spiritualized flesh, nature animated by fauns and nymphs; and we bow in veneration not only before the cross, but also before the divinely beautiful body of Venus. People usually see this golden age as occurring either in the past or in the future, i.e., in empirical existence; but it is in eternity, in extratemporal being, that one should await the resurrection of the earth and the sanctification of the flesh and see the holy path towards it not only up above, but also here below. Till now this has not been understood, but we are beginning to understand something of it.

The man of the new religious consciousness can renounce neither paganism nor Christianity, since he regards both as divine revelation; two turbulent streams of blood flow in his veins, and his thoughts are sundered into two. He can return neither to paganism, the thesis; nor to Christianity, the antithesis: the opposition is too old. The new religious

---

9. Berdyaev is referring to himself and other "new" men of his generation.—Trans.

consciousness desires to achieve a synthesis, to overcome the duality, to attain a higher fullness; it must include something that was not included before; it must unite two poles, two opposite abysses. Historical Christianity does not have any antidotes against the new temptations of the paganism that is being reborn, just as the old paganism did not have any antidotes against the sins of historical Christianity. When we speak of the new religious consciousness, by no means do we intend to say that all the earlier religions were only a temptation and that it is necessary to invent a new religion. If, in general, religion is possible and necessary, the whole cosmic and historical process must then be regarded as a divine revelation, as an intimate interaction between humanity and Divinity. The new religious consciousness is a continuing revelation, the assimilation of a greater fullness of religious truth, since the earlier stages of religious revelation disclosed only a partial truth, not the full truth. Ignorant representatives of historical Christianity assert that God was not revealed in paganism, but this assertion is abhorrent and godless. Christian theologians view the pagan gods in the same way that positivists and rationalists view the Christian God; these theologians are insufficiently mystical and their religious consciousness is insufficiently broad to enable them to see in the pagan gods a revelation, under different masks, of the Eternal Countenance of God the Father, God the Creator, a revelation of Him not less perfect than the Old Testament Jehovah. And is this historically fateful opposition between paganism and Christianity, this implacable warfare between them which has divided our contemporary soul, not due to the incompleteness of that which has been revealed to us? Is it not due to our limitations, which have transformed historical relativity into an eternal conflict between God the Father and God the Son? Will the new religious synthesis not possess a fullness of revelation in which the opposition between the pagan thesis and the Christian antithesis will disappear like a mirage? That is our religious hope.

If the revelation of Divinity has not yet occurred in the world and in the history of humanity, it will never occur and the rationalists and vulgar deists who have invented an unnecessary and remote god would be right. But if the revelation has occurred, it must and will continue to occur, since the fullness of religious truth will be attained only during the entire course of the historical process, and this process must be

The New Religious Consciousness

divine-human in nature. The question of the relationship between relative and temporal historical revelation and eternal and absolute mystical revelation must be reexamined and reworked by a new philosophy, by a mystical as well as critical philosophy of the future, a philosophy which will serve the new religious consciousness. Only the union of religious experience with higher philosophical knowledge will give birth to a true gnosis. The historical limitations of the theological schools will then be overcome; external authority will be replaced by inner freedom; and we will be shown the way to the fullness of the mystical knowledge of God.[10]

There is no Russian or European writer who is more deeply conscious of this dual religious rebirth than Merezhkovsky. No one has plumbed its mysteries more deeply or felt more acutely that the religious duality will inevitably be overcome in the fullness of the new religious synthesis. The fundamental and unchanging theme of all of Merezhkovsky's writings, of all his thoughts and experiences, is the most important and necessary theme, the universal theme of two poles of the religious consciousness, of two opposite abysses: Christianity and paganism, spirit and flesh, heaven and earth, the God-man and the man-god, Christ and Antichrist. In order to resolve the theme of *duality*, which has been handed down to us by universal culture and by the entire religious history of humankind, Merezhkovsky conceived his trilogy, which, though not completely successful in its artistic execution, is remarkable in its intention. The same theme of duality which demands resolution also permeates his most remarkable book, the two-volume *L. Tolstoy and Dostoevsky*, a work on which his future fame will rest. In this book he indicates a pathway towards solving the problem, but he does not yet definitively pass from the separated Two to the united Three. The surface of Merezhkovsky's views changes (which becomes especially

---

10. This significance of philosophy is superbly understood and explained by N. Minsky in his recent book *Religion of the Future*. Vladimir Solovyov did much for the philosophy of religion, and it is impossible to understand how, given his acute philosophical consciousness, he could have subordinated himself to a historically limited external authority.

clear if one reads in order all three volumes of his historical trilogy), but the essence remains the same; we have the same divided thoughts, the same presentiment of the *Third One*[11] reconciling the two abysses, the same yearning for a heavenly earth and an earthly heaven. At the very beginning of his path, Merezhkovsky sensed mystically that salvation does not consist in accepting one of the abysses while rejecting the other. He felt that holiness is not limited to just one of the poles, and that there is no return—either to the pagan earth alone or to the Christian heaven alone. *Merezhkovsky understood that the way out of the religious duality, the way out of the opposition between the abysses of heaven and earth, of spirit and flesh, of the pagan splendor of the world and the Christian renunciation of the world—he understood that the way out of this duality consists not in one of the Two, but in the Third: in the Three.* This constitutes his enormous achievement and his enormous significance for the contemporary religious movement. His torment, which is native to us too, consists in the eternal peril of confusing the countenances of Christ and Antichrist, of replacing the former by the latter; it consists in the eternal horror that you might offer worship not to the True God, that you might reject one of the Persons of Divinity, one of the abysses, one of the poles of the religious consciousness which is not contrary to God, but opposite and equally Divine. This is the torment of the temptation of ultimate religious freedom.

Merezhkovsky is neither a pure artist nor a pure thinker; he often lacks the artistic gift to create images and the speculative gift to create philosophical conceptions, but he is an original artist-thinker who has the gift to create an artistic conception of thoughts as well as the capacity for intuitive knowledge and prevision. He is a special type of gnostic of our epoch, giving astonishing interpretations of Gospel texts and understanding mysteries inaccessible to others. He sets for himself enormous tasks which he does not always have the power to accomplish, and yet he shows us new paths. Merezhkovsky has learned a great deal from Nietzsche and Dostoevsky and to some extent from Rozanov, but one cannot deny the originality of his religious-artistic

---

11. Merezhkovsky preached the advent of a "Third Testament," a kingdom of the Spirit, reconciling and replacing the first two testaments, that of the Father and that of the Son.—Trans.

conception and his enormous ability to see new mystical pathways. He is a radical and revolutionary in his temperament and in his manner of thinking and striving; he always tends towards extremes, not being able to accept merely moderate reforms. He needs not reforms, but a revolution; not transformations, but a transfiguration; and in his religious consciousness, too, his path is a revolutionary one. He is much bolder and more radical that Vladimir Solovyov, who after all sought only to justify the faith of the fathers, was a conservative in too many things, was afraid of new movements, evaded certain fateful and terrifying themes, and agreed with the compromise views of the majority on many questions.

What does the new religious consciousness want? What is its ultimate desire? What differentiates it from the old consciousness? Our ultimate desire in our religious striving consists in the thirst for eternity and the fullness of being, for the conclusive victory over death and the narrowness of life. Every human being will end in death, and all humankind will end in death, and our entire life is filled with partial death. This horror of total non-being we cannot, do not wish to, and must not tolerate. In the final analysis, there are only two religions: the religion of being, of the affirmation of eternal and immeasurably full life; and the religion of non-being, of total death. The world knows one great religion of non-being—Buddhism. It is the most profound and perfect attempt to overcome the horror of death and suffering by total universal death, the mysterious abyss of non-being. But what was the non-religious 19th century positivism that organized life with such fuss and bother? Positivism does not believe it is possible to grasp the meaning of life and to overcome death; it knows that death is the lot of all people and of all things and it reconciles itself to the fact that non-being is the final result, the final word. Above the abyss of universal and total non-being, positivists desire to organize life, to make existence easier, to ameliorate the sufferings of this small, brief, narrow, meaningless, illusory being. The merry positivists, singing the praises of life, must understand life as a "feast in the time of plague,"[12] since a

---

12. Allusion to Pushkin's play with that title.—Trans.

constant, incurable "plague" accompanies human history. Only empty, shallow, insipidly smug souls do not feel the horror of this "plague" and the impossibility of this "feast." Sorrowful positivism converges, in its unconscious religious element, with the religion of non-being; it has a tendency toward asceticism and its voice is weak when it defends the narrowness of being.

We are led to religion not by a thirst for an eternal "feast" *during* the "plague," celebrated above the abyss of non-being, but by a thirst for an eternal "feast" *after* the total victory over all "plague" and all non-being. *Religion teaches that a universal battle against death, against the spirit of non-being, must be waged in the name of absolute and eternal being.* Religion is rooted in the profoundest and most ultimate consciousness that the victory over death in the world and the conquest of absolutely full and eternal life can be attained by every human being and by all humankind only in union with God, the source of all being. Thus, the meaning of life can be realized, death can be defeated, eternity and the fullness of being can be won, and personhood can be affirmed not in a human, non-religious process, but only in a divine-human process, in religious union with Divinity. The human and godless path is the path to non-being. *Religion also teaches that a battle for total and universal liberation, a battle against necessity, enchainment, and limitation, must be waged in the name of absolutely free and unlimited being.* Freedom cannot be attained on a solely human and non-religious path; phantasms of limits imposed by necessity arise everywhere and this path is the path of slavery.

If the total victory over death, the total affirmation of eternal and full life and limitless freedom, could be attained only on the divine-human path, only in the intimate union of man with God, then God had to become incarnate in the world—the God-man had to come. In the history of the world there was one unique and unrepeatable point of convergence of the human with the Divine—a point at which there occurred an unprecedented and triumphant divine-human battle against death, against the spirit of non-being, for life, for joy, for freedom, for the eternity and fullness of being. In Christ, human freedom, the freedom of choice, was limited by God's love, but this did not limit (a word which only exposes the limitations of our language) this freedom, so dear to us; it became even greater, desiring the salvation of man and of the world in the kingdom of God, for only in the latter is salvation from slavery and non-being possible. Human freedom entered into mystical harmony with Divine necessity, or (which is the same thing) with Divine freedom. God Himself died on the cross and was raised from the dead so that He could reveal to the world the truth concerning universal resurrection, the total victory over death, and eternal, joyous, and free life.

From that time the world began to be crucified together with Christ; Golgotha lay like a black shadow over human history; Christ's death cast an enchantment over humankind and His resurrection was not understood or not fully understood. Historical Christianity assimilated only the negative, ascetic half of Christ's religion; it understood heaven as the negation of earth, spirit as the negation of flesh, and it rejected the abyss at the opposite pole as a satanical temptation. The dualism of heaven and earth, of spirit and flesh, poisoned life, transforming the world into nothing but sinfulness. Meanwhile, the life of the world followed its usual course, justifying itself by non-Christian holiness. Sexual life, social life, the whole splendor of world culture, art, and science found themselves at the pole opposite to the religious consciousness of historical Christianity. But suddenly a new religious consciousness has emerged which cannot tolerate this rupture, this dualism, and thirsts for a religious sanctification of life, a sanctification of universal culture; it thirsts for a new holy love, for a holy polity, a holy "flesh," a transfigured earth. This new religious consciousness signifies a return to the deepest sources of all religion, to the overcoming of death in the eternal, full, free being of the personality and to the overcoming of Golgotha in Resurrection. The Christian renaissance will begin when "negation, dying, and death end and affirmation, quickening, and resurrection begin. From the first Countenance of the Lord, sorrowful, dark, and mysterious, Christianity will turn to His second Countenance—joyous and glorious. This great *cosmic* revolution is already taking place, but like all similar cosmic revolutions, it is taking place almost invisibly."[13]

Here are the words with which Merezhkovsky announces a new reli-

---

13. From Merezhkovsky's introduction to the second volume of *L. Tolstoy and Dostoevsky*.

gious consciousness—a new or, more precisely, an eternal religion which is universal and encompasses a greater fullness than historical religion: "Till now it has seemed to us that to be a Christian means to love heaven, only heaven, and to reject and hate earth. But here we have a Christianity that is not a renunciation of earth, not a betrayal of earth, but an unprecedented fidelity to earth, a new love for earth, a kissing of earth. It turns out that not only is it possible to love heaven and earth together, but that, according to Christ's teaching, they cannot be loved except together. Till now we have loved heaven or earth not to the end, not to the extreme limit of heaven and earth, and we have thought, like Tolstoy and Nietzsche, that the one love negates the other. We must love earth to the end, to the extreme limit of earth—*all the way up to heaven*; and we must love heaven to the end, to the extreme limit of heaven—*all the way down to earth*. We will then understand that this constitutes not two loves, but one love, that heaven descends to earth and embraces earth the way a lover embraces his beloved (these are the two halves, the two sexes, of the world), and earth gives herself to heaven, reveals herself to heaven: 'The mystery of earth,' says Dostoevsky, 'touches the mystery of the stars.' This 'touching', this union, contains the essence, if not of historical Christianity, then of Christ's very teaching. Not only does the tree of life ascend with its sticky little leaves[14] in the spring into the innocent blue sky, but it also descends with its roots into the dark, eternally birthgiving, eternally fruitful 'womb' of our mother, the moist earth. Earth is *not yet heavenly*; she is still the old, pagan earth. Heaven is *not yet earthy*; it is still the old, non-Christian, only seemingly Christian heaven. But there will be 'a new heaven and a new earth,' which means a heavenly earth and an earthy heaven. 'Thy kingdom come. Thy will be done in earth, as it is in heaven.' Not only in heaven, but also on earth. Let Thy will unite heaven and earth; let earth and heaven be not two, but one, in the same way that 'I and the Father are one.' That is the salt of the salt in Christ's teaching; we are now baptized not by water, but by fire. When we were baptized only by water, we did not understand this; and only now are we beginning to understand that, if

---

14. The "sticky little leaves" are a favorite vision of Ivan Karamazov in *The Brothers Karamazov*.—Trans.

we have not understood this, we have not understood anything in Christianity."

Merezhkovsky poses the problem of the relation between spirit and flesh with extraordinary acuteness and solves it by a brilliant interpretation of Gospel texts, artistic intuition, and *a mystical presentiment of the future religious culture*. He connects the fate of the new religious movement with a radical solution of the fundamental new theme of the relation of religion to "flesh," to the "earth"—the theme of the religious sanctification of culture, of social life, of sexual love, of the joy of life. "Knighthood did not fulfill its task because it strove towards it prematurely and unconsciously, but the task itself was a true one. To a significant degree, that is still our task: to sanctify that which is not sanctified or insufficiently sanctified by the church; to sanctify that which, from the church's point of view, is too worldly and pagan; to sanctify not just one part of life, but the *whole*, not just one pole, but both of them, not just not-I, the renunciation of personality, but also I, the affirmation of personality in the consciousness of personal dignity and honor, in the ancient heroic and militant love for one's country, for one's land, for one's nation, for the whole Christian world, and in the new extra-marital, extra-familial love for woman." The duality must be overcome in a higher affirmation, not in negation; our pagan rebirth, the rehabilitation of the flesh and of earthy joy, must be recognized as equal in holiness and divinity to Christian rebirth, to the yearning for heaven and the sorrow of the spirit. There is one God in the depths of the two opposite abysses, which are two poles of one religious consciousness united in the fullness of revelation. If this theme loses its intensity, there will be a religious decline and sterility. But the problem of spirit and flesh can also be posed in another way, purely philosophically, ontologically, namely as the questions: What is being? What is the makeup of being? What is its essence? A complete religion cannot fail to have its ontology, its conception of the ontic makeup of the world, and therefore it cannot dispense with a metaphysics. Merezhkovsky speaks constantly of the ascetic metaphysics of historical Christianity and of the opposite metaphysics of paganism, but he never tries to pose and resolve philosophically the problem of spirit and flesh. That is his weak point. Judging by some of the passages in his works, he follows Kant without understanding the extent to which it is necessary for a religious consciousness to philosophically overcome Kant, the extent to which it is impossible for a mystic to be a Kantian.

Merezhkovsky is a fierce opponent of spiritualistic metaphysics; the battle against the spiritualism of historical Christianity is his principal theme. Here, his enormous achievement can easily be marred by an enormous misunderstanding if this problem is not subjected to philosophical analysis. The fact is that the religious problem of the relation of "spirit" and "flesh" does not at all coincide with the philosophical problem of the relation of spirit and matter, soul and body, the physical and the psychical, though the two problems are connected. The "flesh" of which Merezhkovsky speaks is a symbolic concept that personifies the earth in general, all of culture and society (the "body" of humankind), and all sensuous life, including sexual love. This "flesh" contains too little of what philosophers call "matter," which is a physical phenomenon as opposed to psychical phenomena; and too much of what they call "spirit," which is a psychical phenomenon as opposed to physical phenomena. "Flesh" is not defined by physical properties and chemical composition; "earth" does not consist of geological strata. The spatiality and temporality of the empirical world are not necessary conditions for the existence of this "flesh," and impenetrability is not a necessary property of it, as it is of the "matter" that weighs down on us. Nor is "flesh" a phenomenon as opposed to "spirit," noumenon, essence; it contains something noumenal, metaphysically primordial. How can one connect the religious and culturo-historical problem of the "flesh" (the problem of culture, society, sensuousness, sex—in other words, the problem of the incarnate spirit) with the ontological problem of the nature and makeup of being, as well as with the gnoseological problem of the nature of noumena and phenomena, and of the conditions of the formation of the empirical world?

It seems to me that there is only one theory of knowledge that is true and fruitful: the theory that views the empirical, spatial-temporal world not as true being grounded by our noumenal essence, but as something conditional, relative, and apparent. In this "world" which science knows and which positivists regard as the unique and exhaustive world; in this "experience," which we shall call secondary and rationalized, it is possible to discover the noumenal essence of being neither in "physical" nor in "psychical" phenomena, neither in the "body" nor in the "soul."[15] Only in primary, nonrationalized, mystical experience can we discover true being, the really existent, the metaphysical "spirit" and metaphysical "flesh" of the world—not only our mystical "soul," but also our mystical "body." Philosophically critical mysticism teaches that that which is most mystical is most real and most incarnate, though not according to rational laws (this justifies Dostoevsky's "experience"). All those positive "realists" who are fixated on empirical realty live in an illusory world; the world of noumenal essences is not embodied for them in anything:

> If man's soul is to rise
> Out of its lowliness,
> It must enter into eternal union
> With ancient mother-earth.[16]

All great religions speak of fusion with "ancient mother-earth." All the poets of the past yearned for moist mother-earth and saw that the greatest religious experience consisted in union with her. Positivists and rationalists do not know this "earth" who is our Proto-mother, this divine and noumenal element of "earth"; they have forgotten about her; she does not fit into their limited rational experience; they live on another earth, on a planet with a specific chemical composition and made up of geological strata; and this illusory, desiccated, dead earth is the only earth they recognize. This "earth," this lower abyss which Merezhkovsky wants to unite with "heaven," is the noumenal, metaphysical "earth," the transcendent "flesh." The spiritualism of historical Christianity constitutes a fidelity to heaven, to the spirit, but it is a betrayal of the divine earth, of the mystical flesh. On the other hand,

---

15. See my essays "On the New Russian Realism" and "The Crisis of Rationalism in Contemporary Philosophy," which indicate the possibility of this kind of new gnoseology.

16. From Schiller's ballad "Eleusinian Mysteries" in Zhukovsky's translation.—Trans.

the antireligious positivism of the 19th century is a betrayal of both the mystical "heaven" and the mystical "earth." The rationalistic positivists are just as remote from the abyss of the "flesh" as they from the abyss of the "spirit"; they are somewhere in the middle, on a flat plane; they lack both a mystical sense of the "earth" and a yearning for "heaven." This rationalistic culture of the middle is soulless and fleshless; living on the surface of physical and psychical phenomena, it does not penetrate into the depths of noumenal "spirit" and noumenal "flesh." But Merezhkovsky's problem can be posed only in these depths. Whereas the spiritualism of historical Christianity sought to kill the "flesh," a primordial divine element, and thus tended toward Buddhism, the materialism of the antireligious epoch sought to kill the "spirit" without returning to the depths of the "flesh" and thus tended toward total non-being, toward illusory existence on a flat surface. "Flesh" is being rehabilitated, returning us to the "ancient mother-earth," not by materialists, who only know the phenomenon of matter, but by such mystics as Rozanov, who know the ancient mysteries of earthy "flesh." The earth is full of great mysteries only for authentic mystics who have felt within themselves the seething of the ancient chaos; only they are able to dig up the treasures buried in this chaos and to enact earthy mysteries which bring us back to the Eleusinian rites and the festivals of Dionysus.

Thus, for Merezhkovsky and the neo-mystics, for people of the new religious consciousness, "spirit" and "flesh" are not equal to noumenon and phenomenon. Nor are they equal to soul (the psychical) and body (the physical), and certainly not to good and evil. Because he lacks a philosophical critique, Merezhkovsky sometimes gets tangled up in his notions, but his world-view is based on the profound idea of the noumenality, of the metaphysical primordiality not only of "spirit" but also of "flesh," not only of "heaven" but also of "earth," and their religious equivalence. The "flesh" of the world—sensuousness, incarnatedness in society and culture, in sexual love, in orgy—is just as noumenal, metaphysically primordial, and divinely mystical as "spirit" and "heaven." This is clearly connected with spiritualism or panpsychism in ontology, which teaches that being consists of a complex, interacting hierarchy of concrete spiritual entities, of spiritualized monads united into universal unity by the Primary Divine Monad, containing absolute fullness of being and pre-eternally creating, through emanation, the multiplicity of being. One can dispute the quality of the old traditional term "spiritualism," but the new, suprahistorical Christianity, too, must accept this kind of ontology.

The sin of historical Christianity consists not so much in its spiritualistic ontology (which is incapable of solving our problem of "spirit" and "flesh") as in its dualism, according to which "spirit" is regarded as divine and good, whereas "flesh" is regarded as godless and evil. By contrast, a philosophical ontology can exist which rejects the existence of matter and regards the physical world as something conditional and fictitious; and this kind of panpsychism will only help to rehabilitate the "flesh." The roots of the sensuousness and orgiastic character of the "flesh" lie not in the empirical, physical, and material world, but in transcendental, bottomless depths, at one of the poles of "spirit," if the world is spirit.

Metaphysics can teach us to be aware that the being of the world must liberate itself from the fetters of "matter," from the crushing laws of "nature"—it can teach us that space and time must disappear like a nightmare. This coincides fully with the most important and mysterious idea of the new religious consciousness, namely the idea of the transfiguration of "earth," the transfiguration of "flesh." An age-old battle is being waged not against "earth" and flesh," but against the primordial enslavement known as "matter," against the limits imposed by space and time. There will be a transfigured "earth," unfettered by material laws, liberated, extratemporal and extra-spatial; there will be a transfigured "flesh," not physical, but full-blooded, sensuous, mystically lustful and eternal, freed of all material limits. This mystical presentiment can be justified by metaphysics, but only religion can grasp this mystery. By themselves, human beings who are torn away from the Absolute Source of being cannot achieve transfiguration of the "earth," its liberation from space and time, from enchainment by necessity; they cannot achieve transfiguration of the "flesh," the grounding of its eternal, incorruptible individual being. But for God all things are possible; and we believe that transfiguration will occur in union with God, in the divine-human process. *The religious problem of spirit and flesh, of the polarity of the abysses, of duality, is engendered not from the ontological dualism of man's nature, but from the colossal mystery of the separation of God into two Countenances and the relation of this separation to the multiple world emanating from God; and this problem is solved religiously: the duality is overcome in the third Countenance of God.* According to the Christian teaching, this is the apparent and mysterious polarity between God the Father and God the Son, who are really one; and the resolution of all oppositions lies in God the Holy Spirit. We will say more about this below.

But our flesh, the flesh of our world, is corrupted, defective, abnormal. This is so not because flesh is sinful in its essence, not because it is a principle of evil and must be destroyed; but because it dies, decays, grows sick, and suffers; because it is not eternal and free and must be transfigured and resurrected. This brings us to the old and ever new question of asceticism. The curse of humankind, its primordial corruption, lies not in the flesh, but in death; the sinfulness of humanity lies not in free life, but in enslavement and limitation. The abnormality of the flesh lies not in the orgiastic richness of life, but in the poverty, narrowness, and finiteness of the life of the flesh. And religion, conscious of the tragedy of the flesh of the world, battles not against flesh, but against the corruption of the flesh, not against the orgiastic fullness of life, but against death, narrowness, and the supplanting of the whole by a part. One must defeat the non-being in the flesh, not its being. One must defeat its death, not its life; its negation, not its affirmation. Asceticism can be one of the means, but never the goal, never the sole means.

Ascetic religion—Buddhism both ancient and new, historical Christianity's tendency toward black monasticism,[17] religion waging war against life, not against death, against being, not against non-being—is not our religion. The spirit in which every "yes" is swallowed up by an enormous "no" and sinks in the great "nothing"—this spirit repels our religious consciousness. Orgiasm—this tragic excess of life so unfamiliar to our colorless and lukewarm rationalistic culture, a culture which is ascetic and perverted at the same time (these two things always go hand in hand)—is connected by transcendent threads to our final religious goal: affirmation of the fullness of life, union with the Proto-source of all life. Not all orgiasm is a path, but is religious orgi-

---

17. Monasticism which totally rejects life, as opposed to "white" monasticism which rejoices in the transfigured life and world given to man by Christ.—Trans.

asm not a path to the defeat of death, to eternal feasting in the Kingdom of God?

Merezhkovsky feels and understands all this. For him the whole mystery and meaning of Christ's religion are contained in the most enigmatic and incomprehensible words ever uttered: "Jesus took bread, and blessed it, and brake it, and gave it to the disciples, and said, Take, eat; this is my body. And he took the cup, and gave thanks, and gave it to them, saying, Drink ye all of it; For this is my blood of the new testament, which is shed for many for the remission of sins."[18] After this, is it possible to regard the New Testament as a religion of fleshlessness and bloodlessness? Merezhkovsky justly speaks of "the crime of historical Christianity, whose spirit even until now is primarily monastic, bloodless and fleshless, unincarnate—an abstract spirit that has still not responded to Pan's summoning voice, does not celebrate the great feast of Dionysus, has not transgressed that final boundary where heaven converges with earth and spirit with flesh and blood." "What is this feast in which every lustful insect, every sticky little leaf, takes part? Is it not the call of the resurrected Pan? Is it not the feast of flesh and blood, the mysterious 'last supper' of the new Dionysus, who says of himself: 'I am the true vine, and my Father is the husbandman'[19]—the great feast at which wine is transmuted into blood and blood into wine?"

Let us also recall Vyacheslav Ivanov's remarkable work on the religion of Dionysus, the ancient Greek religion of the suffering god.[20] Ivanov's strivings are extremely characteristic for the new religious movement; his experiences must be recognized as a significant contribution to our Christian-pagan renaissance. The view of Dionysus as a mystical presentiment of Christ's appearance in the world is already a pathway to the ardently desired synthesis of Christianity and paganism. The orgiastic rites of Dionysus ripped through the boundaries and liberated and revealed the religious medium in which the suffering god—God the Son—was made incarnate. The god Pan was still only a

---

18. Matt. 26:26–28.—Trans.
19. John 15:1.—Trans.
20. See Ivanov's essay "The Ancient Greek Religion of the Suffering God" in *Novyi Put'*, 1904, No. 8.—Trans.

personification of divine creative power; he lived in the religious atmosphere of God-Fatherhood; but with his feasts of the suffering god, did not Dionysus already represent the religious atmosphere of God-Sonhood that was being born in the world?

The *flesh* of the world is holy and divine not only because it is a creation of God the Father, not only because His eternal nature is reflected in it, but also because God the Son is crucified and suffers in it and, in Him, flesh is resurrected and saved from corruption and death. This religion—the religion of Dionysus which remains pagan and is filled with presentiments and the religion of Christ which has overcome paganism and fulfilled the greatest prophecies—is *the religion of the divinely suffering earth*.[21] In the incarnate suffering God, who is crucified for the earth, the earth is resurrected and comes to life; the flesh of the world defeats death and advances toward the eternal feast of life. As for the fleshless and bloodless asceticism of black monasticism, is this asceticism not a flight from the tragedy of the world, a betrayal of the earth in which God Himself becomes incarnate and suffers? Is it not a temptation from the spirit of non-being?

What needs grounding is not spirit or flesh, but *personhood* in the fullness and specificity of its being, transcendent individuality which is both "incarnate spirit" and "spiritual flesh." The idea of personhood or individuality must occupy the central place in the new religious consciousness; many problems can be resolved only in connection with this idea. Merezhkovsky had to feel the enormous significance of the religious understanding of personhood, but he insufficiently highlighted this aspect of the religious consciousness.[22] After all, God Himself became incarnate in the form of a person, thus affirming the immeasurable value of personhood and grounding it for all eternity.

The problem of flesh in its religious formulation is inseparably connected with the problem of *sex*, and Merezhkovsky justly regards this

---

21. See Ivanov's essay "On the Religion of Dionysus" in the July issue of *Voprosy zhizni*. For Minsky, too, the earth is sanctified by the divine sacrifice of the God suffering in her; see his *Religion of the Future*.

22. In my opinion, it is one of Merezhkovsky's weaknesses that he virtually ignores the religious idea of the absolute value of human personhood, that his mystical sense of it is deficient.

as our most crucial problem and links the fate of religion with its solution. It seems that it is our lot and duty to pose this problem in all its acuteness, to lay it bare, thus throwing down a challenge to that age-old hypocrisy that has attached itself to it like a fungus. It is difficult to discuss this calmly; enormous indignation rises in us not only against the bourgeois and hypocritical attitudes of contemporary society, but also against the repulsive crippling endured by sexual life over the millennia. If it turns out that we talk too much and too candidly about sex, if we go too far perhaps in rehabilitating its rights and like Rozanov bend the bow too far in the opposite direction, not only will the higher judgment forgive this, but it will even regard it as something of a religious achievement. Even the most bourgeois and shallow souls must come to realize and feel in their most intimate depths that *sex* is the source of world history, that the intensity and richness of being are connected with it, that it fills half the life of the world while the other half depends on it, that the tragic nature of life is rooted in it. The most mysterious and enigmatic depths of human existence are connected with sex, and the world's greatest artists knew this. But the most important and terrifying problem of life turned out to the one least posed and least solved, since that which was most intimate was not regarded as necessary for the course of history. This problem still finds itself under a millennial prohibition; it is regarded as shameful, indecent, awkward, and even immoral—as something that should not be studied. Everyone is left to his own devices when it comes to solving one of the most universal problems; everyone must conceal in himself a torment that is familiar to us all but that no one can discuss openly.

Is there much in the world's literature and philosophy on the question of sex and sexual love? Plato's *Symposium*, the most profound and eternal work in this domain; Schopenhauer's Buddhistic reflections; the visions of a few great artists; Solovyov's amazing *Meaning of Love*; and Rozanov—that's it, I think. And soaring above all this are Christ's enigmatic and incomprehensible words. History shows us the fanatical and blasphemous asceticism of the servants of historical Christianity on the one hand and, on the other hand, the eternal temptations of Venus, never dying, always being reborn from the sea foam. A multitude of crimes have been committed around sex over the millennia. Cursed by the religious consciousness dominant in history, sex is driven into an underground realm and unleashes tremors and earthquakes. The ancient goddess Aphrodite takes revenge on her persecutors, destroying the historical religions that do not take into account her divine will. Pseudo-Christian asceticism and spiritualism have poisoned the human soul and body. They have perverted the soul and body by the consciousness of sinfulness, thereby transforming sexual life into something disgusting, filthy, and shameful. They have killed the great religious dream of the holiness of sex, the holiness of love, the holiness of the love-feast of life. Sex (and the divine Eros) have been driven into the prison of the bourgeois family and is suffered only there, though the family is not justified by a single word of Christ. Sex has made a home for itself in café chantants and in brothels, this inevitable corrective of our family structure. Sexual love exists outside of religion; it is unsanctified and is given over to the vicissitudes of fate. A man who is religious in the old sense will inevitably defile the woman he loves, as well as himself, since all desire is regarded as a fall, a weakness, a curse on humanity. Religious preachers, philosophers, scholars, journalists, etc. think it appropriate to write about the most trivial matters, but they never write about sex, this source of torment and suffering. The problem of sex simply doesn't exist for positivists; they are concerned with the question of the abolition of family despotism, which, to be sure, is a very important question of civil law and political economy; or with the medical and hygienic question, which is also very important. But the religious problem of sex doesn't concern them. The majority of the most advanced positivists unconsciously subscribe to the ancient religious asceticism, though God died in them long ago and was replaced by morality. This morality, which is necessary for success in life but not for the religious meaning of life, has been bought at too high a price and must be overthrown by a new religious rebirth, which, in its essence, will be supra-moral.[23] In spite of his extreme views, it is hard to overrate the achievements of Rozanov, who has so boldly and radically formulated the *religious* problem of sex, who has been so revolutionary in breaking with the illegitimate pretensions of morality. I do not agree with Rozanov's solution of the problem; I find profoundly foreign his ancient Judaic divinization of the principle of begetting, his

23. Not immoral.

sanctification of the sexual desire of the begetter; but I am in awe of his mighty attempt to purge our blood of the ascetic poison, to display sex in all its naked Edenic holiness and sinlessness.

There is no doubt that Rozanov influenced Merezhkovsky's entire conception of supra-historical Christianity. Merezhkovsky accepted Rozanov's challenge and took his side, but for him this challenge referred not to the religion of Christ, but to "historical" Christianity. In Merezhkovsky's opinion, historical Christianity did not include sex, but instead cursed it, whereas the religion of Christ includes sex, and the new supra-historical Christianity must reveal itself to us in connection with the solution of this problem, since the whole flesh of the world, the religious truth about the earth, depends on sex. His entire life, Merezhkovsky was tempted and tormented by Aphrodite, "the white she-devil" (no wonder she plays such an important role in his historical novels). And in the statue of Venus he strives to discover features of the ideal of Madonna. In spite of his apparent closeness to Rozanov, Merezhkovsky stands, in essence, at the diametrically opposite end: Rozanov reveals the holiness and divinity of sex and of love-desire as if before the beginning of the world; he wishes to bring us back to the Edenic state before the fall; whereas Merezhkovsky reveals the same thing, but as if after the end of the world, and he summons us to a lustful and holy feast of the flesh in a transfigured world, one that is redeemed and resurrected. Merezhkovsky is right, because he looks forward, not back, but what is the nature of the path from the beginning to the end? What things must be affirmed on this path?

Sex is not just a biological concept, not just an empirical phenomenon that must be abolished in order to establish a realm of the spirit for which there is no place in heaven. Sex is transcendental; love has a metaphysical meaning; love of the sexes, the union of polarly opposite beings, is closely connected with a striving towards eternity, towards the establishment of fullness of individuality. But sex is abnormal, as if tainted in some way; and love is tragic. What is horrifying is not that sexual passion is sinful but that, empirically, this passion leads not to the fullness and eternity of individuality in the world, but instead to a fragmented individuality: Sex leads to child-bearing, and my unfulfilled striving for perfection is passed on to my children, who are condemned to suffer from the same torment. On the other hand, sexual love itself is constantly fragmenting, turns out to be multiple, not unitary, in character; and therefore it cannot attain eternity. Christianity did not invent this tragic, corrupted character of sex, and Rozanov is powerless before this tragedy, as in general he is powerless before the tragedy of death. This is the fundamental antinomy of world history: the continuation of the human race is the result of the imperfection, mortality, and fragmentation of individuality; but this continuation is necessary for the universal victory over death, for the conclusive establishment of the eternity and perfection of individuality. The metaphysical meaning of love, of sexual love, consists in the fact that it grounds metaphysical personhood, eternal individuality, but the corrupted flesh of our world is such that sex, too, dies, is fragmented: we get not the eternity of a single individuality in immortality, but a multitude of mortal individualities in child-bearing; not a single eternal love, but a multitude of corrupted loves. The impersonal instinct of the race is connected with death, but in the eternal and perfect life of individualities there is neither death nor birth. Can there be an individual and eternal sexual love, or must sex always remain an impersonal instinct of the race? Here, as everywhere, the goal cannot be attained solely by human means; it can be attained only on a divine-human path, only through union with God.

The metaphysical meaning of sex is fully actualized only in religion. The fullness of love and its ultimate meaning are actualized only in mystical union, but the pathways to this union are multiple and individual and by no means do they involve the eradication of sex. We are always in great danger of arriving at a new form of asceticism, at negation without affirmation, if we do not recognize that the foundations of sexual love are holy even if this love is manifested outside a church-sanctified union. What we need is rebellion not only against pseudo-Christian asceticism, but also against family unions, which are coercive, non-religious, and opposed to the eternal goals of love, for the family is a union whose goal is earthly prosperity; it is rooted not in individuality, but in the collective character of the race. Christ preached not infinite propagation of the race, which continues imperfection and death, but eternal life and the perfection of personhood. Nowhere do we encounter such insuperable conservatism as here, in the question of sex; nowhere do we encounter such a despotism of the

The New Religious Consciousness

old attitudes and the old morality. Even Merezhkovsky speaks with too weak a voice, is insufficiently rebellious, desires to find common ground with the old Christian doctrine of marriage. Sexual, conjugal love must be a sacrament; it must be sanctified in a religious union if its meaning and goal are to be eternal. There is no doubt about that. But precisely for that reason it is necessary to wage war against the idea of the family union, against any coercion, either outer or inner, against anything that stifles the orgiastic nature of sex. The very notion of fornication is an old, bourgeois notion, a product of abstract moralism, and must be submitted to the court of esthetic and authentically religious judgment.

Through sex there must be accomplished not only the union of two into an eternal fullness of individuality, but also the union of all into a society, since the unsolved mystery of Christian love consists perhaps in the fact that people are united not only by brotherly love, not only by pity and altruism, but also by a mystical conjugal love. Merezhkovsky, too, is close to this view. Sexual love also contains the mystery of individuality, of personhood, and the mystery of universality, of sobornost. In general, Rozanov does not have a good understanding of individuality; this conceals from him the true meaning of love and makes his sexual orgiasm impersonal. On the other hand, he understands like no one else that the path to a unified religious life, to a life of sobornost, lies through sex. Solovyov too writes about mystical erotic love, linking it with many things.[24] It is precisely their attitudes towards sex and love that, more than anything else, distinguish people of the old religious consciousness and of the old non-religious consciousness from people of the new religious consciousness. The new religious people, people of the future religion of freedom, must liberate themselves from hypocritical moralism, throw down a challenge to unions of bourgeois well-being, whether governmental or familial, and become mystical revolutionaries for whom the problem of sex and love is posed and solved religiously, not positively, socially,

---

24. Solovyov's extraordinary, truly mystical ideas about the meaning of love, the eternal feminine, and mystical erotic love sharply contradict the old banal morality which he develops in his weakest work, *The Justification of the Good*, in which he goes astray in relation to "moralism" as an "abstract" principle.

or morally.[25] But too many people are still fettered by cowardice in relation to the old attitudes.[26]

Merezhkovsky has a very radical ideological temperament and he yearns for great universal revolutions. But sometimes he speaks in a false voice, a voice that is not his own; he has two voices, and only one of them is his real voice. It seems to me that his voice betrays him every time he tries to compromise, to find common ground with the old attitudes, with the old governmental structure or with the old church structure. At those times he seems to be afraid of his own radicalism. He has his own *new* and *free* religious point of view; he has his words of prayer, native to people of the new religious consciousness; but sometimes he goes astray: false words appear, old words, of the old church and old government, words that are not ours, as if suddenly he becomes afraid of his own "decadence" and tries to grasp hold of the old stability. It is in this false and strident tone that Merezhkovsky writes about Tolstoy's excommunication from the church[27]: with a voice and words not his own, Merezhkovsky attempts artificially to unite himself with the historical church and with Russia's governing body; he suddenly becomes afraid of heresies, though such fear is not natural to him. These false notes have harmed the great work he is doing.

He clearly went astray when, at one point, attempting to revive a historical corpse, he started to restore the old Slavophile doctrine of the state, when with a voice not his own he spoke of the mystical nature of the state authority. It is amazing that Merezhkovsky—so radical, rebellious, free, and new in his yearnings—failed to realize at once what apparently he is beginning to realize now: that the state is one of the Devil's temptations, that all earthly power, every prince of this world, is not from God but from the Devil, that the new polity must be

---

25. There is much of value on this subject in the essays of Anton the Extreme [pseudonym of Zinaida Gippius] published in *Novyi Put'*.

26. Even Rozanov does not express himself fully, for he is afraid that if he does so, he will no longer be received in the "best houses." This censorship of our contemporary society, this coercion of false conscience and hypocrisy, is detestable.

27. Merezhkovsky has said many true and profound things about Tolstoy. He has spoken justly about the weakness of Tolstoy's consciousness, but he has failed to appreciate the religious significance of Tolstoy's rejection of state authority, of Tolstoy's protest against official falsehood and dissimulation.

established not in a coercive state union but in a free religious union, that there is no place for coercion where the kingdom of love has been proclaimed. Merezhkovsky has been unable to transpose the sense of personhood, so important for the new religious consciousness, into the domain of politics. Sometimes he does approach the true doctrine, the doctrine of mystical statelessness, and then his voice is sincere and in harmony with the new religious consciousness, but more often he is afraid to speak in this voice! The same thing has happened to him that had happened to Dostoevsky, who gave us "The Grand Inquisitor," the most profound and passionate justification in world literature of anarchism on a religious foundation, of unlimited freedom in Christ; but who also defended the old and banal idea of state authority. Even Solovyov never fully understood that the idea of universal theocracy, of the kingdom of God not only in heaven but also on earth, is incompatible with the recognition of earthly power, of coercive state authority. The choice is between two things: to follow Christ, who rejected the temptations of the earthly kingdoms in the name of unlimited freedom and the freedom of love; or to follow the one who tempted Christ in the desert. Merezhkovsky, however, has long been tempted by the *imperium romanum*, the idea of mystical monarchy and the grandeur of Caesar, to whom he was ready to cede part of that which is God's, though this Caesar never existed empirically, but was only a product of Merezhkovsky's romantic imagination. Merezhkovsky venerates Napoleon, a superman, a man-god, and this shows that Nietzsche's influence is still present in him. In Peter the Great, the greatest of the tsars, Merezhkovsky sees an example of a mystical monarch who fulfills a religious vocation, instead of a mere genius, one of those called from above to guide the historical destiny of mankind.[28]

What we have here is Merezhkovsky's old romanticism, motivated by his aversion to bourgeois democracy, to the antireligious politics of our intelligentsia, which has forgotten the grand ideas. There is little grandeur in the contemporary liberal, democratic, or socialist ideas of the state; these are "bourgeois" ideas which are not universal, not con-

---

28. Merezhkovsky's view of Peter the Great startles us with its lack of clarity and ambiguity, and, evidently, this is connected with the lack of clarity and ambiguity of all his notions about the Antichrist.

nected with the religious meaning of life. But what grand universal religious idea of the state can there be in the present day? Certainly, not the old dead idea of the kingdom of earthly power, which has not only been rejected by the contemporary political and moral antireligious consciousness, but which must be even more radically rejected by the new religious consciousness, as the path of the spirit of non-being who tempted God in the desert.

The desired polity must be established not on a foundation of coercive state power but on a new, free, eternal, mystical foundation, just as love can be established not in a family union, but outside of it, in a free mystical union. Should not free love, unlimited freedom in God, be the sole foundation of a new social and sexual union? It is not possible to actualize the great religious idea of the state, such as Merezhkovsky once sought; the epoch of such phantasms and temptations has come to an end. It has been replaced by the great religious idea of statelessness, by a new theocratic, ecclesial union, freely loving, subordinating the individual to the will of God on earth too, in opposition to the coercive state union which subordinated the individual to godless earthly will. Positivists, however radical and anarchistic they might pretend to be, will never free themselves of the temptation of state power, the temptation by earthly kingdoms, since they passionately desire to organize life on earth, are terrified of chaos, and do not know *in the name of what* they should reject the temptation of earthly power.

But how should one view the battle for liberation that constitutes the content of recent history? How should one view the proud rebellion of the individual, the declaration of his rights? Social liberation took place outside of the religious consciousness; it was just as unsanctified as love, as sexual life, but it is necessary to recognize the unconscious religious holiness of this great movement; otherwise, we would have to turn away from the "earth." People of the new religious consciousness must recognize and sanctify the battle for freedom, for the eradication of coercion and tyranny, even though they might feel aversion towards the positive construction of life, towards the cultivation of the instincts of political power which characterize all orientations and parties whose goal is to rule. When in political ideologies the idea of power, of all power, monarchic or popular, begins to be replaced by the idea of absolute rights, of the eternal value of all freedoms, of the lordship of the superhuman good which surpasses random human will, the ground will then be prepared for the idea of universal theocracy, of mystical statelessness. When the fate of human life is placed in dependence on the superhuman good of freedom, on eternal values, on absolute rights which are not subject to human judgment, then this fate will be proffered to the Divine will: in other words, men will thirst for the kingdom of God on earth too. This truth must be disclosed; it must be illuminated by the light of religious consciousness. This light must disclose the unconscious holiness of freedom-lovers, of warriors for the image of God in man; and it must also disclose the godlessness of the hypocritical official servants of religion.

Merezhkovsky has still not solved the political problem in its religious formulation; he has not found the right politics; he has often been led astray in the question of state power, but this question is a crucial one for those who dream of a "heavenly earth." How good it would be if he expressed himself fully on all these tormented themes and found the true path, since we desire strongly to advance with him towards the goal we have in common. For the name Merezhkovsky will be listed in the ranks of the first conscious forerunners of a theocratic union[29] of freedom and love—a union which can be rooted neither in state nor in family, since it is providentially linked with the absence of authority.

Historical Christianity—which is ascetic, preaching individual salvation by flight from the world and cursing the earth—rejects, in essence, not only the religious meaning, but any meaning, of the historical process: the development of the world is ignored by the religious consciousness; universal culture turns out to be nonreligious and even antireligious. But pure, medieval Christian spiritualism died long ago, and people now practice a kind of compromise—they have made a deal with the earth, a deal which leads to a repulsive hypocrisy. Religion has become permissive with regard to history, often looking the other way; it allows the development of culture, but does not sanctify anything; it is not a transfigurative power in the life of the world. Sal-

---

29. In many ways, Solovyov is Merezhkovsky's forerunner here.

vation is now more common outside the church than inside it. Apostates and atheists—and of course the beloved children of God such as Leonardo da Vinci, Goethe, and Nietzsche—are saved more readily than the multitudes of servants of historical Christianity: "whosoever speaketh a word against the Son of man, it shall be forgiven him: but whosoever speaketh against the Holy Spirit, it shall not be forgiven him, neither in this world, neither in the world to come."[30] Historical progress, world culture, and the greatest heroes of this culture are sanctified and saved in accordance with Christ's words, since they do not speak against the Holy Spirit. The magical circle of the mystical church coincides neither with the historical church nor with any other relative human institutions.

Merezhkovsky and people of the new religious consciousness cannot bear this duality; they wish to link their religion with the meaning of universal history and to religiously sanctify universal culture. They yearn for a Church in which the fullness of being would be encompassed and all the sacraments of life would be enacted. But to recognize that universal history has a meaning is to recognize that it has an ultimate goal; it is to affirm that universal history has an end and to judge all the things in history according to this end—to sanctify all things as the path to the universal culmination. The idea of the end of the world can be justified from a purely philosophical point of view, although rationalistically it is just as inconceivable as the absence of an end in time, as an infinite world process, this bad infinity, according to Hegel's expression.[31] Good infinity, eternity, consists not in the absence of an end in time but in the overcoming of any end, in the nullification of time, in extra-temporality. The idea of endless progress, with which the 19th century positivists were so infatuated, is the most boring, tedious, meaningless, and contradictory of ideas. A gray tedium overcomes us whenever we try to imagine the realization of this idea. The infinite multiplication of imperfection and then death again; no dream of eternal life, full in its perfection, unfragmented. Indeed, to deny there is an

---

30. Matt. 12:32.—Trans.

31. Kant regarded this as one of the antinomies and did not allow that rational knowledge could solve the problem of whether the world process has an end or whether it is endless.—Trans.

end is to deny that universal history has meaning as well as to deny the possibility of progress, for meaning requires completion and the tragedy of the world must have not only a first but also a last act. Psychologically, the idea of the end is so deeply ingrained in man's nature that it constantly appears in a masked form: on one hand as the idea of a perfect future society, a golden age, a natural state, in short, a "thousand-year kingdom"; and on the other hand as a dark abyss of non-being, a void of nothingness. Only mystics consciously and joyfully accept the idea of the end, and only a very few thinkers justify it.

Positivists and social saviors of mankind desire to transform the world, to reform and improve it without end, without a radical revolution. But one can desire more than this: one can desire the transfiguration of the world, the end of the present, limited, corrupted, mortal world and its replacement by a new world, by "a new heaven and a new earth." The idea of the end is seductive and beautiful because at the same time it is the idea of the beginning, not of death, but of eternal life; and so this idea must intensify our creative labor, not stifle it. If tomorrow temporal being will end and eternal being will begin, on this last day my labor will be more intense, because there is a greater urge to create for eternity than for temporality. All theories of progress, including the most positivistic ones, have their naïve eschatology, lead with fateful inevitability to the posing of the problem of the end, the problem of the meaning of world history. In particular, Marxism, taken as a religious system, displays such a primitive eschatology, consisting in the fact that it views the socialistic society as the end of history and as the beginning of some supra-historical process. The new religious consciousness too, which is inextricably connected with the meaning of universal history, must inevitably have as its reference point that Christian book which contains mysterious prophecies about the end of the world, about the fulfillment of the meaning of world history, about the final act of the tragedy: the Apocalypse of St. John.

The idea of the end has become Merezhkovsky's principal religious idea; he even calls his understanding of Christianity apocalyptic, opposing it to historical Christianity. Apocalyptic Christianity signifies a break in universal history, *the end of history and the beginning of a supra-historical process*. Till now the religious light has emanated from Christ who died on the cross, from a past in which the complete truth had not yet been revealed; and the light has been growing fainter and fainter, but a new religious light suddenly flares up, emanating from the Coming Christ; a reverse movement of time begins, as it were. Apocalyptic Christianity will reveal the nature of the Holy Spirit, the Comforter promised by Christ; room will be made for what historical Christianity failed to include. There will arise a new, eternal church, the church of St. John; and a new, eternal religion, the religion of the Holy Trinity, the fullness of revelation of all the divine hypostases, which will overcome all duality and include all the values of world culture. The church of St. John, the universal theocracy whose establishment will signify the beginning of the apocalyptic process, will reveal the truth about the "earth" and solve the problems of sex, bread, and society, all the problems that the human historical process could not solve. The great philosopher-mystic Schelling was very close to this kind of religious conception, but Merezhkovsky came to it independently, less philosophically than Schelling, more through life-experience and art.[32]

Thus, the center of the religious consciousness is shifted into the prophetic domain; petrified dogmatism and historical limitation are overcome. But there is the danger that prophecy will again become fettered dogmatically, that it will again become constrained by historical limitation. Does Merezhkovsky recognize freedom of prophecy and new religious creativity? Yes and no. He may take the Apocalypse as his starting point but, after all, this divinely inspired symbolic book can be interpreted in different ways, and its eternal meaning is disclosed only in our inner mystical experience. Merezhkovsky prophesies about the New Jerusalem with great joy and gladness in his heart; his apocalyptic Christianity is of the white kind, whereas for many it is of the

---

32. Schelling speaks of the religion of the Holy Trinity, of a new revelation of the Holy Spirit, of the church of St. John. It is surprising that, in his principal work *Science and Religion*, the dry rationalist Chicherin also speaks of a new revelation of the Spirit in the future historical process, of a Trinitarian religion and of a church of John. The Middle Ages had a heresy of the brotherhood of the Holy Spirit, whose founder, Joachim of Fiore, taught that the world process passes through three periods, according to the three persons of the Holy Trinity. The third epoch will be the epoch of the Holy Spirit, and St. Francis of Assisi was considered to be its herald.

black kind, and their consciousness of the end is primarily a consciousness of the coming Last Judgment, provoking horror and anguish in the heart.

Prophecies are free in nature and are revealed in new mystical experience; herein lies great joy as well as great suffering. Religious dogmatics must develop under the influence of new prophecies and free inner revelation; it must not suppress them. An outstanding example of this is Merezhkovsky himself, whom dogmatists readily call a heretic. But he himself is in danger of falling into a kind of religious schematism,[33] which will cause the flowers of the new, supra-historical Christianity to wither. To grasp the religious meaning of universal history and the inevitability of its end is not the same thing as to squeeze it into schemata which will crush the life out of the great religious truth of freedom. It sometimes seems that, for Merezhkovsky, the fate of the world will be decided by the battle of the Lamb with the Beast coming out of the abyss, by the battle of Christ with Antichrist, while man himself and his creative freedom will be irrelevant. The salvation of the world would then be not a divine-human process but an utterly non-human one, and not at all tragic, since tragedy lies only in ultimate human religious freedom. It is this fatalistic schematism, this degeneration of the new prophecy into the old dogmatics, that frightens me most of all. Indeed, is Merezhkovsky's presentiment that the end is at hand not premature? A great many things still need to happen. Is the world sufficiently free for the last act to occur? Merezhkovsky has uncovered something new and terribly free, but now he is on the verge of covering it up again for himself and for others, and the fear is that the perspective of eternal religious movement will vanish and the phantasm of dead dogmatism will again rise on our path. The formation of the church is an organic process, not an artificial and mechanical one; the church is not a lid that sanctifies any place to which one attaches it; rather, *it grows from the holy places of universal culture*; its walls rise wherever one finds God-given knowledge, art, love, freedom. But the invisible church will become visible when the new religious consciousness intensifies. And every church will then include

---

33. In Merezhkovsky we observe a general tendency towards artistic schematism; few individual nuances can be found in him.

free religious seekings. Is that how Merezhkovsky understands the historical incarnation of the Mystical Church, its realization in time?

When the sole source of religious light is the historical incarnation of the divine principle given in the past, the state of affairs is wholly different than when the chief source of light is transposed into the future and is not yet incarnated in any historical given. In the first case, too, our religious freedom is enormous, since religious truth is grasped in inner religious experience, which alone can give meaning to external empirical phenomena with all their accidents; but in the second case this freedom becomes immeasurable and tragic.

The disclosure of *Spirit* in the divine-human process, in which everyone is called to participate, is an unprecedented recognition of human freedom and also the beginning of humanity's greatest tragedy. Has the Spirit not already begun to disclose itself in the new history, in new experience, in philosophy, in art, in the liberation of the earth? Merezhkovsky seems to understand better than others that the religion of Christ is the religion of freedom, that in Christ everything is permitted in a certain sense; and our great fear is that he might betray this understanding. Our religious tragedy is not the old tragedy of conscience but a new tragedy, the tragedy of freedom; it is not a "moral" tragedy but a religious tragedy of ultimate dualism and ultimate freedom of choice. Merezhkovsky has investigated this tragedy using Dostoevsky's heroes as examples, and we value that more than anything else.

In order for the meaning of universal history to be fulfilled, in order for this history to end, what is needed is the liberation of the world and a terrible intensification of consciousness: Human personhood must rise to its full stature. Only then can the final battle between the two opposite principles of the world's life take place. Merezhkovsky was premature when he proclaimed the end of Russian literature; we still need literature as well as philosophy, the renaissance of culture, and political liberation, because unprecedented freedom and unprecedented consciousness are needed for the end. Positivists, socialists, and their ilk think that people will be happier, calmer, more satisfied, more blissful when they stop being so externally unfree, hungry, and disorganized. That is a very great falsehood. People will be a thousand times unhappier if their consciousness is no longer distracted by external scourges and torments resulting from life's terrible problems. Their life will become unbearably tragic, and their unlimited freedom will thirst for God, yearn for love in God. This, and only this, constitutes the metaphysical and religious meaning of humanity's social liberation. When freedom triumphs in every domain of life, when social reformers succeed in feeding and clothing all mankind, it is then that men will come to a final awareness of their abject poverty and slavish impotence, of their inability to live any longer without God, of the horror of the absolute non-being that will follow this moment of satiety and well-being. Many are called to the feast of eternal life; all are called to participate in the attainment of the goals of universal history; all are equal before God. That is what the truth of democratism consists in. But few are chosen and not all will freely love God, and that is why the fulfillment of the meaning of universal history can be the work only of the few. That is what the truth of aristocratism consists in. The religious aristocratism towards which Merezhkovsky tends is wholly compatible with social democratism and has nothing in common with the rule of the nobility.

Here we come to the most terrifying and most important question. The history of world culture has brought human consciousness to two great ideas: the idea of the God-man and the idea of the man-god. The idea of the man-god tormented Dostoevsky, and this torment was embodied in the prophetic image of Kirillov.[34] Nietzsche went mad because of the idea of the man-god; many positivists in their delirium dream of the man-god, although his image becomes small in their poor imaginations. The idea of the man-god, taken opposition to the idea of the God-man, is reduced by Merezhkovsky to the religious idea of the Antichrist prophesied in the Apocalypse. But in everything that Merezhkovsky wrote on this theme there is a fateful unclarity, an unclarity close to us, our common unclarity. Is this not closely connected with our tragedy of freedom? In his book on Tolstoy and Dostoevsky, Merezhkovsky seems to be inclined to think that "the God-man and the Man-god are one and the same," just as the two opposite

---

34. In the novel *Demons*.—Trans.

religious abysses—above and below, heaven and earth, spirit and flesh—are one and the same. In the final analysis the new religious consciousness tends to view mangodhood, demonism, the war against God, as the same sort of divine principle as the opposite abyss and to regard it as only an apparent evil. As for the Devil, or noumenal evil, the new religious consciousness tends to sees him as the bourgeois middle, the spirit of non-being, banal, flat, insipid. "As long as we do not fully understand the mystery of the final union, 'I and the Father are one,' does the hypostasis of the Son, 'I,' not seem 'demonic' in relation to the hypostasis of the Father, 'not I'; and conversely does the hypostasis of the Father not seem 'demonic' in relation to that of the Son?" Would Merezhkovsky repeat today these mysterious and profound words? Or these: "Perfect love, love unto the end, unto God, and freedom that is just as perfect, these are not two, but one, and therefore you cannot have love without freedom or freedom without love.... The 'whole secret' of the Devil lies in the fact that he does not want 'unto the end'; he does not want two to be one, but wants two always to be two, and for this reason he always pretends to be *one of the two*, either the Father against the Son or the Son against the Father, without being the one or the other, but only the negation of both; he pretends to be one of the two poles, opposite and equal to the other, whereas both poles are contained forever in the bi-unity of the divine Persons, the Father and Son; while the Spirit of the bourgeois middle is only the negation of this mystical polarity, only an 'ape' that, mimicking the bi-unity of the Divine Hypostases, distorts both Persons, confuses them, and laughs." "There is no other Devil... this is the genuine and unique Satan, and... in him we come to know the final essence of noumenal evil." Merezhkovsky attempts to save himself from the temptations of demonism by lowering Satan to the level of a nonentity and vulgar lackey. He develops this point of view further in his remarkable essay "The Fate of Gogol" in which he regards the figures of Khlestakov and Chichikov[35] as representing the noumenal Devil; and in this way he reduces the spirit of evil, the spirit of non-being, to the vulgar bourgeois middle, to insipidity and banality. But

---

35. The protagonists, respectively, of *The Inspector General* and *Dead Souls*.—Trans.

where then is the Antichrist? What makes him terrifying and seductive? The problem of the origin and meaning of evil in the world is the most difficult, terrible, and fateful problem for the future of all religions. There can be two types of solutions to this problem: monistic or dualistic. Either the Devil is a pathetic creature that has incited antagonism between God and the world in the name of non-being, since he cannot ground any being; and then there is no abyss in him, but only the insipid bourgeois middle, and there is nothing seductive in demonism. Or the Devil is an autonomous, pre-eternal, uncreated principle, and we arrive at the dualistic doctrine of two eternal kingdoms, between which we must choose. It sometimes seems that the terrifying words about "the fire of Gehenna" somehow confirm this seductive dualistic doctrine.[36] Merezhkovsky has not yet solved this problem. Freedom is a divine gift, but evil is necessary if the meaning of freedom is to be justified. There is no doubt that the insipid bourgeois middle, banality, vulgarity, positivistic non-being are the Devil. There is also no doubt that the Holy Spirit, not the spirit of the Devil, reposed on God's great enemies, on their profound demonism. But is this not another mystery?

The proud idea of the man-god and all that is contained in it cannot be reduced to the Devil-Khlestakov and the Devil-Smerdyakov,[37] to banality and vulgarity. The grounding of the personhood in its absolute value is a divine work, not a godless one. Merezhkovsky realizes this and says: "Kirillov brings to a culmination Nietzsche's principal religious idea: the kingdom of the 'superman' foretold by Zarathustra turns out to be 'eternal life here,' i.e., 'the coming Jerusalem,' the kingdom of Resurrected Flesh foretold in the Apocalypse: 'we shall reign on the earth.' One of two equal triangles has been reversed, and the two coincide. In the same way, at their extreme points, the first being the idea of the beginning, of divine necessity; the last being the idea of the end of the world, of divine purposiveness—at these points the

---

36. I do not accept the dualistic solution and only wish to indicate the enormous difficulty of this problem, which Merezhkovsky evades. The Devil's element is not only banality and vulgarity, but also (and much more so) malice and extreme arrogance.

37. The vulgar epileptic brother in Dostoevsky's *Brothers Karamazov*.—Trans.

seemingly Antichristic doctrine of Kirillov and Nietzsche coincides with Christ's doctrine; and if two points of two straight lines coincide, the lines themselves must coincide—that is an axiom of geometry." These words are very important for the characterization of the new religious consciousness.

There is an insipid mangodhood that leads us on the path of non-being and is preached by positivists: with vulgar and conceited self-satisfaction man occupies God's place, doesn't respect anything, and rejects all that is superhuman. This is Maksim Gorky's "man." What we have is not a polar abyss, but the bourgeois middle. Meanwhile, God loves His noble enemies, such as Aeschylus' Prometheus, Byron's Cain, Nietzsche, Ivan Karamazov, and Kirillov. There is an abyss here, but perhaps it is the abyss of one of the Persons of God Himself.

The two polarly opposite abysses about which Merezhkovsky speaks are not God and the Devil, not good and evil, but two equally holy and equally divine principles that are reconciled in Trinity. The spirit of non-being, of the bourgeois middle, remains outside of Trinity, which encompasses immeasurable fullness. The doctrine of the Trinity of Divinity is one of the most profound religious-metaphysical doctrines and one that has been defended by the greatest philosophers. Unlike superficial rationalists, Schelling and Hegel did not consider the dogma of the Holy Trinity ridiculous and absurd, and they connected their systems with trinity. Let me note only the following: in the overcoming of Duality through Trinity, the doctrine of the Trinity has a divine dialectic which is admissible only if one accepts the doctrine of the Logos, the metaphysics of the Divine Logos, since the category of number (1, 2, 3) is a rational category and is applicable only to the Being, the Logos, and since the dialectic of division and reconciliation (thesis, antithesis, synthesis) is applicable, too, only to the supreme rational nature—the Logos. Merezhkovsky is insufficiently conscious of this,[38] since he does not follow a philosophical path, but the more philosophical Solovyov understood this very well. In any case, great is Merezhkovsky's achievement: he has re-introduced into our religious consciousness the inexplicably forgotten Third Person of the Trinity, the Spirit, and connected this with our religious dualism. His religion is

---

38. Merezhkovsky says nothing about the Logos.

not historical Christianity and not Christianity insofar as this word was formed from only one of the hypostases; it is a religion of Trinity, which until now has still not been revealed. Some might protest and say that the Christian Creed begins with confession of the dogma of Trinity! And this makes it even more astonishing that Trinity was not included in the Christian religion, that it was not understood, that it was forgotten.

There is some mystery that Merezhkovsky is unable to express, although he agonizingly exerts himself to the utmost in an attempt to do so. Has he collided with something ineffable that is fathomable only in action, in living experience of the mystery? I often think that all human creative effort can be explained by anguished yearning for what is absent. Just let a man become privy to some secret, and he will have everything he needs; he will become terribly rich and joyful and stop all his exertions; he will no longer need to create in the domains of philosophy, literature, art, and politics, these surrogates of true life. Why do we need philosophy, love of wisdom, if we have wisdom itself? Why do we need music, poetry, and sculpture, if life itself is music, poetry, and sculpture? In my writings my only goal is to express my own anguished yearning for true, full, eternal, free, and joyful life and my immeasurable desire to learn the secret of this life—the unique secret. All of us write about what we do not have, yet fervently yearn to have. In music we create sounds of a higher harmony which we do not have; in images of art we create a beauty which we lack. The agony of all genuine creativeness is a religious agony which is born from the fact that we do not yet have a key to the mystery of being, from an agonizing search for this key. Our path now is the path of universal culture, but when we learn the uniquely important secret, all that is finite will end and the eternal will begin. Merezhkovsky appears to be close to the unriddling of some secret; he is circling around it, but does he already know the secret or does he only know *about* it? My yearning is very close to his: we yearn to unriddle the same secret, and therefore our path must be the same.

2

Tolstoy[1]

I never liked Tolstoy's doctrine. I was always repelled by his crude rationalism, and I have always thought (and still think) that his worldview is not a Christian one, but rather Buddhist in character. I always felt closer to Dostoevsky. But in my early youth and adolescence I was drawn to Tolstoy by my first rebellion against the evil and falsehood of the surrounding life, by my first aspiration to actualize truth in personal and social life. *War and Peace* gave me an acute sense of my homeland and of my origins. It has always seemed to me that that book tells the story of my own forebears. Tolstoy's fate is a very remarkable Russian fate, one that is highly significant for the Russian search for the meaning and truth of life. Tolstoy is Russian to the marrow of his bones, and he could have arisen only on Russian Orthodox soil, even though he rejected Orthodoxy. He startles us by his typical Russian face combining nobleman and peasant. It is as if two sundered Russias—the Russia of the noblemen and the Russia of the peasants—were trying to reunite in him. And we cannot renounce this face, because the renunciation of it would signify a terrible impoverishment of Russia. Tolstoy was a favorite of fortune, at least according to the world's understanding of such things; he was given all the goods of this world: fame, wealth, high rank, family happiness. But he came close to suicide, because he sought the meaning of life and God. He could not accept life if it had no meaning. Meanwhile, the instinct of life was exceptionally powerful in him, as were all the passions. In his person, the Russia of the nobility, our highest cultural class, exposes the falsehood of its life.

---

1. First published as part of the essay "Three Anniversaries: Tolstoy, Ibsen, and Fyodorov" in the magazine *Put'*, June 1929, No. 11.—Trans.

[47]

But in his passionate search for God, the meaning of life, and the truth of life, Tolstoy was initially overwhelmed and rendered powerless by a certain contradiction. He began by exposing the falsehood and meaninglessness of civilized life. He believed that truth and meaning could be found among the simple laboring people, the peasants. Tolstoy belonged to our highest cultural class, a large portion of which had fallen away from the Orthodox faith by which the common people lived. He had lost God because he lived the illusory life of external culture. And he desired to believe in the same way as the common people who were not spoiled by culture. But he failed completely. He was a victim of the historical Russian schism between our cultured class and the peasants. The common people believed in the Orthodox manner. But in Tolstoy's consciousness the Orthodox faith came into implacable conflict with his reason. He consented to accept only a rational faith; anything that seemed irrational to him in a faith evoked his protest and indignation. But the reason by which he judged Orthodoxy was entirely assimilated by him from the civilization he hated, from European rationalism, from Spinoza, Voltaire, Kant, et al. However strange this might appear, Tolstoy remained an "Enlightenment" thinker. The whole mystical and mysterious element of Christianity, all of the Church's dogmas and sacraments, provoked in him a violent reaction of the Enlightenment reason. In this respect Tolstoy could never "simplify" himself; he could never s'abêtir, to use Pascal's expression. He did not wish to sacrifice any part of his rationalistic consciousness; the pride of his reason never slept. It was this pride that so wearied the Elder Amvrosy when Tolstoy visited him at Optina. This glaring contradiction between the self-assertion of the Enlightenment reason, the rationalistic consciousness of civilization, and the search for meaning, faith, and God among the peasants is what makes Tolstoy's *Confession* so excruciating. This contradiction exposes the falsehood of religious populism. It is impossible believe in the same way as the common people; it is only possible to believe in what the common people believe in, and one must believe in it not because the common people do, but because it is the truth. Meaning, truth, and God are not the property of any single social class.

Tolstoy is torn apart by the contradiction between his powerful instinctual nature, which is expressed in his art of genius, and his rationalistic consciousness, which is expressed in his religious and moral doctrine. We find this contradiction as early as *War and Peace* and *Anna Karenina*. Tolstoy's fundamental ideas are already present in those two books; one usually exaggerates greatly the revolution in his religious consciousness with which his activity as a preacher begins.

Tolstoy's genius and greatness can be seen, above all, in his powerful feeling that our entire conscious cultural and social life with its innumerable conventionalities is a life that is unreal, illusory, false, and essentially unnecessary, and that behind it is concealed an elemental and unconscious proto-life, authentic, profound, and uniquely necessary. Birth, death, work, eternal nature and the starry sky, man's relation to the divine foundation of life—these are the things that constitute authentic life. The secret of the enchantment of Tolstoy's art consists in a device peculiar to him: a person's thoughts and feelings are different from what he expresses outwardly. There is constantly a kind of double life: (1) the life that reflects civilization and is experienced by the superficial and conventional consciousness and (2) life in its elemental depths, free of conventionalities. Tolstoy's art is always on the side of the elemental power and truth of life against the false and impotent attempts of the civilization-based consciousness to direct life as it wishes. Whence his contempt for great men and heroes who pretend to direct life as they wish. Whence his aversion to Napoleon and his love for Kutuzov.

As early as *War and Peace* Tolstoy is wholly on the side of "nature" and against "culture," on the side of the elemental processes of life that seem divine to him and against the artificial and compulsory organization of life in accordance with reason, consciousness, and the norms of civilization. The truth of life in its immediacy has nothing in common with the conscious and rational norms of life that are established by civilization. A person must give himself passively and elementally to the truth and divinity of the natural process of life. Tolstoy's "non-resistance" already makes its appearance here. One should not resist by conscious effort or by civilization-based activity the direct and simple truth of nature. The common people—who are "nature," not "culture"—possess the wisdom of life. Tolstoy takes the idea of the "non-resistance to evil by violence" not from the New Testament, but from his faith in the beneficence and divinity of "nature," which has been distorted by the violence of civilization; he takes it from his faith in the truth of the elemental depths of life. Tolstoy's works of fiction bear witness to this. But this initial faith was strangely deformed in his religious and moral doctrine, revealing the fundamental contradiction of his life and thought. In his doctrine the truth of life possessed by nature and by the common people, the elemental and irrational truth, is made subordinate to his reason and consciousness, which are entirely engendered by civilization; they are made subordinate to rationalism, which is a type of violence done to the life of the common people.

Tolstoy never noticed that his "reason" was the chief enemy of that meaning and truth of life which he wanted to find in the common people. Tolstoy's "reason," which differs little from Voltaire's "reason," is precisely the violence that civilization wreaks on nature. Faith in the elemental beneficence of nature, which is what produced Tolstoy's doctrine of "non-resistance," collides with faith in reason and consciousness, which turns out to be all-powerful and life-transforming. On the one hand, Tolstoy teaches: be passive and resist not evil by violence, and the truth of nature, which is divine, will reveal itself and triumph. But on the other hand, he teaches: discover in your consciousness the rational law of life, the law of the Master of life, and subject to it all of life and transform by it all of life and the whole world. Tolstoy overcomes this difficulty by assuming that the rational law of life revealed by consciousness is the same thing as the law of beneficent and divine nature. But this is a fundamental rationalistic error. Tolstoy believes that to actualize the true law of life, it is sufficient to apprehend this law. He believes that evil is false consciousness, whereas good is true consciousness. He does not recognize an irrational or volitional source of evil. This is exactly the Socratic point of view. Tolstoy also comes close to Buddhism, for which salvation comes through knowledge. Thus, he not only fails to understand the mystery of redemption, but even feels an aversion towards it. The very idea of redemption seems immoral to him. The doctrine of grace makes him indignant. He preaches salvation, and in this he is close to Buddhism. He has a stony insensitivity towards the person of Christ the Savior.

One other thing made Tolstoy a typical Russian: he was a nihilist. He was a nihilist in relation to history and culture, as well as in relation to his own work. Russian nihilism is a Russian maximalism, an inability to establish degrees and gradations, to justify a hierarchy of values.

Tolstoy

This kind of nihilism easily flourishes even on fully Orthodox soil. No other nation evinces such contempt for cultural values, for human creativity, for knowledge, philosophy, art, and law, for the relative and conventional forms of social life. The Russian tends to regard everything as nonsense and rubbish except the one thing that is needful: for some this is salvation of the soul for eternal life and the Kingdom of God; for others it is social revolution and salvation of the world through a perfect social order. Tolstoy's moral and religious doubt that culture and cultural creativity are justified is a typically Russian doubt, a Russian theme, alien to the West in this form. Tolstoy aspired not towards a new culture, but towards a new life, towards a transfiguration of life. He wanted to stop the creation of perfect works of art and to start the creation of perfect life. Gogol aspired towards the same thing, and so did Fyodorov. These remarkable Russians were tormented by a yearning for a perfect life. And a nihilistic attitude towards culture was often only the reverse side of this yearning. Tolstoy exposed the godless civilization which inevitably results when culture is torn away from life. In this sense, Tolstoy resembles Fyodorov. Tolstoy felt that the goals of life were blocked by the means of life, that the essence of life was being crushed by the accoutrements of life. The exposure of this falsehood of civilization was a great achievement of Tolstoy. But he was not conscious of the original sin that distorts nature. The Christian consciousness of personhood and freedom was absent in him. In this sense, his consciousness resembled the Hindu consciousness, which does not understand personhood and freedom, is impersonalistic and deterministic. For Tolstoy too, neither man nor God is a person; there is only the impersonal divine principle which lies at the basis of life and acts according to an inexorable law. Tolstoy's doctrine is a combination of extreme pessimism and extreme optimism. He also did not believe in personal immortality, just as he did not believe in a personal God; nor did he believe in man's inherent freedom. For Tolstoy, personal being is an illusory and limited being. True being is impersonal. A blissful, happy life is bought at the cost of the rejection of personhood. Tolstoy's doctrine is a typical monism. He viewed suspiciously all that was begotten by personhood. Only the being of the race is genuine. Tolstoy sought the meaning of life and God, and he sought them passionately and in great agony. But he did not believe in God; he was an unbeliever; he was possessed by the fear of death. We cannot regard as God the impersonal law of life discovered by him which will distribute the goods of life. He did not believe in grace; the pride of his reason prevented him from acquiring grace. He never became a Christian and misused the word Christianity. For him the Gospel was nothing more than one of the teachings that confirmed his own teaching.

Tolstoy had an enormous significance for the religious awakening of society, which was religiously indifferent and spiritually empty. It was this society that he addressed. He remains a great phenomenon of the Russian spirit, the Russian genius. We cannot turn away from him and forget him. Tolstoy is great because of his works of fictional art as well as because of his fate and his quest; he is not great because of his doctrine. Tolstoy was never able to actualize his ideas in life; and he revered Fyodorov, who had attained a perfect unity of doctrine and life, of idea and practice. Tolstoy was firmly planted in the earth and full of passions; his nature was more psycho-corporeal than spiritual. That explains why his aspiration towards abstract spirituality was so intense. His positive religious and moral doctrine is weighed down by rationalism and moralism. But there is a greatness in Tolstoy's yearning for the absolute and maximal actualization of truth in life, in his demand that Christianity be accepted and actualized in all its seriousness. Also remarkable is Tolstoy's departure from his old life just before his death. It is painful for us that one of the greatest Russian geniuses was excommunicated from the Church. But he himself excommunicated himself from the Church by attacking and insulting the Church's doctrines, dogmas, and sacraments; and he could not pretend that the Orthodox Church considered him one of its members. We do not know what happened to Tolstoy at the hour of his death; much that had been closed to him during his entire life might have been revealed to him. That is why we should not judge him, but should feel that we are spiritually united with him in his thirst for communion with the Truth. And those external and hypocritical Christians whom he exposes have absolutely no right to judge him.

3

The Old and New Testaments in Tolstoy's Religious Consciousness[1]

Much, perhaps too much, has been written about Tolstoy. It may seem pretentious to desire to say something new about him. It must be admitted, however, that Tolstoy's religious consciousness has never been subjected to anything like a thorough analysis or been analyzed in its substance independently of any utilitarian points of view. Some with tactical utilitarian goals praised him as a true Christian; others, also often with tactical utilitarian goals, anathematized him as a servant of the Antichrist. In both cases Tolstoy was used as a means to one's own goals, and this was an insult to this man of genius. In particular, the memory of him after his death was insulted, and his very death was turned into a utilitarian tool. Tolstoy's life, quest, and rebellious critiques are of great and worldwide importance; they must be assessed from the point of view of eternal value, not from the point of view of temporal utility. Our wish is that Tolstoy's religion be investigated and assessed without any relation to his settling of accounts with the ruling spheres and without any relation to the conflict between the Russian intelligentsia and the Church. Unlike many members of the intelligentsia, we do not wish to recognize Tolstoy as a true Christian just because he was excommunicated from the Church by the Holy Synod; nor, for the same reason, do we wish to regard him as a servant of the Devil. Instead, we are interested in the essential questions: Was Tolstoy a Christian? What was his attitude towards Christ? What was the nature of his religious consciousness? The utilitarianism of the clergy and the utilitarianism of the intelligentsia are equally alien to us and

---

1. First published in the collection *On the Religion of Leo Tolstoy*, 1912.—Trans.

equally hamper our understanding and appreciation of Tolstoy's religious consciousness. Of the extensive literature on Tolstoy one should give special mention to D.S. Merezhkovsky's very remarkable and valuable work, *L. Tolstoy and Dostoevsky*, which was the first substantive investigation of Tolstoy's religious element and religious consciousness, as well as of his paganism. It is true that Merezhkovsky used Tolstoy to further his own religious conception, but that did not prevent him from stating the truth about Tolstoy's religion.[2]

The first thing we need to say about Tolstoy is that he was an artist of genius and a man of genius, but not a religious thinker of genius. He did not have the gift of expressing in words his religious life, his religious quest. The religious element stormed in him, but it was non-verbal. Religious experiences of genius and untalented and frequently banal religious thoughts! All of Tolstoy's attempts to express in words his religious element produced only banal and gray thoughts. In essence, the Tolstoy of the first period, before his conversion, was the same as the Tolstoy of the second period, after his conversion. The world-view of Tolstoy the youth was banal and average: he wanted "to be like everyone else." And the world-view of Tolstoy the man of genius was equally banal and average: he too wanted "to be like everyone else." The only difference was that, in the first period, "everyone else" represented high society; whereas, in the second period, "everyone else" represented the peasants, the laboring people. But in the course of his entire life not only was the banally thinking Tolstoy not like everyone else, but he was like no one else—he was unique, a genius. And the religion of the Logos and the philosophy of the Logos were always alien to this genius; his religious element always remained unexpressed in words, in consciousness. Tolstoy is extraordinarily original and an extraordinary genius, and at the same time he is close to being banal and limited. This contradiction is startling.

On the one hand, we are struck by how organically and naturally he belongs to the world of high society, the world of the nobility. In his early work *Childhood, Boyhood, Youth*, we learn about his origins, his social ambitions, his ideal of the man *comme il faut*. In *War and Peace*

---

2. A psychologically valuable study of Tolstoy can also be found in Lev Shestov's book *The Idea of the Good in the Teachings of Tolstoy and Nietzsche*.

and *Anna Karenina* we see how intimately familiar he was with the "table of ranks" of the nobility, with its customs and prejudices, with all the in's and out's of this special world, and how difficult it was for him to overcome this world. In his short novel *The Cossacks*, we learn of his yearning, as a man imprisoned in the world of high society, to leave this prison and to escape into nature. In Tolstoy we feel the entire weight of the world of nobility, the law of gravitation that pulls this world down to the ground. There is no airiness or lightness in Tolstoy. He yearns to be a wanderer but, imprisoned in his family, his lineage, his estate, his noble world, he does not succeed in becoming one until the last days of his life.

On the other hand, the same Tolstoy, with an unheard-of power of negation and genius, rises against the "world," not only in the narrow sense but also in the broad sense of this word; he rises against the godlessness and nihilism not only of the whole noble society but also of the whole of "cultured" society. His rebellion and critique become a rejection of the whole of history and the whole of culture. Though permeated from childhood with the spirit of social ambition and conventionality, and worshipping the ideals of *comme il faut* and "to be like everyone else," he knew no mercy when it came to attacking the falsehood that lives in society and ripping the veils off all conventionalities. The high noble society, the aristocratic class, had to pass through Tolstoy's rejection to be purified. Tolstoy's rejection remains a great truth for this society.

There is another Tolstoyan contradiction. On the one hand, we are struck by his peculiar brand of materialism, by his apologia of animal life, by his exceptional understanding of the psychical life of the body and his failure to appreciate the life of the spirit. This animal materialism permeates not only his works of fiction, where he displays an exceptional gift, a gift of genius, for penetrating into the primary elements of life, into animal and vegetative processes;[3] it also permeates his religious and moral preaching. He preaches an elevated, moralistic

---

3. Merezhkovsky even called Tolstoy "a clairvoyant of the flesh." There is a great truth in this, although the expression bears traces of Merezhkovsky's peculiar doctrine. I would prefer to call Tolstoy a clairvoyant of the psycho-corporeal sphere of life.

materialism, an animal-vegetative happiness as the actualization of the higher, divine law of life. When he speaks of a happy life, there is nothing that would hint at spiritual life. For him there is only psychical, or psycho-corporeal, life. Nevertheless, the same Tolstoy turns out to be an adherent of extreme spirituality; he rejects the flesh and preaches asceticism. His religious and moral doctrine turns out to be some sort of unheard-of and impossible elevated moralistic and ascetic materialism, some sort of ascetic animality. His consciousness is weighed down and limited by the psycho-corporeal plane of life, and it cannot break through into the kingdom of spirit.

And there is yet another Tolstoyan contradiction. In all things he displayed an extraordinary sobriety, reasonableness, pragmatism, and utilitarianism, an absence of poetry and dreaming, a failure to understand beauty, and a dislike of it bordering on its persecution. And yet this unpoetic, soberly utilitarian persecutor of beauty was one of the world's greatest artists; this rejecter of beauty gave us creations of eternal beauty. Esthetic barbarism and coarseness were combined in him with artistic genius. Equally contradictory was the fact that Tolstoy was an extreme individualist, so antisocial that he never understood the social forms of the battle against evil or the social forms of the creative development of life and culture; he was so extreme an individualist that he rejected history. Nor did this antisocial individualist have any understanding of personhood and, remaining totally in the element of race, he in essence even rejected personhood. We shall also see that this rejection of personhood was intimately connected with his sense and consciousness of the world (here he is close to Buddhism). In *War and Peace* this extreme individualist ecstatically displayed to the world an infant's linen diaper stained green and yellow, thus showing that the consciousness of personhood had not yet overcome in him the element of race. And was it not contradictory that the world and its values were rejected with unheard-of audacity and radicalism by one who was entirely shackled to the immanent world and could not imagine another world? And was it not contradictory that a man so full of passions and rage that when the authorities searched his estate he became so furious that he demanded that the Tsar be informed about this and threatened to leave Russia forever—was it not contradictory that this man preached the meek, vegetarian ideal of non-resistance to evil? Was it not contradictory that, Russian to the marrow of his bones, with a classic Russian face combining peasant commonness with nobility, he preached an Anglo-Saxon religiosity alien to the Russian people? His entire life this man of genius sought the meaning of life, thought constantly about death, and never knew satisfaction; and yet he had virtually no sense or consciousness of transcendence, living a life limited by the horizon of the immanent world.

Finally, the most startling contradiction is that this preacher of Christianity, who was exclusively occupied with the Gospel and teaching of Christ, had no understanding of Christ's religion or of Christ's person. Tolstoy's astonishing, unfathomable contradictoriness, to which not enough attention has been paid, is the key to his genius, to his fate, which cannot be fully unriddled. The hypnosis of Tolstoy's simplicity, his almost Biblical style, conceals this contradictoriness, creating an illusion of wholeness and clarity. He was destined to play a large role in the religious rebirth of Russia and of the whole world; with a power of genius he turned contemporary minds toward religion and the religious meaning of life; he personified the crisis of historical Christianity. And he accomplished all this even though he was a rationalist, an inept religious thinker who, by the nature of his consciousness, was alien to the mysteries of Christ's religion. This rationalist, this preacher of rationalistic-utilitarian well-being, demanded from the Christian world madness in the name of the consistent fulfillment of Christ's teaching and commandments and forced the Christian world to reflect on its false and hypocritical non-Christian life. He was both an implacable foe of Christianity and a precursor of Christian rebirth. The mark of some special mission lay on the personality and life of this man of genius.

In all the periods of his life, Tolstoy's sense and consciousness of the world was non-Christian and pre-Christian. His religion was that of the Old Testament, of the hypostasis of the Father. It was not a new Christianity, but a pre-Christian Old Testament religion, preceding the Christian revelation about personhood, the revelation of the second hypostasis, that of the Son. The consciousness of personhood was alien to Tolstoy as it could only have been alien to a man of the pre-Christian epoch. He did not have a sense of the uniqueness and unrepeatability of every person or of the eternal mystery of every person's fate. For Tolstoy only the world soul existed, not individual persons; he lived in the element of the race, not in the consciousness of personhood. The element of the race, the natural soul of the world, was revealed in the Old Testament and in paganism; and the religion of pre-Christian revelation, of the hypostasis of the Father, was connected with them. The consciousness of personhood and the eternal fate of persons are connected with the Christian revelation of the hypostasis of the Son, the Logos. Every person abides religiously in the mystical atmosphere of the hypostasis of the Son, Christ, the Person. Before Christ there are as yet no persons in the deep, religious sense of the word. Persons have a definitive consciousness of themselves only in the religion of Christ. Only the Christian epoch knows the tragedy of personal fate. Tolstoy had no sense of the Christian problem of personhood; he did not see persons; for him they were swallowed up in the natural soul of the world. For that reason he also did not see the person of Christ. One who does not see any person, also does not see the person of Christ, for every person abides and is conscious of himself in Christ, in His hypostasis as the Son. The very consciousness of a person is connected with the Logos, not with the world soul.

For Tolstoy, an individualist, there is no Logos and therefore there are no persons. Indeed, all individualists, not knowing the Logos, do not know personhood; their individualism is impersonal, abiding in the natural soul of the world. We shall see how alien the Logos is to Tolstoy, how alien Christ is to him. He is not an enemy of Christ-Logos; rather, it is as if he lives in the pre-Christian epoch, or is blind and deaf. Tolstoy is cosmic; he abides entirely in the world soul, in creaturely nature; he penetrates down into the depths of its elements, its primordial elements. That explains his power as an artist, an unprecedented power. How different Tolstoy is from Dostoevsky, whose essence was anthropological, and who abided entirely in the Logos, taking personal consciousness and personal fate to extreme limits, to the point of sickness. With Dostoevsky's anthropologism, with his acute sense of personhood and its tragedy, is connected his extraordinary sense of Christ's personhood, his rapturous love for the Person of Christ. Dostoevsky had an intimate relation with Christ; Tolstoy, on the other

Old and New Testaments in Tolstoy

hand, had no relation with Christ, with Christ Himself. Christ did not exist for Tolstoy; only His teaching and His commandments existed. The pagan Goethe had a much more intimate sense of the Person of Christ than Tolstoy. Something impersonal, elemental, general obscures the Person of Christ for Tolstoy. He heard Christ's commandments, but not Christ Himself. He was unable to understand how uniquely important Christ Himself is and that only His Person, both mysterious and intimate, saves us. The Christian revelation about the person of Christ and about every person is alien to Tolstoy. Tolstoy's Christianity is impersonal, abstract, without Christ, without any persons.

Like no one before him, Tolstoy yearned to fulfill to the end the will of the Father. His entire life he was tormented by an all-embracing yearning to fulfill the law of the life of the Master who had sent him into life. He had an astonishing sense of guilt and an astonishing thirst for justice. No one yearned to fulfill the moral law more than he did. This was the main thing in him. He demanded literal fulfillment of the Sermon on the Mount. Like no one before him, he believed that the will of the Father can easily be fulfilled to the end; he did not want to believe that there was any difficulty in fulfilling the commandments. Man himself, by his own powers, must and can fulfill the will of the Father. This fulfillment is easy; it brings us happiness and well-being. Man fulfills the law of life exclusively in relation to the Father, in the religious atmosphere of the hypostasis of the Father. Tolstoy desired to fulfill the will of the Father not through the Son; he did not know or need the Son. Tolstoy did not need the religious atmosphere of God-Sonhood, the hypostasis of the Son, to fulfill the will of the Father: Tolstoy could and would fulfill the will of the Father by himself. Tolstoy thought it immoral to consider that the will of the Father can be fulfilled only through the Son, the Redeemer and Savior. Tolstoy was repelled by the idea of redemption and salvation; that is, he was repelled not by Jesus of Nazareth, but by Christ-Logos, who offered Himself in sacrifice for the sins of the world. Tolstoy's religion wants to know only the Father and does not want to know the Son; the Son interferes with Tolstoy's desire to fulfill the law of the Father by his own powers. Tolstoy consistently professed the religion of the law, the Old Testament religion. The religion of grace, the New Testament religion, was alien and unknown to him. Tolstoy was more of a Buddhist than a Christian. Like Tolstoy's religion, Buddhism is a religion of self-salvation. Buddhism does not know the person of God, the person of the Savior or the persons of those who are saved. Buddhism is a religion of compassion, not of love.

Many say that Tolstoy is a true Christian, and oppose him to the false and hypocritical Christians of whom there are so many in the world. But the existence of false and hypocritical Christians, who enact works of hatred, not works of love, does not justify a misuse of words, a playing with words that only produces falsehood. One should not call a Christian a man who was repelled by the very idea of redemption, by the very need for the Savior; that is, a man who was repelled by the very idea of Christ. The Christian world had never known such hostility towards the idea of redemption, such aversion to it as to something immoral. In Tolstoy the Old Testament religion of the law rose against the New Testament religion of grace, against the mystery of redemption. Tolstoy wanted to transform Christianity into a religion of rule, law, and moral commandment; that is, into a pre-Christian, Old Testament religion that does not know grace and that does not know or even thirst after redemption, which paganism thirsted after so greatly in its last days. Tolstoy said that it would have been better if Christianity had never existed as a religion of redemption and salvation, for then it would have been easier to fulfill the will of the Father. In his opinion, all other religions are better than the religion of Christ the Son of God, for they teach men how to live and provide them with rule, law, and commandment, whereas the religion of salvation makes everything depend not on man, but on the Savior and the mystery of redemption. Tolstoy hates the dogmas of the church because he wants a religion of self-salvation, believing that it is the only moral religion, the only religion that fulfills the will and law of the Father, whereas the dogmas stipulate salvation through the Savior, through His redemptive sacrifice. For Tolstoy salvation is possible only through Christ's commandments, fulfilled by men by their own powers. These commandments are in fact the will of the Father. The Christ who said about Himself "I am the way, the truth, and the life" is not needed by Tolstoy. Tolstoy not only wants to do without Christ the Savior, but even considers immoral any supplication to the Savior, any help from Him in fulfilling the will of the Father. The Son does not exist for Tolstoy; only the Father exists. In other words, Tolstoy lives entirely in the Old Testament; he does not know the New Testament.

Tolstoy believes it is easy to fulfill to the end, by one's own powers, the law of the Father. He believes this is easy because he does not feel or know evil and sin. He does not know the irrational element of evil, and therefore he does not need redemption and does not want to know the Redeemer. Tolstoy views evil rationalistically, Socratically, regarding it as nothing more than ignorance, as a deficiency of rational consciousness, almost as a misunderstanding. He denies the bottomless and irrational mystery of evil, which is connected with the bottomless and irrational mystery of freedom. He believes that one who has become conscious of the law of the good will, merely by virtue of this consciousness, desire to fulfill it. Evil is done only by those who lack such a consciousness. Evil is rooted not in irrational will and not in irrational freedom, but in the absence of rational consciousness, in ignorance. You can't do evil if you know what good is. Man's nature is naturally good and sinless, and does evil only out of ignorance of the law.

Goodness is what is rational. Tolstoy particularly underscores this. It is stupid to do evil; there is no point to doing evil; only good leads to the well-being of life, to happiness. It is clear that Tolstoy views good and evil in the same way that Socrates viewed it—that is, rationalistically, identifying good with what is rational and evil with what is non-rational. When men achieve rational consciousness of the law given by the Father, this will lead to the definitive triumph of good and to the eradication of evil. This will occur easily and joyfully and will be accomplished by man's own powers. Tolstoy wars against the evil and falsehood of life like no one else, and summons us to moral maximalism, to the immediate and definitive actualization of good in all things. But it turns out that his moral maximalism is connected with his misunderstanding of evil. Naively, as if in a hypnosis of genius, he does not want to know the power of evil, the difficulty of overcoming it, or the irrational tragedy connected with it. To a superficial view it might appear that Tolstoy saw the evil of life better than anyone else, that he penetrated deeper into it than anyone else. But that is an optical illusion. Tolstoy saw that people failed to obey the will of the Father who sent them into life; he regarded people as stumblers in darkness, since they live according to the law of the world, not according to the law of the Father, whom they do not know; he viewed people as irrational and insane. But he did not see evil. If he had seen evil and fathomed its mystery, he would never have said that it was easy to fulfill to the end the will of Father by man's natural powers, that good can triumph without the redemption of evil. Tolstoy did not see sin. For him, sin was only ignorance, only a failure to attain rational consciousness of the law of the Father. He did not know sin and he did not know redemption. This naïve ignorance of evil and sin led to Tolstoy's denial of the burdensomeness of world history; it led to his maximalism. Here, we arrive at where we began. Tolstoy did not see evil and sin because he did not see personhood. Consciousness of evil and sin is connected with consciousness of personhood, and consciousness of the selfhood of persons is attained in connection with the consciousness of evil and sin, in connection with persons' resistance to the natural elements, with the setting of limits. The absence of personal consciousness in Tolstoy equals absence of the consciousness of evil and sin. He did not know the tragedy of personhood—the tragedy of evil and sin. Evil cannot be defeated by consciousness and reason; it is rooted in man's deepest depths. Man's nature is not a good nature, but a fallen one; man's reason is a fallen reason. Evil can be defeated only by the mystery of redemption. But Tolstoy was filled with a kind of naturalistic optimism.

Rebelling against the whole of society, against the whole of culture, Tolstoy arrived at an extreme optimism, which denied the corruptedess and sinfulness of nature. Tolstoy believed that God alone accomplishes good in the world, and that man's only role is not to oppose His will. Everything that is natural is good. In this, Tolstoy approached Rousseau and the 18th-century theory of the natural state. Tolstoy's doctrine of the non-resistance to evil resembles the theory of the natural state as good and divine. Resist not evil, and good itself will be accomplished without any need for your activity; it will be the natural state in which the divine will, the higher law of life, which is God, is directly actualized. Tolstoy's doctrine of God is a particular form of pantheism, for which neither the personhood of God nor the personhood of man exists (or, for that matter, any personhood at all). For Tolstoy, God is not a being, but a law, the divine principle present in all things. For him, neither a personal God nor personal immortality exists. His pantheistic consciousness does not admit the existence of two worlds: an immanent natural world and a transcendent divine world. This kind of pantheistic consciousness presupposes that good, i.e., the divine law of life, is actualized in a natural and immanent way, without grace, without the intrusion of transcendent powers into this world. Tolstoy's pantheism confuses God with the world soul. But his pantheism is not consistent, and sometimes it verges on deism. After all, the God who gives the law of life but does not bestow grace, this God is the dead God of deism. Tolstoy had a powerful sense of God, but only a weak consciousness of God; he abided elementally in the hypostasis of the Father, but without the Logos.

Just as Tolstoy believed in the goodness of the natural state and in the possibility of actualizing the good by natural means in which the divine will acts, he also believed in the infallibility of natural reason. He did not see that his reason was a fallen reason. He viewed reason as sinless. He did not know that there is a reason that had fallen away from the Divine Reason and that there is a reason that is united with the Divine Reason. Tolstoy believed in naive, natural rationalism. He always appealed to reason, to the rational principle, not to will and not to freedom. In Tolstoy's rationalism, which is sometimes very crude, we find the same faith in the goodness of the natural state, in the goodness of nature and the natural. Tolstoy's rationalism and naturalism are powerless to explain deviations from reason and the natural state, but such deviations are ubiquitous in human life and they produce the evil and falsehood of life that Tolstoy attacks so powerfully. Why did humankind fall away from the good natural state and the rational law of life that reigns in that state? There must have been a falling away, a fall into sin. Tolstoy would say: all evil is caused by the fact that people walk in darkness and do not know the divine law of life. But where do this darkness and ignorance come from? We inevitably come back to the irrationality of evil as the ultimate mystery—the mystery of freedom. Tolstoy's sense of the world has something in common with Rozanov's sense of the world: Rozanov, too, does not know evil and does not see personhood. He, too, believes in the goodness of the natural; he, too, abides in the hypostasis of the Father and in the world soul, in the Old Testament and paganism. With all the differences between them, Tolstoy and Rozanov both oppose the religion of the Son, the religion of redemption.

To show the correctness of my characterization, I don't need to expound Tolstoy's doctrine in detail and systematically. His doctrine is sufficiently known by everyone. But people read books in a prejudiced way and see only what they want to see. And so, for that reason, I will present a number of vivid passages from his writings which serve to confirm my view of his doctrine. Let me first present several quotations from his fundamental religious-philosophical treatise, *What I Believe*: "It has always seemed strange to me that Christ, if He knew in advance that his teaching would be impossible to fulfill by human powers alone, would have given such clear and beautiful rules that refer directly to every individual human being. When I read these rules, it always seems to me that they refer directly to me and must be fulfilled by me alone."[4] "Christ says: I find that the way you provide for your life is very bad and stupid. I propose for you a wholly other way."[5] "It is characteristic of man's nature to do what is better. And every teaching about the life of people is only a teaching about what is better for people. If people are shown what it is better for them to do, how can they say that they want do what is better, but cannot? People can refrain from doing only what is worse, not what is better."[6] "As soon as a man reflects, he is aware that he is rational; and aware that he is rational, he cannot fail to recognize what is rational and what is not rational. Reason does not command anything; it only illuminates."[7] "Only the false idea that nonexisting things exist and existing things do not exist can cause people to so strangely deny the possibility of fulfilling what, in their own view, is good for them. The false idea that causes this is what is called dogmatic Christian faith—the faith that is taught from childhood to all those who confess the ecclesial Christian faith according to the various Orthodox, Catholic, and Protestant catechisms."[8]

---

4. From *What I Believe*, the Posrednik edition, 1906, p. 13.
5. Ibid., p. 75.
6. Ibid., p. 88.
7. Ibid., p. 89.
8. Ibid.

Also: "It is asserted that the dead continue to be alive. And since the dead cannot confirm whether they are dead or whether they are alive, just as a stone cannot confirm whether it can speak or not, this absence of denial is taken as proof, and it is asserted that people who died did not die. And it is asserted with even greater solemnity and certitude that, after Christ, by faith in Him, people are liberated from sin, i.e., that, after Christ, people do not have to illuminate their lives and choose what is best for them by their reason. They only need to believe that Christ redeemed them from sin, making them sinless, i.e., perfectly good. According to this teaching, it is necessary for people to believe that their reason is powerless and that they are therefore sinless, i.e., infallible."[9] "What this teaching calls true life is life that is personal, blissful, sinless, and eternal, i.e., a life that no one has ever known and does not exist."[10] "Adam sinned for me, that is, he *erred* [the italics are mine]."[11] Tolstoy says that, according to the teaching of the Christian Church, "true and sinless life consists in faith, i.e., in imagination, i.e., in *madness* [the italics are mine]." And after a few lines he says about the teaching of the Church: "this is complete madness."[12] "The Church's teaching gave fundamental meaning to the lives of people in the sense that they have a right to a blissful life and that this bliss is attained not by human powers, but by something external; and this world-view became the foundation of our entire science and philosophy."[13]

Also: "Reason, the thing that illuminates our lives and forces us to change our conduct, is not an illusion, and there is no way its existence can be denied. *The necessity to follow reason in order to achieve what is good—that has always been the teaching of all the true teachers of humankind, and that is the whole of Christ's teaching* [the italics are mine]; and it, reason, can in no way be denied by reason."[14] "Before and after Christ, people said the same thing: that, in human beings, there lives a

9. Ibid., pp. 91–92.
10. Ibid., p. 92.
11. Ibid.
12. Ibid., p. 93.
13. Ibid., p. 93
14. Ibid., p. 97.

divine light, come down from heaven, and this light is reason; and that it alone should be served and that in it alone is the good to be sought."[15] "People have heard and understood everything, except one thing: the teacher's message that they should by themselves make their happiness here, in this house where they have gathered. Instead, they imagine that this house is just an inn for wayfarers, and that the real house will be somewhere else."[16] "No one will help us if we do not help ourselves. . . . Do not expect anything from heaven or from earth; just stop harming yourself."[17] "In order to understand Christ's teaching it is necessary, above all, to take stock, to come to our senses."[18] "Christ never spoke about personal resurrection in the flesh."[19]

Also: "The notion of a future personal life came to us neither from Jewish teaching nor from Christ's teaching. It entered church doctrine from the side. However strange this might appear, we must say that *belief in a future personal life is a very low and crude idea, based on a confusion of sleep with death and characteristic of all primitive peoples* [the italics are mine]."[20] "To personal life Christ opposes not the afterlife, but the past, present, and future life of all humankind."[21] "Christ's entire teaching consists in the fact that His disciples, having understood the illusory character of personal life, renounced this life and transposed it into the life of all humankind, into the life of the Son of Man. However, the doctrine of the immortality of personal life not only does not summon people to renounce their own personal life, but it even establishes this personhood for all eternity. . . . Life is life, and it must be used as well as possible. It is irrational to live for oneself alone. Therefore, since the time people have existed, they have sought for life goals outside themselves: they live for their children, for their nation, for humankind, for other things that do not die with personal life."[22]

15. Ibid., p. 98.
16. Ibid., p. 102
17. Ibid., p. 103.
18. Ibid., p. 104.
19. Ibid., p. 112.
20. Ibid., p. 115.
21. Ibid., p. 118.
22. Ibid., p. 125.

"If a man does not grab hold of that which saves him, this can only mean that he has not understood his situation."[23] "Faith is produced only by a consciousness of one's situation. Faith is rooted only in our being rationally conscious of what it is best for us to do given our situation."[24] "It is a terrible thing to say, but if neither Christ's teaching nor the church teaching that is based on it existed, those who now call themselves Christians would be much closer than they are now to Christ's teaching, i.e., to a rational teaching about the good of life. The moral teachings of the prophets of all humankind would not be closed to them."[25] "Christ teaches us how to free ourselves from our misfortunes and live happily."[26]

In enumerating the conditions for happiness, Tolstoy could barely find a single condition connected with spiritual life; they're all connected with material, animal-vegetative life, such as physical work, health, and so on. "Christ does not teach us that we should be martyrs in his name. He teaches us to stop being martyrs in the name of the false teachings of the world.... *Christ teaches people not to do stupid things* [the italics are mine]. That is the simplest and most accessible meaning of Christ's teaching.... Do not do stupid things and your life will be better."[27] "Christ... teaches us not to do what is worse but to do what is best for us here, in this life."[28] "The rupture between the teaching about life and the explanation of life began with the sermons of Paul, who, not knowing the ethical teaching expounded in the Gospel of Matthew, preached a metaphysical-kabbalistic theory alien to Christ."[29] "Sacraments are the only thing a pseudo-Christian needs. But sacraments are not performed by the believer himself; they are performed over him by others."[30] "The concept of law that is indisputably rational and obligatory for all according to their inner consciousness, this concept has vanished in our society to such an extent

23. Ibid.
24. Ibid., p. 132.
25. Ibid., p. 135.
26. Ibid., p. 142.
27. Ibid., p. 150.
28. Ibid., p. 152.
29. Ibid., p. 168.
30. Ibid., p. 169.

that the existence in the Jewish nation of a law which determines their entire life and is obligatory not by coercion but by everyone's inner consciousness, is regarded as the exclusive property of the Jewish nation."[31] "I believe that the fulfillment of this teaching [of Christ] is easy and joyous."[32]

I will now present some passages from Tolstoy's letters: "I pray 'Lord, have mercy upon me, a sinner', and now my love is weaker because this prayer is an egoistical one, a prayer of personal weakness and ineffective for that reason."[33] He writes to M. A. Sopots'ko: "I have a great desire to help you deal with the dire and difficult situation in which you find yourself. I am referring to your desire to hypnotize yourself into the faith of the church. This is very dangerous because, through such hypnosis, *you will lose the most precious thing a man possesses—his reason* [the italics are mine]."[34] "One cannot introduce with impunity anything into one's faith that is irrational, anything that is unjustified by reason. Reason is given from above in order to guide us. We cannot stifle it with impunity. *To lose one's reason is the most terrible loss*" [the italics are mine].[35] "The Gospel miracles could not have occurred, because they violate the laws of that reason by means of which we understand life. Miracles are unnecessary, because they can't convince anyone of anything. In that savage and superstitious environment in which Christ lived and acted, there necessarily had to be a tradition of miracles, just as such a tradition exists today among our superstitious peasants."[36] "You ask me about theosophy. I myself had been interested in this doctrine but, unfortunately, it admits the miraculous, and to admit the miraculous even to a very slight degree deprives religion of that simplicity and clarity which characterize a true relation to God and to one's neighbor. Thus, this doctrine might contain much that is very good, as is the case with the doctrines of the mystics and even spiritism, but one should be wary of it. The main thing, in my

---

31. Ibid., p. 178.
32. Ibid., p. 186.
33. From Tolstoy's Letters, vol. 1, p. 193.
34. Ibid., p. 240.
35. Ibid., p. 246.
36. Ibid., p. 288.

opinion, is that people who need the miraculous do not yet fully understand the true, simple Christian teaching."[37]

Also: "In order that a man know what is required of him by the One who sent him into the world, the Latter placed reason in him, by which the man could always (if he desired it) know the will of God, i.e., that which is required of him by the One who sent him into the world.... If we obey what reason tells us, we will all unite, because the reason of all is one, and only reason unites people and does not hamper the manifestation of the love of one another that is characteristic of people."[38] "Reason is older and more reliable than all scriptures and traditions, and it was given to each of us directly from God before there were any scriptures or traditions. When the Gospel says that all sins will be forgiven except the blasphemy against the Holy Spirit, these words assert, in my opinion, that reason should not be believed. But if one should not believe God-given reason, then whom should one believe? Should one believe those people who want to force us to believe what does not accord with God-given reason?"[39] "We should not pray for our inner improvement, because we are given everything we need for our improvement and do not need to add anything to it."[40] "To ask God and to invent means for our improvement would be possible only if there were obstacles to this work and we were not able to accomplish it by our own powers."[41] "In this world we live as if in an inn for wayfarers where the owner set up everything that we, pilgrims, need, and then departed, leaving guidance on how we should conduct ourselves in this temporary refuge. Everything we need is here. What else is there for us to invent or to ask for? All we have to do is fulfill what has been prescribed to us. It is the same way in our spiritual world: everything we need has been given to us, and now we must accomplish the work by ourselves."[42] "There is no teaching more immoral and harmful than

---

37. Ibid., p. 327.
38. From Tolstoy's Letters, vol. 2, p. 188.
39. Ibid., p. 190.
40. Ibid., p. 191.
41. Ibid., p. 197.
42. Ibid., p. 198.

the one that says that people cannot improve themselves by their own powers."[43]

Also: "The repellent and absurd notion that human reason cannot come to the truth by its own efforts originates in a horrible superstition, just as horrible as the superstition that a man cannot fulfill God's will without help from outside. The essence of this superstition lies in the fact that the complete and perfect truth is supposedly revealed by God Himself.... This superstition is horrible.... A man stops believing in the sole means by which knowledge of the truth can be attained—the efforts of his own reason."[44] "Without reason no truth can enter a man's soul."[45] "The rational and the moral always coincide."[46] "The belief that one can commune with the souls of the dead... violates my rational world-view to such an extent that, if I heard the voices of spirits or saw them appear, I would go to see a psychiatrist and ask him to treat my obvious mental disorder."[47] "You say," he writes to the priest S.K., "that since a man is a person, then God too is a person. But it seems to me that a man's consciousness of himself as a person is a consciousness of his limitation. No limitation is compatible with the concept of God. If one allows that God is a Person, a natural consequence of this will be (as was always the case in all primitive religions) the attribution to God of human qualities.... The conception of God as a Person ... is completely impossible for me."[48] I could cite many other passages from various works to confirm my view of Tolstoy's religion, but these are sufficient.

It is clear that Tolstoy's religion is a religion of self-salvation, of salvation solely by natural and human powers. Therefore, this religion does not need the Savior; it does not know the hypostasis of the Son. Tolstoy wants to be saved by virtue of his personal merits, not by virtue of the redemptive power of the bloody sacrifice offered by the Son of God for the sins of the world. Tolstoy is guilty of pride because he does

---

43. Ibid., p. 199.
44. Ibid., p. 200.
45. Ibid., p. 201.
46. Ibid., p. 205.
47. Ibid., p. 215.
48. Ibid., p. 264.

not need God's grace to fulfill God's will. He does not need redemption, for he does not know sin and does not see that evil cannot be overcome by natural means. He does not need the Redeemer and Savior and feels like no one else that the religion of redemption and salvation is alien to him. For him, the idea of redemption is the main obstacle to fulfilling the law of the Father-Master. Christ, as the Savior and Redeemer, as "the way, the truth, and the life," is not only unnecessary; He hinders the fulfillment of the commandments that Tolstoy considers Christian. Tolstoy understands the New Testament as the law, commandment, and rule of the Father-Master; that is, he understands it to be the same as the Old Testament. He does not know the mystery contained in the New Testament—the mystery that in the hypostasis of the Son, in Christ, there is no law and no subordination to the law, but only grace and freedom. Abiding exclusively in the hypostasis of the Father, in the Old Testament and paganism, Tolstoy could never grasp the mystery that "the truth, the way, and the life" reside not in Christ's commandments, not in His teaching, but in Christ Himself, in His mysterious Person. Christ's religion is the teaching *about* Christ, not Christ's teaching. For Tolstoy, the teaching about Christ. i.e., Christ's religion, was always madness; he regarded it as would a pagan.

Here, we come to another aspect of Tolstoy's religion which is quite clear. His religion resides within the limits of reason; it is a rationalistic religion which rejects all mysticism, all sacrament, all miracle, as contrary to reason, as madness. His rational religion is close to rationalistic Protestantism, to Kant and Harnack. Tolstoy is a crude rationalist with respect to the dogmas; his critique of the dogmas is sophomorically rationalistic. He rejects with an air of triumph the dogma of the Holy Trinity on the grounds that 1 cannot equal 3. He says straight out that the religion of Christ the Son of God, the Redeemer and Savior, is madness. He is an implacable foe of the miraculous and mysterious. He rejects the very idea of revelation as meaningless. It's hard to believe that such an artist and man of genius, such a religious nature, could have been possessed by such a crude and elementary rationalism, such a demon of rationality. It seems monstrously incredible that a giant like Tolstoy could have reduced Christianity to the assertion that Christ teaches us not to do stupid things, that he teaches us how to be happy on earth. Tolstoy's religious nature, a religious nature of genius, finds itself in the grip of elementary rationalism and elementary utilitarianism. In his personal religious life, he is a mute genius, deprived of the gift of the Word. And this unfathomable mystery of his personhood is connected with the fact that he abides entirely in the hypostasis of the Father and in the world soul, outside the hypostasis of the Son, the Logos. Tolstoy was not only a religious nature who his entire life was burning up from religious thirst; he was also a mystical nature in a special sense. There is a mysticism in *War and Peace* and in *The Cossacks*, a mystical attitude towards the primary elements of life; there is also a mysticism in Tolstoy's life and fate. But his mysticism never encountered the Logos; that is, he never consciously understood his mysticism. In his religious and mystical life Tolstoy never encountered Christianity.

It is very easy to confuse Tolstoy's asceticism with Christian asceticism. It has often been said that, in its asceticism, Tolstoy's doctrine is indistinguishable from historical Christianity. Some have said this in defense of Tolstoy, others in order to castigate him. If we take Christian asceticism in its mystical essence, it has never been a preaching of the impoverishment of life, of simplification and abasement. Christian asceticism has always had in view an infinitely rich mystical world, a higher level of being. But in Tolstoy's moral asceticism, there is nothing mystical, no trace of the riches of other worlds. Just consider the degree to which the asceticism of the "little poverino" of God, St. Francis of Assisi, differs from Tolstoy's simplification. St. Francis' religion is full of beauty, and there is nothing in it resembling Tolstoy's moralism. From St. Francis the beauty of the early Renaissance was born. For him, poverty was the Beautiful Lady. Tolstoy did not have the Beautiful Lady. He preached the impoverishment of life in the name of a happier and more prosperous organization of life on earth. Alien to him was the idea of the messianic feast which mystically animates Christian asceticism. Tolstoy's moral asceticism is an asceticism of populism, so characteristic for Russia. In our land a special type of asceticism has evolved, not a mystical asceticism but an asceticism of populism, an asceticism in the name of the well-being of the people on earth. We encounter this type of asceticism in an aristocratic form, among repentant noblemen, as well as in a form typical of the intelligentsia, among populists. It is typically associated with attacks against beauty, metaphysics, and mysticism as impermissible and immoral luxuries. In religion, it leads to iconoclasm and the rejection of cultic symbolism.

Tolstoy was an iconoclast. Icon-veneration and the associated cultic symbolism seemed to him an immoral and impermissible luxury, forbidden by his moral-ascetic consciousness. He did not admit the existence of sacred luxury and sacred riches. This artist of genius regarded beauty as an immoral luxury, as riches forbidden by the Master of life. The Master of life gave us the law of the good; and only the good is valuable; only the good is divine. The Master of life did not place before man and the world the ideal image of beauty as the supreme goal of being. Beauty is from the Devil; only the moral law is from the Father. Tolstoy was a persecutor of beauty in the name of the good. He asserted that the good is superior not only to beauty but also to the truth. In the name of the exclusivity of the good he rejected not only esthetics but also metaphysics and mysticism as ways to know the truth. Both beauty and truth are luxuries, forbidden riches. The feast of esthetics and the feast of metaphysics are forbidden by the Master of Life. People must live exclusively according to the simple law of the good, the moral law. Moralism had never been taken to such extremes. Moralism begins to scare and stifle us. After all, beauty and truth are not less divine than the good, not less valuable. The good has no right to proclaim itself superior to beauty and truth; beauty and truth are just as close as the good to God, the Source of all things. Abstract moralism taken to the final extreme makes us think that there can exist a demonic good, a good that devitalizes and destroys being. If demonic beauty and demonic knowledge can exist, then demonic good too can exist. Taken in its deepest mystical depths, Christianity not only does not reject beauty, but it creates an unprecedented new beauty; and not only does it not reject gnosis, but it creates a higher gnosis. Rationalists and positivists are more apt than others to reject beauty and gnosis, and they often reject them in the name of an illusory good. Tolstoy's moralism is connected with his religion of self-salvation, with his rejection of the ontological meaning of redemption. However, though one side of Tolstoy's ascetic moralism is directed at the impoverishment and suppression of being, another side of it is directed at a new world and boldly rejects evil.

THE BRIGHTEST LIGHTS OF THE SILVER AGE

In Tolstoy's moralism there is an inert, conservative element as well as a revolutionary element. Tolstoy rebelled with unprecedented power and radicalism against the hypocrisy of the pseudo-Christian society and against the falsehood of the pseudo-Christian state. He brilliantly exposed the monstrous untruth and moribund character of the official Christianity; he placed a mirror before the hypocritical and moribund Christian society and horrified those with an acute conscience. As a religious critic and seeker, he will remain forever great and dear to us. However, in our religious renaissance his main achievement was his negative criticism. He labored immeasurably to awaken us from our religious hibernation, but he did not deepen our religious consciousness. It should be remembered, however, that his seekings and criticism were directed at a society that was openly atheistic or hypocritically Christian or simply indifferent. It was impossible to cause any religious harm to this society; it was already thoroughly harmed. And it was useful and important to shake up our moribund and over-ritualized Orthodoxy.

Tolstoy is the most consistent and extreme anarchist-idealist in the history of human thought. It is very easy to refute his anarchism, which combines extreme rationalism with outright madness. But the world needed his anarchistic rebellion. The "Christian" world had become so false in its foundations that there was an irrational need for such a rebellion. I think that, though it was irrational, Tolstoy's anarchism, serving to purify society, was enormously important. His anarchistic rebellion signified a crisis of historical Christianity, a watershed in the life of the Church. This rebellion prepared the way for the coming Christian rebirth. And it remains a rationally unfathomable mystery why the task of Christian rebirth should have been served by a man who was alien to Christianity, who abided entirely in the pre-Christian, Old Testament element.

His final fate remains a mystery known only to God. It is not for us to judge. Tolstoy himself excommunicated himself from the Church, and the fact of excommunication by the Holy Synod paled before this fact of self-excommunication. His excommunication was abominable because the Synod excommunicated the man who did more than anyone else to awaken the religious sense in Russia. But we do not dare say

Old and New Testaments in Tolstoy

anything about the mystery of his final relations with the Church and about what happened at the hour of his death. We do know that with his criticism, seekings, and life, Tolstoy awakened a world that was religiously asleep and moribund. Several generations of Russians passed through Tolstoy and grew under his influence; and God forbid that this influence should be equated with "Tolstoyism," which is a very limited phenomenon. Without Tolstoy's criticism and seekings we would have been worse and would have awakened later. Without Tolstoy the question of the living (not rhetorical) significance of Christianity would never have been posed so acutely. The false and hypocritical "Christian" world needed Tolstoy's Old Testament truth. We also know that, without Tolstoy, Russia is inconceivable and that Russia cannot renounce him. We love Tolstoy as we do our motherland. We find our forebears and our land in *War and Peace*. Tolstoy is our riches and our luxury—he, who hated riches and luxury. Tolstoy's life is a unique fact of genius in the life of Russia. And every fact of genius is providential. Tolstoy's "departure" before his death agitated all of Russia and the whole world. It was a "departure" of genius. It was the culmination of Tolstoy's anarchistic rebellion. Before his death, Tolstoy became a pilgrim; he tore himself away from the earth in which he had been rocted with all the weight of everydayness. At the end of his life, the great elder returned to mysticism; mystical notes sounded more strongly and drowned out his rationalism. He was preparing himself for the final revolution.

4
Vladimir Solovyov's Fundamental Idea[1]

Everyone more or less agrees that Vladimir Solovyov was the greatest Russian thinker. But our generation[2] does not feel any gratitude for his heroic spiritual accomplishments; nor does it understand and revere his spiritual image. And it must be acknowledged that Solovyov's image remains enigmatic. His philosophy, theology, and social and political writings served more to hide the contradictions of his spirit than to reveal his spiritual image. There was a Solovyov of the daytime and a Solovyov of the nighttime. And the contradictions of the nighttime Solovyov were reconciled only outwardly in the consciousness of the daytime Solovyov. It would be correct to say about him that he was both a mystic and a rationalist, both an Orthodox and a Catholic, both a man of the Church and a free gnostic, both a conservative and a liberal. Opposite movements regarded him as an adherent. But during his lifetime and after his death he was, and remains, a solitary and misunderstood figure. He had a universal mind and attempted to overcome contradictions in a concrete all-unity. His creative labor was rich with ideas and embraced a great multiplicity of problems.

But he had a single central idea which was the passion of his life and with which his understanding of Christianity was connected. This idea permeated both his nighttime mysticism and poetry and his daytime philosophy and social writings. This idea was divine-humanity. Solovyov was, above all, a defender of man and of humanity. The

---

1. First published in 1925 in the magazine *Perezvon*, nos. 178 and 179, on the occasion of the 25th anniversary of Solovyov's death.—Trans.

2. Written in 1925.—Trans.

entire originality of the Christian task of Solovyov's life consisted in the fact that he returned to the faith of the Fathers and became a defender of Christianity after the humanistic experiment of modern history, after the self-assertion of human freedom in knowledge, creative activity, and social and political organization. He assimilated this experiment into his own depths and, after overcoming its evil fruits, he brought what had been experienced into his Christian world-view. For him, human freedom and activity are an inalienable part of Christianity. For him, Christianity is a religion of divine-humanity, presupposing not only faith in God but also faith in man. Into Christianity he introduced the principle of development and progress, and he defended freedom of mind and conscience to the same degree as the Slavophiles, differing in this respect from Catholicism. For him the essence of Christianity consists in the free union of two natures, divine and human, in divine-humanity. Man is the connecting link between the divine world and the natural world.

There were several periods in Solovyov's creative activity, and they must be distinguished if we are to understand the complexity of his world-view. But at the center of all the periods stood the problem of the active expression of the human principle in divine-humanity. The first period, which includes his *Lectures on Divine Humanity*, is characterized by an extremely optimistic view of world history and of the pathways of the actualization of universal theocracy. He does not notice the tragic character of world history and believes that the Kingdom of God can be realized through progressive evolution. His starting point is the crisis of contemporary atheistic civilization, the crisis of positivism which this civilization engendered in human consciousness and the crisis of socialism which it engendered in social life. He desires to religiously overcome this crisis and believes that the key to overcoming it lies in free theocracy. But he also believes that the falling away of natural human powers from God had a positive significance, for after this falling away the *free* union of man with God became possible. The Kingdom of God cannot be realized by compulsion and violence. Compulsory theocracy had to fall, and man had to enter onto the path of the free disclosure of his powers. Solovyov thinks that the world must pass through freedom and freely come to God. He himself passed through the school of German idealism, which was a school of the freedom of thought and which was as important for Russian religious thought as Greek philosophy, especially Platonism, had been for eastern patristics.

Solovyov always understood Christianity not only as something given but also as a task that man needs to accomplish through his freedom and activity. That is Solovyov's great achievement. Christ's work in the world consists, above all, in love. And it is Solovyov's belief that works of love are needed not only for justification by works or by faith but also for the realization of the Kingdom of God. "Humanity," he wrote, "must not only receive the grace and truth given in Christ; it must also actualize this grace and truth in its own personal and historical life." "The establishment of the Church and of Christian culture in the world requires, in addition to government by a universal authority, the free activity of personal human forces." In divine-humanity there must occur collectively the same union of two natures that occurred individually in the God-man, Christ. In his initial schema Solovyov thought that divine-humanity would result from the union of the divine principle, which has found its preeminent expression in the East, with the human principle, which has found its preeminent expression in the West. He asserted this when he was still close to Slavophilism. His attraction to Catholicism was determined by his conviction that organized human activity is stronger in Catholicism, whereas Orthodoxy is too passive. This attraction was determined outwardly, not inwardly, by the dogmatic system of Catholicism. Solovyov placed a great value on the idea of the dogmatic development of the Church, in which he saw a manifestation of human activity; and he saw more of this development in the West than in the East. In his attraction to the idea of dogmatic development he resembled Cardinal Newman, the most remarkable Catholic personality of the 19th century. "The essential and fundamental difference between our religion and other eastern religions, particularly Islam," Solovyov wrote, "consists in the fact that Christianity is a divine-human religion, presupposing divine activity while also requiring human activity. In this respect, the realization of the Kingdom of God depends not only on God but also on us, for it is clear that the spiritual regeneration of humanity cannot occur apart from humanity itself; it is a work that has been assigned to us, a problem we must solve."

Solovyov believed that humanity is a real being. This is connected with the most intimate side of his religious philosophy, his doctrine of Sophia. For him Sophia is, above all, ideal and perfect humanity. Humanity is the center of the world's being. And Sophia is the soul of the world. Sophia, the world soul, humanity, is dual in her nature: divine and creaturely matter. There is no sharp distinction between the natural and the supernatural, as is the case in Catholic theology, in Thomism. Humanity is rooted in the divine world. And every individual human being is rooted in the universal heavenly man, in the Adam Kadmon of the Kabbalah. The sophianic world soul is free. She pre-eternally fell away from God and must freely return to God. God is that which exists absolutely. Humanity, which in and through Christ becomes the divine-humanity, is an absolutely becoming entity. The appearance of Christ is the appearance of the New Adam, the new spiritual man; His appearance is the new day of creation, an anthropological and cosmogonic process. Solovyov finds completely alien the judicial concept of redemption which plays such an important role in official Catholic theology. With respect to redemption, he is closer to eastern than to western patristics. Before Christ the world process was advancing toward the coming of the God-man. After Christ the world process is advancing toward the coming of divine-humanity. Solovyov introduces an evolutionary element into the concept of the God-man as well as into the concept of divine-humanity. A series of theophanies prepared the way for the coming of the God-Man. The fructification of the divine mother, the Church, by the human principle had to produce the deified humanity. For Solovyov the idea of the incarnation of God was always more significant than the idea of redemption. He never understood Christianity exclusively as a religion of personal salvation; he always understood it as a religion of the transfiguration of the world, a social and cosmic religion. The Church is *not only* the divine-human foundation for the salvation of *individuals*; she is also the divine-human economy for the salvation of "this world." Solovyov ascribed an enormous significance to Judaism precisely because it expresses the activity of the personal human principle, because its religious life is a drama between man and God.

Solovyov's religious affirmation of the human principle is connected with his understanding of the *prophetic* ministry, with the idea of free prophetic activity which is necessary for the fullness of the Christian life. His conception of theocracy presupposes the existence of prophets and of the prophetic ministry. The prophetic function in spiritual life is what constitutes free spiritual creativity. The prophet is a divinely inspired human being, and his prophetic mission constitutes a free inspiration without which religious life stagnates. Priesthood is the conservative foundation of religious life, the eternal foundation of the Church's life. Prophecy, in contrast, is the creative principle, the principle of movement directed at the future. The theme of the possibility of prophecy in Christianity was an intimate theme of Solovyov's entire spiritual life. He was conscious of himself as being called to the free prophetic mission. He was solitary and misunderstood because of his prophetic ministry. A prophet is always solitary, always in conflict with the religious collective. In his deepest depths a prophet dwells in the Church and in sobornost. But he is the organ of creative development in the Church and he therefore breaks with the inert forms of the Church's collective life. He is directed toward the unknown future. The dogmatic development of the Church is connected with the prophetic function of her life.

Solovyov regarded progress as a Christian principle opposed to inertia in the Church. In his essay "On the Decline of the Medieval Worldview," a essay which had stirred up a commotion and provoked harsh attacks against him, he exposed the semi-pagan character of Medieval Christianity and asserted that humanitarian progress and political reforms which produce social truth and justice are forms of the realization of Christian principles. He always demanded that Christianity be accepted in its full seriousness and actualized in all aspects of life, personal as well as social. This is a fundamental theme of his, and he remained faithful to it his entire life. He could never reconcile himself to the fact that Christians found it possible to be guided by Christian principles and commandments in their personal lives, whereas in social and historical life they were guided by zoological principles, by principles diametrically opposed to Christianity. He preached an indisputable truth of Christian morality, namely that Christians must, above all, strive to improve themselves and to fulfill Christ's commandments, instead of hating and persecuting non-Christians. He applied this Christian truth to the Jewish problem. Christians must treat Jews in a

Christian manner, showing them an example of Christianity being realized in life. In an essay entitled "The Idea of Humanity in Auguste Comte," Solovyov insists again on his favorite idea that humanity is half of divine-humanity and that veneration of humanity is part of the Christian religion. He affirms that Comte's cult of the Higher Being, or Humanity, is similar to the cult of the Madonna and to the cult of Sophia in Russia, which is reflected in Russian iconography. Comte's sin was a sin against the Son of Man (which will be forgiven), not a sin against the Holy Spirit (which will not be forgiven). "When the empowered representatives of Christianity concentrate their attention on the fact that our religion is, above all and par excellence, a divine-human religion and that *humanity* is not an appendix but an essential and formative half of *divine-humanity*, they will then resolve to exclude from their historical pantheon various inhuman things that got into it by accident over the centuries and to include a few more things that are human." And Solovyov proposes that the name Auguste Comte be included in the Christian pantheon. There is much truth in Solovyov's fundamental idea here. But he does not notice that, whereas humanity is half of divine-humanity, the cult of humanity torn away from God and directed against God is not half of divine-humanity, but a religion opposed to Christianity.

Solovyov was a particular kind of Christian humanist. Christianity, as the religion of divine-humanity, is immeasurably higher than humanism; but, nevertheless, humanism is immeasurably higher than bestialism. Many Christians, however, defend a politics of bestialism. Solovyov battled against this attitude his entire life, but in doing so, he sometimes simplified the complexity of the problem. He was not completely free of the illusions of progress, underrated the power of evil in the world, and had too evolutionary a view of the realization of the Kingdom of God. When we conceive of the actualization of theocracy as the result of a necessary development, we reject human freedom, which can be produced not only by good but also by evil. Solovyov's universal theocracy is a compete utopia, which he himself rejected in the last period of life. Toward the end of his life he wrote his most profound work, "A Short Tale about the Antichrist," in which the historical perspective vanishes, the boundary between the two worlds is obliterated, and everything is seen in an apocalyptic light. An eschatological conception of Christianity replaces the historical conception. Solovyov stops believing in historical tasks and no longer expects the historical actualization of theocracy. An extreme optimism is replaced by an extreme pessimism. Solovyov conceives of the Antichrist as a philanthropist, a lover of mankind, who establishes socialism and universal peace and happiness. This is reminiscent of Dostoevsky's Grand Inquisitor. Solovyov sees the growth of evil under the guise of good, evil that tempts and seduces good. All power passes to the Antichrist. The unification of the churches takes place at the end of time beyond history, in the apocalyptic plane. The Orthodox elder John is the first to recognize the Antichrist, thus confirming the special acuteness of the mystical sense in Orthodoxy.

The entire task of Solovyov's life sets an excruciating problem before the Christian consciousness. Christians must actualize Christ's truth in the world with all the powers of their spirit, not only in their personal lives but also in social life; they must aspire toward the Kingdom of God not only in heaven but also on earth; but the Kingdom of God on earth can easily turn out to be a trick and deception, the kingdom of the Antichrist, a temptation in the form of good. After all, communism too tempts people because it appears to aspire toward the actualization of social truth, whereas it is actually a work of the Antichrist, an ape mimicking the Christian truth. It would seem that the modern period has not produced any heresies comparable to those of the early centuries of Christianity, that this period has been indifferent to dogmatic questions. But it has in fact produced one great heresy, the heresy of *humanism*, a heresy of religious anthropology which is possible only within the Christian world. Each heresy has left a particular important and unresolved problem in the Church's consciousness, a problem to which it offered a false solution; and each heresy has provoked a creative development of the Church's thought, leading to a positive resolution of the problem. The truth about man and about his creative vocation in the world had not yet been fully disclosed in Christianity, and this provoked a free self-assertion of man in modern history. This problem is also one of Christian culture and Christian society. Solovyov accomplished a great deal when it came to formulating the religious problem of man and mankind, but he did not always solve it correctly. He was among those who believed in the prophetic mission of Christianity, and he prepared the way for a positive resolution of the problem of religious anthropology.

When the hour comes when the Church will find a solution which overcomes humanism inwardly, not outwardly, in that hour Solovyov will be remembered differently than he is remembered now; and he will be recognized as a great laborer on the pathways of the actualization and fulfillment of Christ's Church.

5

The Problem of East and West in the Religious Consciousness of Vladimir Solovyov[1]

I

There is something enigmatic and ambiguous about Solovyov. He captivates and repels us at the same time. We recognize that his immeasurable, prophetic significance is a great phenomenon in the life of Russia and of the world. All you have to do is look at his portraits to see how extraordinary, otherworldly, and unique he was. But we feel annoyance and repulsion when we read his philosophical and theological treatises. We are struck unpleasantly by how rationalistically this mystic writes, by how he blunts all contradictions and smooths over anything that is thorny or paradoxical. Everything is too smooth, precise, and schematic in his philosophy and theology. Religious life, however, is full of contradictions; it is antinomic by its very nature. And the paradoxicality of one's philosophizing can be an accurate reflection of the antinomic character of one's religious experience. Solovyov wrote as if he was unaware of abysses and contradictions, as if his inner life was in perfect order. But we know that, deep down, he was a mystic, full of contradictions in his religious experience and paradoxical in his disordered private life. We know that there was a Solovyov of the daytime and a Solovyov of the nighttime. It is very clear to us that in his philosophical and theological schemata Solovyov did not disclose himself, but closed himself up. The real Solovyov must be sought in individual

---

1. First published in the collection *On Vladimir Solovyov*, Moscow, 1911.—Trans.

lines of his writings and between the lines, in individual verses and in his essays. His genius is revealed most clearly in his poems, in the "Tale about the Antichrist," in such amazing essays as "The Meaning of Love" and "Tyutchev's Poetry," and in portions of such larger works as *The History and the Future of Theocracy;* in these writings, instead of an extreme schematism, we find profound mystical insights. Though they are more celebrated and contain much that is brilliant and useful, his longer philosophical, theological, and socio-political writings are not works of genius; they do not speak of ultimate things but instead rationalistically conceal the irrational mystery of Solovyov's life.

We are struck by a particular contradiction in Solovyov, a fundamental one for him. There was something ethereal about him; he was detached from everyday life. He was not organically connected with anything; he did not grow out of the earth, had no roots in its soil. He came to us from other worlds; he was a foreigner to almost everyone, not kindred in the flesh to anyone. He knew kinship only in the spirit, not in flesh and blood. How earthy and organic, as if he had climbed out of the deepest recesses of Russian life and Russian history, seems Tolstoy in comparison to the foreigner and wanderer Solovyov, about whom one sometimes wondered whether or not he was Russian. And here Tolstoy anarchically rejects all that is historical, organic, earthy, inherited from our ancestors, throwing down a challenge to all that which is born in the womb of his native land; whereas Solovyov justifies everything and finds a place for everything: for the Russian state, for nationality, for war, for everything. He accepts the traditions of the ancestors, wants to be faithful to those traditions, does not rebel against anything, does not break with anything. His book *The Justification of the Good* contains a virtuoso justification and defense of all that is organically created by history, of all historical institutions. But it remains an enigma why such an ethereal, unearthly man is justifying and defending all the historical things that have grown out of the earth and are organically connected with the soil. Rational and irrational motives are mysteriously interwoven in Solovyov.

Solovyov's life and work can be divided into several periods. The last period differs sharply from the preceding ones. In the first period, when he wrote his large, more systematic philosophical and theological treatises, he was very much a gnostic-idealist, and his Christianity was rosy and optimistic. He did not yet feel the whole horror and power of evil; he did not see the tragedy that was connected with evil. His understanding of evil was not mystical but overly rationalistic; interpreting it gnostically, he had not yet come to the final mystery of evil, of bottomless, foundationless, irrational, unfathomable evil, engendered from freedom. It even seems that he almost regarded evil as something of a misunderstanding, as a deficiency of perfection, as an error of consciousness, and therefore as something that could be easily defeated. Typical of this period are his *Lectures on Divine Humanity*, a highly scholastic work in which mysticism is rationalized, a work which interweaves a theory of humankind's progress with the profound mystical idea of divine humanity and presents a theological interpretation of optimistic progress, as it were. In *The Lectures on Divine Humanity*, things are still too perfect; there is no tragic end or horror before the end. An optimistic attitude towards evil colored the entire first period of Solovyov's work. In this period, rational philosophy and rational theology eclipsed his mysticism. His religious consciousness was enriched with a progressive humanism. He believed that the Christian truth can be easily achieved on earth, in human life; believing in a Christian politics and summoning people to implement it, he developed a theory and practice of Christian progress towards the good. Solovyov underrated the power of evil and sin. But life struck him with blow after blow, with wound after wound, destroying all his rosy hopes. Evil took revenge on him for not sufficiently recognizing and respecting it. His solitude in this world grew and grew. He could not make common cause with anyone or with anything.

In his middle period he primarily devoted himself to the writing of militant social criticism, in which he battled against empirical evil. In the last period of his life, a period when he returned to his fundamental religious and philosophical themes, he was filled with an apocalyptic horror of the growing power of evil and of the imminent and final incarnation of evil. He felt that history was falling into a dark abyss, destroying his rosy faith in the possibility of a Christian politics and in the actualization of Christ's truth on earth—his faith in theocracy. Even the idea of divine humanity was shaken in him, creating a rupture in this idea between transcendental Christianity and immanent humanism. Most typical for this period are the *Three Conversations* with their

"Tale about the Antichrist." His consciousness was filled with apocalyptic nightmares and he posed eschatological problems. We shall see that Solovyov posed his fundamental problem of East and West differently in the different periods. It is always important to remember that, just as there is a Solovyov of the daytime and a Solovyov of the nighttime, there is also a Solovyov of the first period and a Solovyov of the last period.

Solovyov's most striking characteristic—a deep-seated characteristic which he retained his entire life—was his sense of *universality*, his universalism. He had no individualism in him, no particularism. All schism, all splintering, was abhorrent to him. He could never belong to any school or party, to any movement or circle. Russian life and thought of the second half of the 19th century did not know another man so universal, who concerned himself only with Russia, humanity, the world soul, the Church, and God, and not with parties and movements. Because of his universality, people still don't know what camp to stick Solovyov in; they are still debating whether he was a Slavophile or a Westernizer, Orthodox or Catholic, conservative or liberal. The truth is that he was a universalist; that was his distinguishing characteristic. He was neither a Slavophile nor a Westernizer, neither Orthodox nor Catholic, because his entire life he truly abided in the universal Church. He lived in unity with the world soul, which, like a faithful knight, he wished to liberate from captivity.[2] Dostoevsky's words that the Russian is preeminently a universal man are most applicable to Solovyov.

This Russian longing for universal humanity, for universality, serves as the basis for posing the problem of East and West. The problem of East and West, the problem of unifying the two worlds into a Christian all-unity, into a divine humanity, was Solovyov's fundamental problem, and it tormented him his entire life. But what makes Solovyov great, as well as greatly significant, is the fact that the problem of East and West is not only his fundamental problem, but also Russia's fundamental

---

2. See Alexander Blok's essay "The Knight-Monk."

problem: it is a problem not only of the Russian philosophy of history, but also of Russian history. The Russian national consciousness of self was born in the posing of the problem of East and West. And, in the course of the entire 19th century, Russian thought struggled with this problem. The centrality of this problem is attested by the struggle between the Slavophiles and the Westernizers, a struggle which permeates Russian literature, Russian philosophy, and Russian political and social life. Slavophilism was our first Russian experiment at a national consciousness and national ideology. The Slavophiles posed the problem of East and West as, above all, a religious problem; and Russian creative thought followed the direction set by the Slavophiles. Russia is the third Rome. This proud consciousness passes through almost all of Russian history. And in the 19th century, the century of national consciousness par excellence, Russia—in the persons of her greatest thinkers and creative geniuses—tried to understand her sense of herself as the third Rome. The problem of East and West is connected with Russian messianism, which takes different forms. For Solovyov, Russian messianism was connected with his longing for the unification of the Churches. Though his starting point was the Slavophiles and Dostoevsky, he fundamentally diverged from them here.

Solovyov became well known as a critic of Slavophilism and its sins, as a foe of nationalism. His *National Question* was more widely read than any of his other books and gained for him wide popularity. In this book he is Westernizer, a reputation that was further confirmed by his Catholic sympathies. Nevertheless, in his origins Solovyov is a Slavophile. From the Slavophiles he inherited his themes and his faith in Russia's great mission. Like the Slavophiles, he emphasized the centrality of the Christian faith; the religious theme became the dominant theme of his thought. And the Slavophile problem of East and West became his fundamental problem. At the center of his world-view and his relation to life he placed the Slavophile rejection of "abstract principles" and the affirmation of the integral life of the spirit. With respect to his basic ideas and themes, Solovyov belongs to the Slavophile current in the history of our thought. By contrast, the Russian Westernizers did not share these themes. Russian messianism is always a form of Slavophilism, even if it has a Westernizing flavor. Solovyov had a family quarrel with the Slavophiles. He published his new conception of Russia's mission in Aksakov's *Rus'*.[3] He represented a new consciousness in Slavophilism, a more developed form of the latter. If Solovyov had not introduced this new development in Slavophilism, the latter would have gradually died out. It was dying out in its faithful epigones and finding a new development only in Dostoevsky and Solovyov, who had assimilated everything that was great and vital in Slavophilism.

It must be stated, however, that Solovyov's conception differs profoundly from the traditional Slavophile conception and he solves the problem of East and West in a different manner. In the person of Solovyov, Russian messianism thus entered into an utterly new phase. Solovyov's attitude towards the West and towards Catholicism was completely different from that of the Slavophiles. He was closer to Chaadaev. The Slavophiles believed that the fullness and integrity of the Christian truth were contained in the East, in eastern Orthodoxy, in Russia, as the guardian of Orthodoxy. In the West and in Catholicism the Slavophiles saw only a betrayal of the Christian truth, a violation of spiritual integrity, a rationalistic sundering. They had no need of a unification of the eastern Orthodox world with the western Catholic world, since Orthodoxy contained the fullness of truth, whereas Catholicism was nothing more than a deviation from this truth. The higher type of Christian culture was possible only in the Orthodox East, in Russia. Western culture is anti-Christian, rationalistic, and therefore false and in the process of degeneration. We can learn nothing from the West. For the Slavophiles, Russian messianism meant that only Russia was destined to have a great future, since she was the only Christian country. They believed that the Russian people were God's chosen people, and at times their messianism was reminiscent of ancient Jewish messianism. Slavic culture was destined to supplant the western cultures, which were declining and dying out. The only unification that could be considered was the return of Catholicism to the Orthodox Church, the return of the lost sheep into the womb of the Church. The West does not possess independent principles that have significance for the fullness of the truth. The Slavophiles regarded the eastern Christian world as universally human. Solovyov sensed the

---

3. A Slavophile journal.—Trans.

danger in this Slavophile national self-assertion; he knew where this conceited self-assurance was leading. He understood that Slavophilism's fundamental error and one-sidedness consisted in a false relation to Catholicism, in ecclesiastical particularism and nationalism. The identification of the Orthodox Church with the Russian nationality seemed monstrous to him. He saw the great truth of Catholicism and felt a longing for Catholicism. For him the problem of East and West was the problem of mutual fulfillment, the problem of uniting two one-sided truths into a higher fullness. Russia's great mission was to overcome by love and self-renunciation the sin of the millennium-long conflict between East and West, to overcome this enmity which more than anything else was preventing Christ's work from being accomplished on earth. Solovyov always opposed the universal Logos to the power of the national element. Ecclesiastical nationalism and particularism always result from the dominance of the national element, the feminine element, over the Logos, the universal, masculine element.

Solovyov's great truth consisted in the fact that his longing for western Catholicism was a longing for a free and militant Church. He yearned for a Church that would have an active relation to history and to society. He was captivated by the activeness of Catholicism and repelled by the passiveness of Orthodoxy. In one of his poems he wrote:

> But before the dragon's open jaws
> You understood: the cross and the sword are one.

Holy war was dear to Solovyov's heart. He justified with great force the religious and moral meaning of war. But the "sword" is not a just a symbol of war in the strict sense; it also symbolizes a militant struggle against evil and a militant defense of truth. Solovyov possessed this spirit of knighthood, and he was tormented by the absence of the knightly spirit in the Orthodox East. With his usual tendency toward schematic thinking he saw the East as the realm of an inhuman god and the West as the realm of godless man. This had its origin in the pre-Christian separation of East and West but also left its mark on the schism between eastern and western Christianity. The East and eastern Christianity retained the dominance of divinity over humanity, whereas the West was marked by the dominance of humanity over divinity. But the religion of Christ is a perfect union of the divine and the human; it is a religion of divine humanity. Solovyov was tormented by what he considered the Monophysitic tendencies of the East. He yearned for the fullness of the Christian truth about divine humanity, about the perfect transformation of human will into Divine will, about the perfect deification of humanity. The union of the human and the divine that was accomplished in the person of Christ had to be accomplished in all of humanity. Christ is the God-Man and the Church is the divine humanity. Before Christ the world was advancing toward the God-man; after Christ it is advancing toward divine humanity. Christianity saves not individual souls, but humanity and the world. To Solovyov it seemed that the idea of divine humanity was more clearly expressed in the West, in Catholicism, than in the East. It seemed to him that Catholicism's ecclesiastical organization was adapted to the active divine-human process of history. He was captivated by Catholicism's anthropologism and by the West's humanism. The East's passiveness, the complete absence of human activity in it, led to Byzantinism and to the Russian Old Believers, and even in Russian Orthodoxy it led to nationalism and particularism, to the enslavement of the universal Church by the state and by the national element. Solovyov saw the East as exclusively possessing a religiosity of contemplation and prayer and the West as possessing a religiosity of activeness and toil. The East does not possess an ecclesiastical organization and unity that make possible the active and militant actualization of Christ's truth on earth, in the earthly history of humanity—that is, that make possible the divine-human process. The West, in Catholicism, does possess such a unity and organization, and that was what most attracted Solovyov and convinced him of the truth of Catholicism. Peter, the rock of the Church, is necessary for the actualization of Christ's Kingdom. And Solovyov bowed down before the Peter of the Catholic Church, before the high priest of Rome, before the active and militant hierarchical order of the West. He decisively and triumphantly rejected as a heresy the Slavophiles' national-Orthodox view of Catholicism. The opinion of the theologians is not the opinion of the Church. The universal Church could not have condemned Catholicism as a heresy if only because, after the schism of the Churches, no ecumenical councils took place.

But Solovyov's fundamental error was that he ascribed too much significance to a formal agreement between the Vatican and the Russian Synod[4] and Russian government. He saw the unification of the Eastern and Western Churches, first and foremost, as the union of the Christian Tsar with the Pope of Rome, as a theocratic union of kingdom and priesthood. He worked out plans for such a union. In his French book *La Russie et l'église universelle* he defended the papacy with the usual Catholic arguments, such as could be found in the works of any Catholic theologian. The only original thing was that these arguments were made by a Russian. In this book Solovyov is essentially an adherent of the Medieval papal theocracy.[5] In this book, which is remarkable because of the universal spirit which permeates it, one is unpleasantly struck by the abundance of scholasticism, of scholastic schematism and formalism. Solovyov understands the Church's hierarchical order too formally and likens it unduly to a secular government. He shared this Catholic tendency to liken the Church to a secular government. In the depths of his mystical experience he was a member of the universal Church; he was both Orthodox and Catholic, aspiring toward the Church of the future. But on the surface of his consciousness and in practice he was a "Uniate," i.e., an adherent of formal contracts and agreements. First and foremost, he wanted the Orthodox Church to be formally subordinate to the Pope, the vicar of Peter. The unity of the universal Church depended for Solovyov on the formal subordination of the ecclesiastical hierarchy to the Pope. He was lead astray by his conception of the Church as a priestly authority. Solovyov's letter to Archbishop Josef Strossmaier is typical of his Uniate leanings. In this letter he wrote that in the Russian people the Pope would acquire a pious people. But Khomiakov was right when he said that a Uniate was impossible. The formal contracts and agreements of a Uniate, mutual concessions and claims made to

---

4. The Most Holy Governing Synod was the highest governing body of the Russian Orthodox Church between 1721 and 1918.—Trans.

5. In an unpublished letter Solovyov wrote to L. P. Nikiforov: "I have nothing to say about my French books. Their fate doesn't interest me much. Though they contain nothing contrary to objective truth, I have long outgrown the subjective mood, feelings, and yearnings I experienced while writing them."—Trans.

achieve as much as possible for oneself, are possible only in politics, only in relations between states, not in the Church. No political horse-trading is admissible in the life of the Church. The Church cannot make any concessions: the Church is one. Strictly speaking, we cannot talk about the unification of the Churches; we can only talk about the unification of two human worlds, of the eastern Christian world and the western Catholic world. The Church is one; it contains fullness. Only humanity, only human history, knows schism and lack of fullness. And the schism between Orthodox and Catholic humanity is a human sin and limitation. But the redemption of the human sin and the overcoming of the human limitation will be attained not by formal Uniate agreements, not by mutual concessions or claims, but by a transformation of the mutual relations of the two Christian worlds in the very depths of their religious experience. Khomiakov was right when he rejected the Uniate, but he was not right in his lack of love for the Catholic world, in his human one-sidedness and limitation. The unity of the Church as the Body of Christ does not have any formal attributes, and the Church never split apart and cannot split apart. There is one Church both in the East and in the West. Only people split apart, and people must be unified. But Solovyov leaned toward a formally Catholic understanding of the unity of the Church and therefore had to believe that Orthodoxy represented a schism. Khomiakov had a more accurate sense of the essence of the Church and was right when he rejected the Uniate. But his antipathy toward the western Catholic world was his religious sin and falsehood. Solovyov had an inaccurate sense of the unity of the Church and was not right when he asserted that the Uniate was possible. But his loving relation to the western Catholic world constituted his great truth. Solovyov was also right when he recognized the possibility of dogmatic development, when he saw the divine-human process occurring in the Church. He did not agree that Orthodoxy had achieved perfection. It would almost be a blasphemy against the Holy Spirit to assert that Orthodoxy was perfect Christianity, that religious development had stopped and there was nothing more to wait for. That was what Solovyov's great importance consisted in. He saw in Christianity not only priesthood but also prophecy and reign. In this, he had advanced far beyond the Slavophiles. His whole being was permeated with Christian prophecies of the City of God, the Coming City. In this, he was a new man, a man of the new religious consciousness.

II

The Churches can be united only by the mutual love of the Orthodox world and the Catholic world, a love in which these two types of religious experience interact and permeate one another. These two Christian worlds will be truly united only by mutual love, not by any formal agreements. The Churches will be united and the universal Church will triumph in every Orthodox and in every Catholic who loves not only his own world but also the other world and who feels universal brotherhood in Christ, a brotherhood which has overcome one-sided self-assertion. True union will take place in the depths of ecclesial mysticism, not on the surface of agreements between ecclesiastical authorities. To achieve this union there will be no need to leave the Church of one's fathers, to change one's denomination. Every Orthodox must, from within Orthodoxy, love Catholicism and recognize the truth of Catholicism, and every Catholic must do the same in relation to Orthodoxy. That is the task. Converting from Orthodoxy to Catholicism will not lead to union, to the triumph of the universal Church. The conversion of Russian Orthodox to Catholicism cannot lead to a solution of the problem of East and West; it would only remove, not solve, the problem and it would weaken Russians' consciousness of their messianism. Solovyov overly supported converting to Catholicism, even though he himself never became a Catholic, of course. But his view that this great problem (which justly tormented him) could be solved by converting to Catholicism distorted his labors. To be sure, he spoke not of the union of the Eastern Church to the Western Church but of the unification of the Eastern and Western Churches. But he was always tempted by Catholic formalism in the understanding of the unity of the Church and by Catholic imperialism in the understanding of the hierarchical order of the Church. He was so easily tempted because of his just yearning for a militant Church. But the time is coming for a new kind of militancy. Solovyov's great truth consists in his genuine love for the western Catholic world, for an entire half of the Christian world. To our great grief, this love, this sense of brotherhood, this sense of the unity of Christian humanity, is rarely encountered in the Russian Orthodox world. This love of his was a much greater unifier of the Church, of East and West, than all of his ideas about formal Uniate agreements. The mystic was always at war with the scholastic-rationalist in Solovyov.

Nevertheless, Solovyov did not penetrate to the bottom of the difference between Orthodoxy and Catholicism; he did not get down to the final, mystical experience of East and West. For the sources of the separation between the Orthodox East and the Catholic West and of their mutual unification must be sought not in dogmatics and not in hierarchical order, but in the depths of mystical experience. The handbooks of dogmatic theology and of canonical law can yield nothing that could help us solve the problem of East and West. Nor do the debates between official Orthodoxy and official Catholicism concerning dogmatics and ecclesiastical government have much value. They shed no light. Differences of dogmatics and hierarchical order are secondary differences which are derived from differences in religious experience related to different types of mysticism in the communion with God. The Orthodox world and the Catholic world are so alienated from each other and so poorly understand each other not because they are separated by Filioque, purgatory, the immaculate conception, the Pope, etc., but because their religious experiences are profoundly different, because the two worlds have a different relation to Christ, because Orthodox mysticism and Catholic mysticism, i.e., the mysterious roots of religious life, are profoundly dissimilar. Solovyov showed little interest in Catholic mysticism; he was not drawn to it. What interested him most in Catholicism was its hierarchical order and the papacy as an active organization adapted to the struggle for Christ's truth on earth. Solovyov never carefully studied the mysticism of Catholicism in general or the lives of the Catholic saints in particular. Nor was he much interested in eastern ascetic mysticism, which he understood poorly and valued little. When Solovyov spoke of the Orthodox East, he never mentioned St. Seraphim of Sarov, that peak of eastern Christianity and the key to understanding the mystical mission of Orthodox Russia. Solovyov was much more preoccupied with the false relation of the Church to the state in Russia, the passiveness of the Orthodox hierarchy, and so on. But, after all, the Catholic West con-

The Problem of East and West

sists not only of the militant hierarchical order of the Church, not only of Peter, not only of ecclesiastical authority, but also of St. Francis of Assisi, of St. Teresa of Avila, of *The Imitation of Christ*, of heightened mystical sensitivity, of romantic hunger, of stigmata, of rapturous delight in the Lord's passion. As for the Orthodox East, it is characterized not only by the passiveness of the Church hierarchy, not only by a Byzantine subordination of the Church to the state and a conservatism that hampers the divine-human work on earth, but also by St. Isaac the Syrian, by St. Macarius of Egypt, by St. Maximus the Confessor, and by the courageous and white mysticism of St. Seraphim, this deification of man's nature from within. One cannot underscore strongly enough that, when he wrote about the excruciating problem of the interrelation between the Orthodox East and the Catholic West, Solovyov over-emphasized the political aspect of the problem. In his French book *La Russie et l'église universelle*, which was intended for the western world, he was unable to give an idea of the sacred world of the Orthodox Church, though only this sacred world can justify Russia's universal mission. He confined his characterization of the Orthodox East to practically nothing more than excerpts from Ivan Aksakov which vividly expose the sores of our ecclesiastical structure and to his own condemnations of our false relation between Church and state. Readers of his book might get the idea that the Orthodox East consists of nothing more than false relations between the Church and state which would be rectified by hierarchical subordination to the Pope of Rome. Solovyov does not show what the unique religious path of the East consists in. Western readers of his book will not understand what constitutes Russia's mission, the great calling of the Orthodox East. For Solovyov, eastern ascetic mysticism is something like Hinduism, almost Yogism, i.e., a deviation from Christian religious experience.

    He underrated the sacred world of Orthodoxy; he failed to understand that, in the Orthodox East, in the lives of the saints, in a special mystical experience, a Divine work is being done that will transfigure the world. Solovyov is a thousand times right when he exposes the sores of our ecclesiastical structure, our false relation between Church and state, and the non-Christian nature of our national self-assurance. But there are things immeasurably more profound with which the solution of the problem of East and West is connected, and Solovyov did not touch on them in *La Russie et l'église universelle*: he did not inform the West about the East's truth, without which the world cannot arrive at a good end. We must penetrate deep down into the mystical differences between Catholicism and Orthodoxy and seek there the sources of the conflict and the possibilities of reconciliation.

In the West, in Catholicism, God is an object that is outside and above man. Man stretches himself towards God; he strives towards God. This striving is filled with hunger and agony. This stretching is felt in the Gothic architectural style. In Catholic cathedrals man's stretching upward, toward God, is so intense that in the cathedral itself it is cold. Christ is an object in Catholicism, an object of love and imitation. Catholic mysticism is a sensual mysticism, full of rapture, ecstatic delight in suffering, the sweetness of agony. Man's nature feels an agonized yearning for the divine nature. The stigmata are a common characteristic of Catholic mysticism. Imitation of the Lord's passion and the being in love with Christ are possible only when Christ is an object that is outside and above man, when He is an object of striving and is not received inwardly. Also characteristic of Catholicism is a romantic yearning to find the Holy Grail. Catholic mysticism is full of hunger and passionate striving. The sensuality of Catholic mysticism is clearly visible in the case of someone like Teresa of Avila. There is something feminine in Catholic mysticism. Almost all the Catholic mystics and saints speak of the almost sensual sweet agony of the experience of the imitation of Christ and love for Christ. This hunger and striving, this stretching upward, beget Catholic creativity and produce the beauty of Catholic culture. The mystical experience of Catholicism is anthropological in character; the human element is stretched and vibrates in it; man stretches toward the object of his love, toward God, and attains an intoxicated and passionate ecstasy. Catholic mysticism is feverish and cold at the same time; it is both passionate and disciplined, combining ecstatic intoxication with strict discipline.

In Catholic cathedrals one feels both the coldness and the agony; there is much in them that is human, but there is also escape upward from the human, toward God. We never feel that God has descended to us in the cathedral, warming us. God does not descend to us; we must stretch upwards toward Him, the way Gothic cathedrals stretch upwards. The Gothic style is present in all of Catholic mysticism, in the whole religious experience of the West. The Gothic religious experience has engendered the whole of western Catholic culture. All the great achievements of western Catholic culture, all of its enchanting beauties, are due to this passionate striving, this Gothic stretching upward. Within the Catholic religious experience there is a dynamic process directed outward, toward the object of striving. This experience begins with human hungering, with sweet agonizing love for the object. This is a creative, dynamic love. Without it we would not have all the riches of the Divine world; we would not have Divine art. This love has engendered all of the West's activity and anthropologism. The West has never been religiously satisfied; it has always striven to find the Holy Grail, filled with Christ's blood. The West has never found a point of departure in Christ as an inner fact of mystical experience; it has never found a point of departure in the givenness of Divinity, but instead it has striven in love towards Christ, rising from man to God. St. Augustine already evinces this type of religious experience, this anthropologism and psychologism, this lover's passion. In the West, in Catholicism, the emphasis was not on the marriage between man and God but on man's being in love with God. And the great mission of the Catholic West consisted perhaps in revealing the mystical truth of being-in-love as a creative power. This being-in-love created western culture; the West's knightly power is connected with it. Knights intoxicated with love went on the Crusades and created beauty. The West's militant power and creative culture were born in this special type of religious experience, in this striving toward God as an object.

The Orthodox East followed a different religious path; it had a different kind of mystical experience. In the Orthodox East, God is a subject, residing within man. God descends to man; man receives Christ into himself. In Orthodoxy, man does not stretch upwards towards God; he prostrates himself before God. In Orthodox churches, God descends to people, thereby making these churches warmer than Catholic cathedrals. In eastern Orthodoxy, people are not in love with Christ and they do not imitate Him, for He is not an object, but a subject, a fact of inner experience. Orthodox mysticism is not sensual but primarily volitional in character; it is characterized by a particular spiritual sobriety. In eastern Orthodox mysticism the divine is the point of departure from within, not an object of agonized striving. Eastern mysticism is characterized by the idea of the theosis or deification of man's nature from within by the reception of Christ into oneself. Romantic longing engendered by mystical hunger is absent in eastern Christianity; instead, the latter is characterized by mystical satiety. In the Christian East, activity is directed inward, toward the illumination and deification of man's nature, not outward, toward the creation of culture and the manifestation of itself in history. The history of the East does not know the West's knightly courage; the East's activity and courage have been transposed into inner spiritual creativity, a creativity that is invisible on the surface of history.

Inwardly, in its type of communion with God, eastern mysticism is more masculine that western mysticism. Eastern religious experience is not favorable for creative activity in history, for it is entirely directed at the inner adaptation of man to God, at the creation of a new nature in Christ. Less anthropological than the West, the East preserves the Divine and does not objectify the human in the dynamics of history. St. Seraphim of Sarov is not a great creator, but a great creation of God, a great fact of existence, a great achievement of life. Man's relation to God is more profound in the East; the West is stronger in the relation of man to the world. Its creative culture is much stronger than that in the East. Eastern Orthodox mysticism is not a being-in-love, but a marriage, the marital union of man and God. Eastern theosis actualizes the marital mystery, permeating man's nature with Divinity. That is what constitutes the East's great truth and great mission. Only the Orthodox East has preserved the mystical mystery of fusion with God, i.e., the principle of the transfiguration of the world. In the West, God remains outside of man. Through the mystical fullness of the East, man's nature is deified, but this Christian deification has nothing in common with Hindu pantheism; it does not annihilate the individual, but saves him. The West's mystical hunger has created a great culture. In the East there is no cultural-historical dynamics, but there is a dynamics of inner communion with God. Being-in-love seems more dynamic and creative than marriage. The mystical experience of being-in-love has its great mission and its unique creative achievements. But the mystical experience of marriage also has a great mission, and it has a unique inner dynamics. Gothic culture is a culture of creative being-in-love, and the historical path of the West is connected with it. Eastern, or Russian, culture is a culture of divine marriage, and the historical path of the East is connected with it. The historical fate of the Orthodox East is determined by the relation to God as a subject. Because of the mysterious goals of Divine Providence, the religious life of humanity split apart into two experiences and two paths. Each of these experiences and paths has its own mission, and it complements the other experience and path. It would be dishonest and godless to say that the truth is found exclusively on one side or the other. The Father's house has many mansions. These different experiences and paths remain within the limits of universal Christianity, of one Church of Christ; the conflict and schism are due to human limitations, to historical relativity. Why does the East relate to God as to a subject, while the West relates to Him as to an object? That is a mystery that we are not destined to fathom; it is the mystery of human freedom and Divine grace. But we can and must understand the differences between these two experiences and overcome the conflict on our different paths.

Solovyov recognized the great mission of the Slavic world and of Russia; he was the philosopher of Russian messianism. Everything that was creative and significant in the history of 19th century Russian thought was connected with the recognition of Russia's mission. But faith in the universal mission of Russia presupposes a belief that in the depths of her spirit Russia has preserved a great truth and that she is called to communicate this truth to the world. This truth can only be a religious truth, a Christian truth, the truth of the mystical experience of the Orthodox East. The great Russian literature attests to the existence of this religious truth, a truth increasingly betrayed by the West. All of Dostoevsky's works document the Russian soul and disclose its religious agony. All Russians agonize over the question of the religious meaning of life and, from childhood to the grave, are tormented by God. All the spiritual energy of Russians is pushed inward in an effort to foster the inner relation of man to God; they have no energy left for historical activity, for the practical organization of life, or for cultural development. Even our politics is one of dreamy exaltation and religious maximalism. This may alarm us about the future of Russia, but we cannot fail to recognize here the special Russian religious character.

Solovyov devoted his entire life to the ultimate religious questions, the Russian questions; his entire life he dreamt of an organic religious culture. Nonetheless, in his projects and schemata, in his rational consciousness, there remained almost no room for an independent mission of Russia. His great achievement was that, rebelling against Slavophile limitations, he overcame the Slavophiles' self-assurance and nationalism and turned lovingly toward the West, toward the Catholic Church. From Russia he demanded Christian love and Christian self-renunciation. In him, the Slavophile consciousness was dynamic, not static. He summoned Russia to become conscious of her sins and to repent. In his thought, the recognition of Russia as the third Rome was interwoven with the sense of Russia's sinfulness and the call for her to repent. That was Solovyov's great truth. In this, we must follow him and accept his tradition in relation to the Catholic West, not the Slavophile tradition. Russia must become conscious of her sins; she must repent and renounce her excessive national pride and national hatred. That would be a preliminary stage, a necessary asceticism and purification preparatory to a great, positive labor in the world. What will Russia contribute to solving the tragedy of world history? What truth will she communicate to the world? This truth must be positive and creative, and it cannot be exhausted by repentance alone, by the overcoming of sins. The truth of the third Rome, the truth of Russian messianism, cannot be exhausted by unification with Catholicism, by the subordination of our ecclesiastical structure to the Pope. The truth of Russia cannot be only a recognition of the truth of Catholicism. Russia will have a universal mission only if she introduces her own truth into the world, a truth that is unknown to the West and preserved only in the East. If Russia cannot live and fulfill her task without the truth of the West, the West, in turn, needs Russia's truth, the truth of eastern Orthodoxy. The very formulation of the problem of East and West presupposes that the two experiences and two paths be mutually complementary. Russia is incubating a sacred mystery without which the goals of world history will not be attained and its religious meaning will not be fulfilled. To be sure, Solovyov was full of such messianic hopes but, in his consciousness which was formulating projects and formal agreements, he was led astray and thought that Russia's sole task was to subordinate herself to the hierarchical order of the Catholic Church. But Solovyov was more than his rational schemata and projects. Immeasurably more. And this made itself known in the last period of his life. The very existence of Vladimir Solovyov represented an enormous dynamics in solving the problem of East and West.

III

In the last period of his life, Solovyov's view of the problem of East and West changed. All his works of this period lacked the rationalistic character that was so unpleasant in the earlier periods. In the last period, he was full of apocalyptic horror before the growing power of evil. He no longer formulated optimistic projects and orderly schemata; instead, he prophesied. Potentially, he always possessed a prophetic consciousness and always affirmed the prophetic element in Christianity, but only at the end of his life did prophetic madness overwhelm in him the rationality of this world. He dared to write "A Short Tale about the Antichrist," which is filled with symbolic realism, every word having a profound and unique meaning. The prophetic power of this Tale has already been revealed and will be increasingly revealed. It represents the end to all of Solovyov's rosy hopes, a total collapse of his idea of history as the divine-human process on earth. The "Tale about the Antichrist" contains chiliasm and Christ's thousand-year reign, but this reign is disconnected from history; it is not so much the good result of history as the radical rejection of history as evil. The very idea of divine humanity was shaken in Solovyov. He stopped believing in the divine-human work on earth. If he began by underrating the power of evil, he ended by becoming overly terrified by it, and evil took revenge on him for his earlier failure to recognize it. He sensed that not the kingdom of Christ's truth but the kingdom of the Antichrist's falsehood was the principal result of the historical process. His prophetic consciousness sensed the approach of the end of history. Eschatological themes began to dominate his prophetic consciousness. The *Lectures on Divine Humanity* did not have any real eschatology; the divine-human process was too successful.

But now, in the "Tale about the Antichrist," he saw the problem of East and West in a new, apocalyptic light, in the light of the end of history. He lost faith in the good, divine-human, Christian works of history. He no longer believed that his most cherished dream, the unification of the Churches, would be realized within the limits of history. In the Tale, the unification of the Churches takes place beyond history, in a supra-historical process, in the apocalyptic plane. The unification of the Churches and Christ's chiliastic reign are not immanent to history, but transcend it. In the past, Solovyov had optimistically introduced chiliasm as an immanent element into humanity's historical process: the unification of the Churches was to take place in history and Christ's truth was to triumph on earth in theocracy. Now, the chilastic element was pessimistically separated out from history and became transcendent with respect to it; theocracy no longer seemed realizable in earthly history. The idea of theocracy collapsed. It had already begun to collapse when he was writing the "National Question" and exposing with his liberal criticism the falsehood of nationalism and reactionary politics. In the end, the royal function of theocracy belongs to the Antichrist. The kingdom is now not the kingdom of Christ, but the kingdom of the Antichrist.

The horror of the Antichrist leads to the unification of the Churches beyond history. Here, Solovyov achieves a profounder understanding of the sacred mystery of Orthodoxy. The mission of the Orthodox Church, which had been unclear for him within the limits of history, now became clear beyond history, in the eschatological plane. It became clear why the Orthodox Church has preserved the divine truth. In a few lines of the "Tale about the Antichrist," Solovyov comes to a better understanding of the differences between Orthodoxy and Catholicism than he had in his large philosophical-theological treatises. The Elder John is the final, good result of the eastern Orthodox path, just as Pope Peter II is the final, good result of the western Catholic path.[6] It is clear from the very names that, for Solovyov, Orthodoxy is preeminently the Christianity of St. John, whereas Catholicism is preeminently the Christianity of St. Peter. The Elder John possesses the gift of mystical clairvoyance. Having come out of the depths of the Orthodox East, the Elder John is the first to recognize and name the Antichrist. The whole mystical experience of the eastern Church, with its elders being the highest peaks, has made it possible to attain that final and highest vision which recognizes the Antichrist in the world. Without the Christian East, the Antichrist could not be recognized. The West does not possess

---

6. The Elder John and Pope Peter II are the heads of the beleaguered Orthodox and Catholic remnants in "A Short Tale about the Antichrist."—Trans.

John's vision; that is not the path of the West. In the East, with all its passiveness in history, an apocalyptic consciousness of the end flares up. It is Pope Peter II who actively condemns the Antichrist, thus manifesting the militant spirit of Catholicism; but in the recognition of the Antichrist, he follows the Elder John. The Elder John's mystical clairvoyance and vision is the sacred mystery of the East, the truth of the East; and this truth does not depend on John's hierarchical subordination to Peter II. Having recognized and condemned the Antichrist, the Elder John and Peter II unite. Here, Solovyov attains a prophetic vision of genius. How much more profound are these images of the last elder of the East and the last pope of the West than is the entire scholasticism of his French book. This apocalyptic light illuminates Russian messianism with new meaning.

The apocalyptic horror before the approaching end was connected for Solovyov with the horror of the approaching eastern-Mongol peril. The problem of East and West now rose before him in its entirety: besides Russia and the West, Orthodoxy and Catholicism, the Far East, Mongolism, was now introduced into this problem. The role of the Mongol East in the historical destiny of humankind is usually foolishly ignored; the Far East has been forgotten. The movement of the Mongol East, which Solovyov calls Pan-Mongolism, was for him the herald of a divinely appointed fate, indicating the apocalyptic destiny of humankind.

> Pan-Mongolism! Although the word
> Is strange, it caresses my hearing
> As though it were filled
> With premonition of some mighty Divine fate. . . .[7]

As punishment for their sins, for betraying Christ and the Christian revelation about man, Christian Russia and Christian Europe are threatened by Pan-Mongolism, by the Far East, which till now was slumbering and had been forgotten by us. Solovyov's poem "Pan-Mongolism" has turned out to be prophetic for Russia, predicting as it does the war with Japan and the defeat of Russia. I think that this will

---

7. From Solovyov's poem "Pan-Mongolism." Solovyov uses these four lines as the epigraph to "A Short Tale about the Antichrist."—Trans.

not be the only confirmation of Solovyov's prophecies. The approaching peril of Pan-Mongolism contains a mystical terror, a presentiment of the end. The great significance of Pan-Mongolism consists, above all, in the fact that it poses in all its acuteness the question: What does Russia want to be, a Christian country and an organic part of Christian humanity, or part of the non-Christian Far East? Has Russia preserved the Christian revelation about personhood or has she betrayed this revelation and subordinated herself to eastern-Mongol impersonality? Only Christian Russia, united with Christian Europe, has the power to defeat Pan-Mongolism. Eastern-Mongol impersonality has already crept into western civilization in the form of all-leveling Americanism. The far East and the far West have clandestinely converged. The problem of the Orthodox East and the Catholic West has now become the problem of the relation of Christian humanity which has remained faithful to the Christian revelation about man and humanity to the non-Christian humanity which has not accepted the Christian revelation or which has betrayed it. The Christian Churches or, more accurately, the two Christian worlds will be united by the external peril from the impersonal element of the far East and the inner peril from the impersonal anti-Christian civilization. Solovyov's question confronts Russian messianism:

> O Russia! In profound foresight,
> You are preoccupied with a proud thought:
> What kind of East do you want to be:
> The East of Xerxes or the East of Christ?[8]

Russia is in danger of becoming the East of Xerxes if she does not defeat the Mongolism that has crept into the depths of her soul. In order to achieve the Christian and cultural defeat of Mongolism, Russia must first change her relation to the Christian West. Christian Russia must overcome her conflict with the Christian West and learn to love the latter; she must learn to see the one truth of Christ, the truth of the universal Church that resides both in Orthodoxy and in Catholicism. The universal Christian culture must be opposed to all Mongolism, both external and internal; to all impersonality, both barbaric and

---

8. From Solovyov's poem *"Ex Oriente Lux."*—Trans.

civilized. Confronting the spirit of Antichrist, the elder John recognizes the truth of Pope Peter II, while the latter follows John's vision. Pan-Mongolism will serve the task of the unification of East and West.

Solovyov was the prophet of the new religious consciousness, an apocalyptic consciousness. In the light of this new consciousness he prophesied about Russian messianism, continuing the work of Dostoevsky. The mystery of the unification of East and West was closed to his formalistically scholastic consciousness; it was revealed only to his apocalyptic consciousness. Solovyov prophetically overcame both the Slavophiles and the Westernizers. The problem of the prophet was the fundamental problem of Solovyov's life. His entire life he felt that his calling was the prophetic ministry, not the priestly one. He was a potential prophet; he was tormented by a prophetic spirit and his entire being was dedicated to prophecy. At the end of his life this took an extreme form and led to a dangerous deviation. But it is impossible to understand Solovyov and the task of his life if we view his idea of the prophet (as opposed to the high priest and the king) as nothing more than a product of his tendency to formulate abstract schemata. His entire religious sense of the world was such that for him the Christian religion had not only a priestly side but also a prophetic side. He had always lived in the prophetic spirit, but this spirit found full expression only at the end of his life.

Solovyov stood at the threshold of a new cosmic religious epoch. He already saw the colors of the new dawn. And the tragedy of his life was the tragedy of this cosmic crisis. He sensed, like Dostoevsky and all the other heralds of Russian messianism, that Russia stands at the center of the world and that, through her, the world is advancing toward a new cosmic epoch. It is not by chance that the image of Sophia, the Wisdom of God, is preserved primarily in the East, in Orthodoxy. In his sense of Sophia, the sense of the cosmic character of Christianity, Solovyov was more connected to eastern Christianity than he realized. With his sense of the world soul, of the eternal feminine, he belonged to the new religious consciousness. But his apocalyptic consciousness was overly biographical and therefore overly pessimistic. After all, the apocalyptic consciousness will contain the revelation of the new earth, the new Jerusalem, the city of God; and this joyous expectation overcomes in us the horror of the looming kingdom of the Antichrist. Dostoevsky felt more profoundly than Solovyov this joy of the new earth, of the city of God. In his "Legend of the Grand Inquisitor," a work of genius, he reveals the immeasurable freedom in Christ, and he sees the great mission of Russia as the preserver of Orthodoxy in the fact that it is destined to communicate to the world the mystery of freedom.

Catholicism has equated the Church with the city of God, with a kingdom on earth. We find this deviation as early as St. Augustine, who considered the Church to be the beginning of Christ's thousand-year reign on earth. The whole papacy grew out of this confusion of the Church with the city, with the kingdom. This belief that the city of God, the Kingdom of Christ, has already been realized in the hierarchical order of the Church obscures in the Catholic world the apocalyptic vision of the Coming City; it shuts off the prophetic future. The Catholic world does not seek the Coming City; it already has its city in the hierarchical order of the Church and in its claim to be the kingdom. But the priestly hierarchism is an angelic hierarchism, not a human one. The kingdom of divine humanity cannot be built on the hierarchical priesthood alone; the latter lacks the anthropological revelation concerning the City. Therefore, Catholic priesthood's claim to be the kingdom of divine humanity on earth gives rise to a demonic deviation, creating not a divine-human order but an angelic-bestial one. Orthodoxy has never confused the kingdom with the City; the Orthodox hierarchy has never claimed to be a human kingdom; Orthodoxy has never had the sense that the City could be realized on earth. For that reason the hunger for the Coming City, the apocalyptic consciousness, is more easily born in the Orthodox East. There is more of the prophetic spirit in Orthodoxy than in Catholicism. And Solovyov's prophetic spirit was not a Catholic spirit.

In *The Brothers Karamazov* Dostoevsky with the lips of Father Paissy prophesies from out of the depths of Orthodoxy about the Church as the kingdom, as the City of God: "From the East this earth will glow with light." Solovyov's entire life and work were directed toward the Coming City, the new earth. The errors of his consciousness are negligible before the prophetic fact of his existence. The phenomenon of Vladimir Solovyov in our life teaches us and leads us forward. But our following of him must be not a static condition but a dynamic process toward the solution of the problem of East and West.

6
Christ and the World: In Response to Vasily Rozanov[1]

Rozanov is one of the greatest Russian prose writers, a true magician of the word. He frightens all Christians, both old and new. They are stung by his blows and consider him to be Christ's most dangerous opponent, as if Christ could have dangerous opponents, as if Christ's work could be hit with stinging blows. Furthermore, Rozanov is an enemy not just of Christianity, of "historical" Christianity; he is, above all, an enemy of Christ himself. Christianity per se is not that repulsive to Rozanov. He finds many good things in it resulting from its compromise with the "world": It promotes a firm family structure and a married priesthood and permits the eating of "jam"[2] and the begetting of children. Into itself it has assimilated nearly the whole "world." For Rozanov, Christ is worse than Christianity. Christ is merciless toward the world; He is terrifying in His negation of the world. Christianity, by contrast, is humanly pliable and tolerant toward human weaknesses. In history, Christianity did not pose so acutely the dilemma, "Christ or the world"; it took in some of Christ and some of the world. Rozanov is not an enemy of how Christianity has arranged everyday life. He is devoted to many of these arrangements; for instance, that is where his somewhat unctuous love of family life comes from.

Rozanov is an enemy of Christ, and only a lack of courage compels him to mask this enmity and lead astray good people, who continue to think that he demands only corrections to Christianity, that he is only a reformer, that he is ready to accept Christianity if it accepts divorce,

---

1. First published in the magazine *Russkaya mysl'*, July 1908.—Trans.
2. Jam was one of Rozanov's favorite treats.—Trans.

[109]

theater, and jam, the sweet things of this world. Two things need to be debunked: that Rozanov is a reformer of Christianity and that he is a dread and invincible foe of the faith of Christ, a foe more dread than Nietzsche. We are astonished and almost hypnotized by Rozanov's brilliant and bewitching literary talent, by the audacity and sensuous concreteness of his manner of posing problems, by his intense mystical sense. But the Devil is not as frightening as he is painted.[3] A clear philosophical and religious consciousness easily detects how muddled his formulation of his theme is, and this is not an accidental muddle due to the weakness of his thought but a fateful muddle, sent by higher meaning for goals similar to Rozanov's.

Rozanov's theme (which to a significant degree is also the theme of *Novyi Put'*[4] and of the Religious-Philosophical Meetings)[5] is Christ and the world, the relation between Christ and the world. Rozanov develops this theme with extraordinary talent and brilliance in his essay "Sweetest Jesus and the Bitter Fruits of the World" (1907); it is to this essay that I primarily address my response to Rozanov in the present essay. God has two children: Christ and the world. For Rozanov, these two children of God are in irreconcilable conflict. Those who find Jesus sweet, find the world bitter. In Christ, the world has become bitter. Those who love Christ have lost their taste for the world; Jesus' sweetness has made bitter all the fruits of the world. All this is written beautifully, vividly, boldly, and (at first impression) dangerously. One must choose between Jesus and the world, between the two children of God. It is impossible to unite Jesus with the world, to love both of them, to taste both the sweetness of Jesus and the sweetness of the world. Family, science, art, the joy of earthly life, all these things are bitter or tasteless for those who have tasted Jesus' heavenly sweetness. According to Rozanov's marvelous expression, Christ is the

---

3. Russian saying.—Trans.

4. A Russian religious, philosophical, and literary magazine, founded in Petersburg 1902, which published important writers of the "Russian religious renaissance," including Rozanov and Berdyaev.—Trans.

5. The "Religious-Philosophical Meetings," held in Petersburg in 1903–1904 and partly organized by Rozanov, were designed to promote encounters between religiously interested Russian writers and theologians and bishops of the Russian Orthodox Church.—Trans.

Christ and the World: In Response to Vasily Rozanov

"mono-flower," and all the flowers of the world pale before him. *The Imitation of Christ* praises this sweetness of Jesus and this bitterness of all the fruits of the world. St. Augustine's *Confessions*, too, are full of love for Christ and hatred of the world. Rozanov does not like to dot his "i's"; he is ambiguous and never draws decisive conclusions, leaving it up to the reader to guess what they are. But here is the dilemma: If Jesus is divine, the world is demonic. If the world is divine, Jesus is demonic. Rozanov is attached to the world with his entire being; he is in love with the world and with all worldly things, and feels the divinity of the world and the sweetness of its fruits. Sweetest Jesus became demonic for him; Christ's image is dark.

Rozanov's formulation of this problem makes a very strong impression; all the objections of Christian apologists seem weak and pathetic. Rozanov argues concretely and (at first glance) clearly; astonishing and hypnotizing us, he makes us feel the entire acuteness of the problem. He can be coarse, especially when he drags the monk to the "theater," but the monk really does seem helpless. The babbling of the official defenders of the Church is not convincing; the impression remains that Rozanov has clearly shown that there is an absolute opposition between Christ and the world, that the sweetness of Christ is absolutely incompatible with the sweetness of the world. For Rozanov, Christ is the spirit of non-being, the spirit of the diminution of all the things of the world, and Christianity is the religion of death, an apologia for the sweetness of death. The religion of birth and life must declare unending war against Sweetest Jesus, the poisoner of life, the spirit of non-being, the founder of the religion of death. Christ has hypnotized humanity, filling it with hatred of being and with love of non-being. Christ's religion has recognized only one thing as beautiful: dying and death, sorrow and suffering.

Rozanov is very gifted; he writes beautifully and says much that is true. His point of departure, however, is false; his formulation of the problem is muddled and incorrect. *Rozanov is a brilliant petty-bourgeois*; and in the final analysis his problem, though formulated with amazing talent, is a petty bourgeois one. Rozanov astonishes precisely because he expresses something that is dear to the petty bourgeois heart of the average man, because the problem of the sweet and bitter fruits of the world preoccupies the average men of this world and is a stumbling block for official Christianity, which has long been a petty bourgeois religion. Rozanov's family, jam, theaters, all the sweets and joys of a prosperous life, are understandable and dear to the entire petty bourgeois kingdom of the average man, which sees in all this the essence of the "world" and would like to rescue this "world" from the hypnosis of Sweetest Jesus. For Rozanov, being is identical with average, everyday existence, and the "world" is identical with the sweetness of average, everyday life. This is very deep; it is a force.

Rozanov assumes that every average petty bourgeois man knows what the "world" is and experiences it as everyday things that bring joy: the family, jam, life's adornments, and so on. The average man knows, whereas the philosopher does not know. The problem of the *world* is very unclear and indefinite, and Rozanov's entire trick, as well as the key to his apparent power, consists in passing off what is unclear and indefinite as what is clear and definite, in passing off the undetermined unknown as what is already known. What is this world? What world are we talking about? What content does Rozanov put in the word "world"? Is the world the totality of empirical phenomena or is it the positive fullness of being? Is the world the totality of all the things that are given, both real and illusory, both good and evil? Or does it consist only of that which is real and good? If the world is conceived as the totality of all the things that are empirically given, where the sweetness of jam is on the same level as the sweetness of the greatest works of art, this conception of the world is almost uninteresting. That which is eternal in the world cannot be placed on the same level as that which is perishable; and it is inadmissible to formulate the problem of the world without any qualifying valuations. That kind of world is a "world" only in quotes. The *de facto* world, given to us and experienced by us, is a mixture of being with non-being, of reality with illusion, of eternity with transience. What world does Rozanov love? Which of the worlds does he choose? In what world does he want to live? I am worried that, from religion, Rozanov demands a *de facto* mixing of what is real and valuable with what is false and worthless. The term "religious," however, is applicable not to the problem of the world, but to the problem of the authentic and real world, to the problem of the fullness of being, of the values of the world, of the extratemporal and imperishable content of the world. To merely assert this

Christ and the World: In Response to Vasily Rozanov

"world" is to assert the law of corruptibility, of slavish necessity, of need and sickness, of deformity and falsification. The world lies in evil, and the positive fullness of being is the highest goal and good, and real being consists in what is valuable and joyful in the world. Rozanov can do nothing more than helplessly observe this evil of the world; he cannot deny its existence; nor can he understand its origin. Where did death come from, this death which Rozanov hates as much as the rest of us? From where did death enter the world, and how is it that it has taken possession of the world? Will Rozanov consent to recognize death as an essential element of the world which he loves so much and which he defends against Christ? It is not from Christ that death came into the world. Christ came to save us from death, not to subject the world to death.

Christ came to separate what is real and valuable in the world from what is false and worthless, the divine from the demonic. Christ is the Savior of the real world, of the world that is full of being, the Savior of the sin-damaged divine cosmos, not of chaos, the kingdom of the prince of this world, non-being. Christ condemned the corrupt, illusory, chaotic world. The kingdom of Christ is not of this world. Christ taught men to love not this world, nor the things of this world. But the empirical content of the world is neither this world nor that one; it is a mixture, a mixing of that world with this one, a sickness of creation, being and non-being, value and worthlessness. Christ had to come, because the old world, the sinful world that had fallen away from God, was decaying and dying; corruption had eaten away at its foundations and it was gripped by anguish. The old, immanent sense of life, which Rozanov finds so captivating in paganism and Judaism, has been replaced by a transcendental sense. This has always happened in tragic periods of history and at the threshold of every religious revolution. The old world could not, by its own powers, save itself from destruction; the old world did have within itself the power that could save it from universal death. Self-divinization is self-destruction; deification of the world by the Son of God is salvation. Rozanov desires an immanent salvation of the world and rejects transcendental salvation because he identifies it with non-being and death. He senses the divinity in creation but is deaf and blind to the tragedy connected with the rupture between creation and the Creator.

Rozanov's sense of the world can be called *immanent pantheism*. It contains a very powerful sense of the divinity of the world's life and of the immediate joy of life, but only a very weak sense of the transcendental. It lacks transcendental longing, the longing for a transcendental way out. Rozanov's sense of the world consists in an original mystical naturalism, a divinization of the natural sacraments of life. In the 20th century, as human history is ending, Rozanov is experiencing the naturalistic phase of religious revelation: he longs for universal-historical childishness and simplicity and does not notice the ancientness and decrepitude of his restoration of the first days of humankind. Rozanov's naturalistic pantheism is old age that has fallen back into childishness. It is old age remembering and delighting in the pleasures of childhood and youth. And Rozanov, the mystic Rozanov who has had visions of genius, divinizes the joys of this life, venerates family happiness, gazes at the sweet jam with the lusty greediness of a child, and imperceptibly arrives at an apologia for everyday petty-bourgeois contentment. He identifies a happy, natural life with the world. He wants to achieve a total divinization of the natural life. But we have already seen that this "world" so dear to Rozanov is totally subject to the law of corruption, and Rozanov is incapable of dying as Abraham, Isaac, and Jacob died, blessing their descendants; he lacks the power of impersonality that was good only in that epoch; even he will not consent to live only in his descendants; he is deeply affected by the following phases of religious revelation in the world, and his blood is poisoned with Sweetest Jesus. Restoration is never what it tries to restore.

And however good the religion of Babylon might have been in its own time (although we know that even in its own time it was bad, since there were higher forms of religion then), there is no doubt that, after Christ and the whole of experience of Christian history, any attempt to restore the religion of Babylon would amount to madness or infantile idiocy. Historical science has sufficiently us disabused of the notion that a golden age once existed, and our religious consciousness regards the sweet memory of a golden age not as evidence of the existence of a certain epoch in the past history of humankind, but as a sign of man's pre-temporal and pre-earthly closeness to God, a closeness damaged by sin. We have lost paradise, but this paradise was, despite what Rozanov may think, not Babylon, not Judaism, not paganism, or any other element of

Christ and the World: In Response to Vasily Rozanov

the earthly past of humankind. Rather, this paradise was man's heavenly origin. But, as we shall see, Rozanov not only looks back into the past; he also looks forward and yearns for an earthly paradise in the future. Unexpectedly for himself, he is not averse to accepting a mystical interpretation of the building of the Tower of Babel, and he justifies the divinization of the old, natural world by social builders of the future. Imperceptibly, his yearnings start to converge with the dreams of positivists and naive, green radicals; and he rapidly advances toward Pisarev's doctrine,[6] though he does not become a craftsman, but remains an artist.

Rozanov is a man immersed in everyday life. He has an acute sense of the everyday environment and a very weak sense of personhood. Personal consciousness is virtually absent in him, as absent as it can be in a contemporary man. Therefore, he has no sense of the tragic nature of life that ends in death, no sense of the tragic nature of personal fate, of the horror of individual annihilation. Rozanov's sense of life has something in common with Tolstoy's; to a certain extent, they both have an Old Testament view of the life of the world. Like Tolstoy, Rozanov unfurls "an infant's diaper linens, stained green and yellow,"[7] before the world, wishing with those linens to defeat death and personal tragedy. *The Kreutzer Sonata* is only the reverse side of those linens. Both Tolstoy and Rozanov have a love of ordinary, everyday, petty-bourgeois existence that doesn't accord with their religious seekings. This is how Rozanov solves the problem of death: there were a man and a woman who had eight children; the man and the woman died, but life triumphs and multiplies in the eight children. Salvation from death lies in birth, in the fragmentation of every human being into a multiplicity of parts. It lies in bad infinity, and the only consolation for a person is to disintegrate. To death Rozanov opposes not eternal life, not resurrection, but birth, the emergence of new and different lives without end, without any way out. But this type of deliverance from the tragedy of life can be achieved only by beings for whom only

---

6. Allusion to Dmitry Ivanovich Pisarev (1840–1868), radical writer and social critic. Pisarev held that artists are nothing more than craftsmen whose labor satisfies the needs of society.—Trans.

7. From *War and Peace*.—Trans.

the species, not the person, is real. This type of consolation resembles the breeding of cattle.

In the Old Testament and in the primitive pagan world, personhood was slumbering, barely awakening from the sleep to which sin had condemned it. All world history had represented a gradual awakening of the personhood; and, in our epoch of agonizing complexity, it awoke with a scream of horror and helplessness and tore itself away from the species, and now for the first time it can attach itself to something new. Rozanov is pulling personhood back into the species, and he is assuring the world that a return is possible if Christ is rejected and forgotten. He is telling us that Christ is responsible for this hypertrophy of personal sensation, and if there were no Christ, there would be no tragedy of death, death would not be feared with such agony, and the horror of death and annihilation would dissipate as soon we glimpse the diaper stained green and yellow. For Rozanov the world consists in the species and the life of the species; as for personhood, he does not see its presence in the world; it is somewhere beyond the world, with Christ. The sense of personhood and of its tragic fate is transcendental: it transcends what Rozanov calls the "world," and that is why the fate of personhood is so tragic and agonizing in this world.

And all the things that have been real and valuable in the history of the world have been *transcendental*: they represent a yearning to go beyond this world, to break through the closed circle of immanence and bring another world into our world. The transcendental becomes immanent to the world: that is the meaning of world culture. All human creative activity has represented an anguished longing for the transcendental, for another world; this activity has never praised the natural life of the species or expressed contentment with this world. Creative activity has always been an expression of discontent, a reflection of the agony of dissatisfaction with this life. Art, philosophy, cult, and many other types of cultural creativity are manifestations of humanity's transcendental longing; but sexual love, too, so dear and central to Rozanov, represents a yearning for transcendence, an anguished desire to break though the limits of this world. Sexual love is more than this "world"; it is dissatisfaction with this "world." Rozanov does in fact recognize the transcendental character of sex.

To justify love, art, philosophy, and other examples of creative

Christ and the World: In Response to Vasily Rozanov

activity is to disclose their transcendental character, to see in them the possibility of transcending this world. The family is still this world, a closing of the horizons, whereas love is already another world, an infinite expansion of the horizons. Positivism is this world, a forever-closed horizon, whereas metaphysics is another world, an expansion of distances. Rozanov's immanent pantheism is actually a poeticized positivism, a particular form of mystical positivism. Every effort at the social reorganization of the human kingdom is a thing of this world, the world of closed horizons, whereas the dream of the unification of people in the Kingdom of God on earth is already another world, a world in which the horizons are wide open. It is common, when speaking of Greek culture, to oppose its affirmation of the world to the negation of the world in Christianity. But the greatest achievements of Greek culture—Plato's philosophy and Greek tragedy—were connected with transcendence of this world, with a consciousness of the insufficiency of the immanent world, and already represented a pathway to Christianity. The entire Medieval culture, full of creativity and beauty, was based on the sense of transcendence. In this culture we find love and the cult of the Beautiful Lady, as well as art, philosophy, knighthood, and folk festivals. In Rozanov's terms, was all this an affirmation or a negation of the world? I have presented all of these examples in order to show clearly all the uncertainty related to the formulation of the problem of the "world." The "world" that Rozanov is making such a fuss over does not exist.

To religiously justify history, culture, the flesh of the world is not the same thing as to justify the family, our ordinary everyday environment, and "jam." Rather, it is to justify the transcendental yearning for another world, a yearning embodied in world culture; it is to affirm in this world the yearning for a universal escape from the natural order, which is evil and corrupted.[8] I even dare to think that there exists a profound opposition between the world and the family, in the name of

---

8. In order to see the erroneousness of the view that Christianity is hostile to the flesh of the world it is sufficient to read Justin the Philosopher, Irenaeus, and other apologists and teachers of the Church. It was Christianity that defended the flesh of the world and the earth against the spiritualistic negations formulated by Platonism, Gnosticism, etc.

which Rozanov rebelled against Christ. The family often becomes a law unto itself and supplants the world; it separates one from the world, fostering indifference to the world and all the things of the world. Between the world and the family there exists a much greater antagonism than between the world and Christ. It has been sufficiently shown and proved that family ties have no equal when it comes to hampering the universal sense of the world's life and historical tasks. Furthermore, there exists an opposition between the family and love; it often happens that love is buried in the family.

Every settled and closed form of existence is opposed to creative activity, is in eternal opposition to the universe and to that which is universal. But Rozanov wants to make us believe that the family and habitual existence constitute the universe, the whole of God's great world. We do not need to offer any particular proof that the family and habitual existence are in conflict with universal creative impulses, since this conflict is a fairly obvious fact. That is why Rozanov's "world" seems to me a fiction that is clearly recognizable by the habitual, everyday consciousness. This "world" is a mixture of being and non-being; and, religiously, the important thing is not the question of the "world" but the question of the universal-historical triumph of *being* in this "world." The immanent religion of this "world" consists in an apotheosis of petty-bourgeois ordinariness, to which one part of Rozanov is greatly attached. Taken in itself, this "world" deserves only to be destroyed; but in its history we can recognize the affirmation of another world, the real world, which contains divine-human connections, creative aspirations toward a divine cosmos, a universal pathway toward a new heaven and a new earth, and liberation from evil, and with all of this is connected the religious question of the affirmation of the world.

Our increasingly decaying monasticism does not reject the world; instead, the world finds its way like contraband into the everyday life of the monks. There is too much "jam" in the monasteries, and too little "grieving in ashes." Our monasticism rejects creativity, the penetration of another world into this world; it rejects the history of liberation from the evil of this world. But our monasticism has become enmired in this "world"; it is losing its connection with ascetic Christian mysticism; official Christianity has settled into a routine existence, dear to Rozanov's heart. Our monasticism continues to reject what is valuable in the world, hates all creative impulses, is hostile toward all attempts at liberation from the power of this world, and values the evil of the world because its own existence is justified by this evil. Monks, bishops, princes of the Church, the historical masters of religion are, for the most part, ordinary and worldly men placed in power by the kingdoms of this world. We do not believe that these men are not of this world; their rejection of the world is only another example of the cunning of this "world." And we are ready to rise up against the hierarchs of the Church, against official Christianity, not in the name of the world, but in the name of another world, in the name of creativity and freedom, in the name of the yearning to break through the limits of this world.

The universal-historical meaning of ascetic Christian mysticism consists in a challenge to the whole order of nature, in opposition to natural necessity, in the deification of man's nature through union with Christ, in the victory over death. This asceticism of the Christian saints was not a misunderstanding or an evil; it had a positive mission as well as cosmic consequences in the work of the salvation of the world. But where are today's saints? Does ascetic mysticism even exist today? The fact that we have gone beyond Christian asceticism does not mean that we reject its great mission and accept this world. The new religious consciousness[9] affirms not this chaotic and enslaved world, but the cosmos, the holy flesh of the world. The flesh of the world, which must be religiously sanctified, liberated, and saved, is transcendental, as transcendental as spirit. This flesh is not the matter of this world; this flesh will result from the victory over the weight and enchainedness of the material world. The chiliastic hope that history will culminate in the Kingdom of God on earth, in a visible kingdom of Christ, is not an expectation of the kingdom of this world; chiliasm is the kingdom not of this world, but in this world. And with chiliasm is connected the universal-historical resurrection of the flesh, the religious affirmation of the flesh of the world. Which flesh does Rozanov love? The religion of which flesh does he preach?

For Rozanov the problem of the origin and essence of evil is unsolvable and even incomprehensible. Pantheism is always one-sided, containing only part of the truth: it does not grasp the tragedy of the

---

9. See the first essay in the present collection.—Trans.

world. If the world is good and divine, if it contains its own immanent justification, if it is not necessary to transcend world history, then it becomes unfathomable where the evil of this world and the horror of our present life came from. For Rozanov, evil is a misunderstanding, an accident, a fateful error of history which has taken the wrong path. Where did Christ come from? Where does the power of His dark (in Rozanov's view) Countenance come from? Why does the religion of death have such a hypnotic power over human hearts? Why does death mow down the life of the world? Rozanov cannot answer any of these questions. He hides from evil in the joy of family life, in the sweetness of everyday life: he tries to sweeten with jam the bitter pill of life. He shouts: I'm sick and tired of tragedy and of suffering; I don't want to hear about death; I can no longer tolerate the dark rays; I want the joys of life; I want only the divine world. We're all sick and tired of it, but nothing can be done: evil is a reality, not a hypnosis of misunderstanding. Sex, shouts Rosanov, is our salvation; it is divine and overcomes death. He wants to oppose sex to the Logos. But sex is poisoned at its roots; sex is corrupt and fosters corruption; sex is dark. Only the Logos can save it.

To view Christ as a dark principle of non-being hostile to the divine world signifies a profound collapse of pantheism, a collapse the latter cannot withstand. But Rozanov is too much of a mystic, too fascinated by the person of Christ, to try to explain rationalistically the power of this person. Rozanov senses an irrational mystery here. But the evil of the world, too, is an irrational mystery, and pure pantheism stands petrified before this mystery with a sense of helplessness and awkwardness. Rozanov tells us that the religion of death came from Christ. But let him also tell us where death came from and how it is compatible with the immanent divinity of the world.

Rozanov's beloved "world" is a graveyard, in which all things are corrupted by poisons secreted from the dead. In this graveyard he wants to grow flowers of divine life and to console himself with the fecundity of decomposing corpses. He deifies the biological fact of birth; however, the mystical riddle of life is linked not with biological birth, but with the mystery of death. It is as if Rozanov does not want to see *the duality of man's nature*, the fact that this nature belongs to *two worlds*; he shuts his eyes to the contradiction between the potential of

Christ and the World: In Response to Vasily Rozanov

the eternal and absolute life contained in man and the relativity of man's present life, the limitedness of all his present accomplishments. But man's religious hunger is rooted in this duality of his nature; it is the metaphysical-anthropological basis of religion. The religion of Christ rejects the world's limitedness and enslavement in the name of absolute unlimitedness and freedom. If Rozanov had a deep sense of personhood, of the tragic antinomy of all individual human existence, he would not insist on the dilemma: the "world" or Christ. Another dilemma must first be posed: *the world or personhood*. In "Rozanov's world," personhood perishes with all of its absolute potential. Christ comes: in Christ personhood is saved and all of its absolute potential, its divine-sonhood, is realized; it is summoned to participate in the divine harmony. And thus the dilemma "Christ or the world" loses all religious meaning or acquires another meaning, not Rozanov's.

True being is personhood, not species. The true universal union of persons is divine-human sobornost,[10] not impersonal nature. To affirm the fullness of being in the world is to affirm another world, the real one, not the natural order. But Rozanov does not believe in the supernatural; he erases all distinctions between mystical sensuousness and empirical sensuousness (the latter is what we have called immanent pantheism), and he therefore regards the religion of Christ as an illusory consolation, not as a real solution. Let me ask Rozanov the question upon which everything depends: Did Christ rise from the dead, and if Christ did rise from the dead, what happens to the dilemma "the world or Christ"? If Rozanov believed in the reality of the resurrection, would he insist on calling the religion of Christ the religion of death? But together with all the rationalists and positivists Rozanov is compelled to see in the resurrection either a deception or a myth; he believes that, in Christ, death triumphs, not life. That is why Rozanov's attack against Christ is not mystically terrifying. The attack would be terrifying if Rozanov believed in the reality of the resurrection but nevertheless kept portraying the religion of Christ as the religion of death. We have heard the positivists' refrain that "real" social reforms have a much greater efficacy in life than Christ's "illusory" resurrection, but it does not scare us one bit. Rozanov is imperceptibly rolling

---

10. The fellowship of deified human beings.—Trans.

down an inclined plane toward vulgar positivism; like a youth, he is growing his first whiskers of positivism. Indeed, his youthful infatuation with radical social ideas makes a strange impression. That which Rozanov is proclaiming at his age is commonly proclaimed by much younger men. It's as if this is his honeymoon period with positivism and socialism, the final results of atheistic European culture.

Formerly a conservative, almost a reactionary, Rozanov has begun to flirt with revolution and has gradually turned into a radical. But his ignorance and even illiteracy when it comes to politics prevents him from understanding the existing political movements; he remains alien to politics in the strict sense of the word. To the great chagrin of all those who revere this first-rate writer, something ambiguous has crept into him: his radicalism seems to lack seriousness, to be nothing more than a caprice of his temperament. But I think his attraction to social radicalism, his love of the "lefties," has deeper roots. He senses that the task of immanent pantheism and naturalistic mysticism can be furthered by a union with the burgeoning religion of socialism, the progressive social reorganization of this life. Socialism promises to organize and divinize the natural world and natural humanity. Rozanov's type of pantheism could enrich and poeticize the prose of social reorganization and spiritualize the joys of material life. Rozanov can make common cause with socialism and even with positivism because of his immanent relation to this world and to the joys of this life and his hostility toward the transcendental. But the "lefties" despise artists to such an extent that they don't wish to use Rozanov, and he continues to bear many insults from them. Rozanov will always remain a mystic, of course; his direct mystical sense of the world is too strong. He would never consent to do the work that the "lefties" would assign him; his overflowing talent would always be more powerful than his silly "leftism," than his dilettantish and philistine radicalism. The radicalism of Rozanov's formulation of the problem of sex and the flesh is much more authentic, sincere, and significant than his flirtation with "leftism."

Rozanov deserves enormous credit for his critique of official Christianity and the official ecclesiastical structure; with his themes he has greatly served the new religious consciousness. He has with unprecedented radicalism posed before the Christian consciousness the problem of our relation to the life of the world and especially to the source

Christ and the World: In Response to Vasily Rozanov

of life—sex. He has had a great influence on Merezhkovsky[11] and *Novy put'*, and he has been instrumental in defining the themes of the "Religious-Philosophical Meetings."[12] He has done much to improve the plight of illegitimate children. Rozanov has been much feared and much toasted; and his influence has been both beneficial and creative and harmful and oppressive. He has hypnotized everyone with his dilemma "Christ or the world," even though this dilemma does not exist in the way that he poses it. His dilemma is a product of the confusion and darkness of his consciousness. Rozanov's theme is a powerful one that helps sweep away a lot of our official Christian and ecclesiastical rubbish, but it has nothing to do with Christ. Only a weak and tottering consciousness could believe that it has anything to do with Christ. When Rozanov says that Christian marriage does not exist and that the Church vilifies love; when he says that if the sacrament of marriage truly exists, then let the union of man and woman take place in the church—he is powerful, radical, brilliantly audacious, and important to us. The official Church could not and did not find any way to answer him. But what does this religiously profound question have in common with the divinization of this immanent world, with the attempt to suppress Christ with the trite pleasures of routine existence? The historical Church has a high regard for routine family life, and in general is nourished by routine life; but it does not recognize the sacrament of love and denies the transcendent character of the sacrament of marriage. The official ecclesiastical structure does not oppose this world and the routine existence that crystallizes in it; it opposes the cosmos, the divine flesh of the world, and that is the tragedy of the Church. It is as if the Church opposes the very idea of the Church as a cosmic organism. We are seeing the birth of a new religious consciousness that yearns for a transfigured flesh, not for the original flesh. The original, pagan, corrupt flesh continues to live as contraband in the Church; but the new, resurrected flesh has not yet appeared in the Church. Rozanov pronounces his judgment on the Church as the representative of this old, pagan, corrupt flesh, which is already too prominent in the Church.

---

11. See the first essay in the present collection.—Trans.
12. See notes 4 and 5 above.—Trans.

That is why it is not good for the "Religious-Philosophical Meetings" to be overly influenced by Rozanov.

Christ is God's perfect, divine child, the image of the Cosmos. The Christ-child is the absolute norm for the world-child. In the name of His Son, the Logos, God created the world; through the Son the world becomes a child of God, returns to the Father. Christ is the divine intermediary between God and the world: if there were no Christ, the world would not be a child of God and the pantheist could not have his partial truth, i.e., the divinity of the world. Only the world that has received Christ and entered Christ becomes divine—a child of God. Our world, the one without Christ, is a world fallen away from God, a world that lies in evil; and its divinity is therefore a damaged and sick divinity, a dubious divinity. But there still remains a link between this fallen world and God; in the mystical order of being, this link is the Son of God, the God-Man, the eternal intercessor. This link became incarnate in history in the person of Christ. Through the God-Man and the God-World, the world becomes divine; it is deified. Between God and the world there is only an apparent opposition, caused by the weakness of human consciousness; beneath this opposition is concealed a mystically real union. Within the historical limits of Christianity the union of Christ and the world, the divinity of humanity and of the world, is not sufficiently visible, inasmuch as the cosmic epoch of redemption is not yet complete. The union of the world with God will be complete only in the divine dialectic of Trinity; the flesh of the world will be resurrected only in the coming Church. In the Spirit, all opposition disappears between the two children of God, between the world-child and the Christ-child. Christ revealed in Himself the God-Man; the Holy Spirit will reveal divine humanity. In divine humanity the deification of humanity and the deification of the world's flesh will take place. But the new, holy flesh will not be the same flesh as the old, pagan, corrupt flesh; it will not be the flesh that Rozanov is so concerned with. Instead, when they enter into the new world, all the elements of our world will be transfigured; nothing will be destroyed, but everything will be illuminated. We look forward to the coming Kingdom of God, not back at the lost paradise of the past. We want to be religious revolutionaries, not reactionaries. (Because of a strange irony of history, religious reactionaries sometimes make common cause with social revolutionaries.)

Christ and the World: In Response to Vasily Rozanov

Rozanov strives toward not the kingdom of the Spirit, not toward the kingdom of the One and Trinitarian God, but toward the kingdom of God the Father; but the kingdom of God the Father can now not arise, for it is incompatible with the mystical dialectic of Trinity, which completes the union of Creator and creation. This kingdom is virtually indistinguishable from atheism, from which pantheism is separated by an imperceptible barrier.

A new religious soul is being born in the world. This new soul is intimately linked with the old soul, with what was eternal in the old soul; but new horizons are opened in the new soul. For the new religious orientation and consciousness, a consciousness which has experienced all of modern history and all of its doubts and negations, the question of the Church is posed differently than it is for the old consciousness. We seek a Church that would contain the whole fullness of life, the whole experience of the world, a Church that would contain all that is valuable in the world, all that was authentic being in history. Nothing but non-being must remain outside the walls of the Church. The Church is a cosmic force, the deified world-soul. The Church is the divine world, the imperishable link between God and the world. To enter the Church is not to exit the world but to enter the true world. People of the old religious consciousness go into the Church in order to be saved from the life of the world, to atone by prayer for the sins accumulated in the world; and they leave outside the entrance to the Church all that is most dear to them in the world. All their creative impulses, all their raptures of love, all the complexity of their experience, the whole path of world history—all this they dare not bring with them into the Church. But we can no longer tolerate this dualism; it is godless and kills off all religious life; it is a blasphemy against the Holy Spirit. The Church must include all that is dear and valuable to us, all that we have gained through our suffering in the world—our love, our thought and poetry, all our creative works which the old consciousness has excluded from the Church. The Church must include all the great men of the world, all of our rapturous impulses and dreams, all that is transcendent in our life and in the life of the world. Ecclesial life is fullness of life, richness of being, not the uninspired existence of seminarians, priests, and monks who kowtow to the powers that be. Dostoevsky and Solovyov—these greatest of Russians, our teachers—

furthered the new religious movement more than anyone else, but they were not completely free of the old religious consciousness. Dostoevsky and Solovyov were very complicated men; they assimilated the whole experience of modern history, enduring all the temptations and doubts connected with it; and many new riches were accumulated in their souls. But, as before, they remained members of the Church; they did not bring all their riches into the Church; their wide experience did not make the Church more accommodating and capacious; in the Church they negated what they were. Solovyov's religious-philosophical system is much broader than his ecclesial religiosity; his system includes the idea of *divine humanity*, but the Church does not yet have a divine-human life. "In the Legend of the Grand Inquisitor," Dostoevsky widens the religious horizons and senses an amazing religious freedom, but he continues to go to Church with a consciousness that closes off all horizons. That is why I think that none of the existing historical churches is the Universal Church; none of them contains the fullness of revelation. The world, however, is advancing toward the Universal Church and yearning to sanctify its life in her.[13]

Rozanov will say that we are pantheizing the idea of the Church, but this pantheizing has nothing in common with his immanent pantheism. The Universal Church, encompassing the fullness of being, is the Church of the One and Trinitarian God, the Church of the Holy Trinity. In this Church, the apparent opposition between the world and Christ disappears for good. In the light of the new consciousness, a different dilemma is born: "official Christianity or Christ." Official Christianity is the old, inert world; Christ is the new world, opposed to all inertia.

---

13. I do not deny, of course, that the path to the total fullness of the Universal Church lies through the historical Churches, through their sacraments.—*A later note.*

7
The Fundamental Idea of Lev Shestov's Philosophy[1]

I have already had occasion to write about Lev Shestov in the pages of *Put'*. But now it is necessary to write a different kind of article about him and to honor his memory. Shestov was a philosopher who philosophized with his whole being; philosophy for him was not an academic specialty but a matter of life and death. He was obsessed by a single idea. And his independence from the dominant currents of the time was astonishing. He sought God; he sought the liberation of man from the power of necessity. That was the problem that obsessed him personally. His philosophy was a type of existential philosophy; that is, it did not objectify the process of cognition or separate this process from the subject of cognition, but linked it with the integral fate of the human being. Existential philosophy emphasizes the existentiality of the philosophizing subject who puts his existential experience into his philosophy. This type of philosophy presupposes that the mystery of being is knowable only in human existence. For Shestov, the human tragedy, the horrors and suffering of human life, the experience of despair constituted the source of philosophy. There is no need to exaggerate the novelty of what today is called existential philosophy thanks to certain currents of contemporary German philosophy. This element was possessed by all authentic and significant philosophers. Spinoza philosophized by means of the geometric method, and his philosophy can produce the impression of a cold, objective philosophy; but philosophical cognition was for him a matter of salvation, and his *amor Dei*

---

1. First published in the magazine *Put'* (No. 58, 1938) on the occasion of Shestov's death.—Trans.

[127]

intellectualis is by no means an objective, scientific-like truth. By the way, Shestov's attitude towards Spinoza was very interesting. Spinoza was Shestov's enemy, with whom he struggled his entire life as with a temptation. Spinoza was a representative of human reason, a destroyer of revelation. Nevertheless, Shestov loved Spinoza, remembering him constantly and quoting him frequently. In his last years, Shestov had a very significant encounter with Kierkegaard. Before this, Shestov had never read him and knew of him only by hearsay; thus, we cannot speak of any possible influence of Kierkegaard on Shestov's thought. But when Shestov read him, he was profoundly shaken and agitated by the closeness of Kierkegaard to the fundamental theme of his (Shestov's) own life. And he added Kierkegaard to the list of his heroes. His heroes were Nietzsche, Dostoevsky, Luther, and Pascal; and from the Bible—Abraham, Job, and Isaiah. As in the case of Kierkegaard, the theme of Shestov's philosophy was religious; and, as in the case of Kierkegaard, his principal foe was Hegel. Shestov went from Nietzsche to the Bible. He was increasingly preoccupied with Biblical revelation. The conflict between Biblical revelation and Greek philosophy became the principal theme of his reflections.

To the principal theme of his life Shestov subordinated all that he thought, said, and wrote. He viewed the world and judged the thought of others solely from within his own theme; he referred everything to his theme and divided the world according to his theme. His theme shook him to his very core. What was his theme? He was shaken to his very core by the power of necessity over human life, of necessity which produces the horrors of life. He was interested not in crude forms of necessity, but in its subtle forms. Philosophers had idealized the power of inexorable necessity in the form of reason and morality, in the form of self-evident and universally obligatory truths. Necessity is engendered by knowledge. Shestov is obsessed with the idea that the fall of man is connected with knowledge, with the knowledge of good and evil. Man stopped being nourished from the tree of life and started being nourished from the tree of knowledge. And, in the name of the liberation of life, Shestov wars against the power of knowledge which subjects man to the law. This signifies a passionate striving towards paradise, towards the free life of paradise. But paradise is attained when the conflict is intensified; it is attained through disharmony and despair.

The Fundamental Idea of Lev Shestov's Philosophy

Fundamentally, Shestov was not against scientific knowledge, against the use of reason in ordinary life. But that was not the problem that concerned him. He was opposed to the claim of science and reason that they could solve the problem of God and liberate man from the tragic horror of human fate, whereas reason and rational knowledge actually want to limit possibilities. God is, first and foremost, unlimited possibilities; that is the fundamental definition of God. God is not constrained by any necessary truths. The human person is a victim of necessary truths, of the law of reason and morality—a victim of the universal and universally obligatory.

God stands in opposition to the kingdom of necessity, the kingdom of reason. God is not constrained by anything, not subordinated to anything; for God, all things are possible. Here, Shestov poses a question that preoccupied thinkers as early as the scholastic philosophy of the Middle Ages: Is God subordinate to reason, truth, and the good, or are they established by God? The first opinion originated with Plato and was shared by Aquinas. The second was defended by Duns Scotus. The first opinion is associated with intellectualism, the second with voluntarism. Shestov is on Scotus' side, but his posing of the problem is much more radical. If God exists, then everything is possible and the truths of reason stop being inexorable and the horrors of life stop being invincible. This is the most important element of Shestov's theme, the element responsible for the profound agitation that marks his entire thought. Can God undo that which has been done? Reason finds this extremely unfathomable. It is very easy to understand Shestov incorrectly here. The poisoned Socrates can be resurrected; Christians believe that. Kierkegaard can regain his bride and Nietzsche can be cured from his horrible illness. That is not what Shestov means. God can make it so that Socrates was never poisoned, Kierkegaard never lost his bride, and Nietzsche never contracted his horrible illness. Absolute victory can be achieved over that necessity which rational knowledge imposes on the past. Shestov was tormented by the unchangeabilty of the past, by the horror of that which had been.

This theme of necessary and obligatory truth is connected with Shestov's opposition of Jerusalem to Athens and of Abraham and Job to Socrates and Aristotle. All attempts to unite with revelation the reason discovered by Greek philosophy led to nullification of faith; theology was constantly guilty of this. The God of Abraham, Isaac, and Jacob was supplanted by the God of the theologians and philosophers. Philo was the first betrayer. God was subordinated to reason, to necessary and universally obligatory truths; and Abraham, the hero of faith, perished. Shestov is very close to Luther, to Luther's salvation by faith alone. The liberation of man cannot come from man himself, but only from God. God is the liberator. Liberation comes not from reason, not from morality, not from human activity, but from faith. For the necessary truths of reason, faith is miracle. The mountains move. Faith demands madness. We already learn this from the Apostle Paul. Faith fosters conflict and paradox, as Kierkegaard liked to say. With great radicalism Shestov expressed an essential and eternal problem. Shestov's writings were full of paradox and irony, and that prevented readers from understanding him correctly. Sometimes he was taken to mean the opposite of what he actually meant. This happened for example with the remarkable thinker Unamuno, to whom Shestov felt very close.

Shestov had great difficulty expressing his philosophical thought, and this led to many misunderstandings. He was unable to express his thoughts on what was most essential for him, his thoughts on the fundamental theme of his life. He was most successful when he used a negative form of expression. It was clear what he was battling against. By contrast, the positive form of expression was difficult for him. Human language is too rationalized and too adapted to the thought that is a product of the fall of man, a product of the knowledge of good and evil. Directed against that which was universally obligatory, Shestov's thought itself took on, unintentionally, the form of the universally obligatory. And this provided much ammunition to his critics. We encounter here a profound and little studied problem: to what extent can creative thought be communicated to others? Can the most primary and important things be communicated, or only secondary and ephemeral things? This problem is posed most profoundly by existential philosophy, which formulates it as the problem of passing from "I" to "thou" in authentic communion. Philosophy that regards itself as rational is not troubled by this problem because it assumes the existence of universal reason. One and the same universal reason makes possible an adequate transmission of thought and knowledge from one

The Fundamental Idea of Lev Shestov's Philosophy

person to another. But, in reality, reason has different degrees and qualities and depends on the character of human existence, on existential experience. Will determines the character of reason. Thus, there arises the question of the possibility of the transmission of philosophical thought not through rational concepts. Indeed, rational concepts do not establish communication from one person to another. Shestov was not directly interested in this problem and did not write about it; his attention was entirely absorbed by the relation of man and God, not by the relation of man and man. But his philosophy poses this problem very acutely; he himself becomes a problem of philosophy. His contradiction was that, although he was a philosopher, i.e., a man of thought and knowledge, he knew the tragedy of human existence and rejected knowledge. He battled against the tyranny of reason, against the power of knowledge which expelled man from paradise; but he battled against it on the territory of knowledge itself and with the weapons of reason. This constitutes the difficulty of philosophy that desires to be existential. I credit Shestov with the achievement of making this difficulty as acute as possible.

Shestov battled in defense of personhood, in defense of the individually unrepeatable against the power of the general. His chief enemy was Hegel and the Hegelian universal spirit. In this, he shows his kinship with Kierkegaard, with Belinksy (in the letters to Botkin), and especially with Dostoevsky. It is in this battle that Shestov's great truth consists. In this battle against the power of the universally obligatory he was so radical that what is true and salvific for one person he considered untrue and not obligatory for another person. He thought, in essence, that every man has his own personal truth. But this led to the same problem of communication. Can people communicate with one another on the basis of the truth of revelation, or is communication possible only on the basis of the truths of reason, adapted to common, everyday life—that is, on the basis of what Shestov (following Dostoevsky) called "all-ness"?

Until the last days of his life Shestov retained a fiery intensity of thought. He manifested in himself a victory of the spirit over the frailty of the flesh. It was in this last period of his life that he wrote what are perhaps his best books, *Kierkegaard and Existential Philosophy* and *Athens and Jerusalem: An Endeavor at Religious Philosophy*. Now is not the time to criticize the philosophy of my old friend Lev Shestov. I only want to say one thing. I am in great sympathy with Shestov's problematic and with his theme of the battle against the power of the "general" over human life. But I always diverged with him in the assessment of knowledge; I do not consider the latter to be the source of the necessity that oppresses our life. Only existential philosophy can explain the true nature of the matter here. Shestov's books help provide an answer to the fundamental problem of human existence; they have an existential significance.

8
Lev Shestov and Kierkegaard[1]

Lev Shestov's book on Kierkegaard is perhaps the best of his books. Like most of Shestov's books, it is written brilliantly. Its fundamental thought is expressed with extreme concision and clarity, ironically enough by a thinker who rejects thought and wars against knowledge. I consider him to be a highly remarkable and original thinker; I greatly value his problematic and greatly sympathize with his battle against the power of the "general" over human life, his battle against necessity, his thirst for freedom. But only his negative philosophy is rich and extensive; his positive philosophy is meager and brief—it could fit on half a page. It could not be otherwise: what he wants can't be expressed in thought or word; it is pure apophatics. He remains, however, on the territory of thought and reason. In the book on Kierkegaard, I even find a whole cosmogony, though expressed briefly. It is nevertheless an intellectual construction, though one that is based on the tragic experience of Shestov himself and of his favorite heroes.

As could have been expected, the book is more about Shestov himself than about Kierkegaard. Kierkegaard is only a splendid excuse to develop a theme that has tormented Shestov himself and to which he has dedicated all his creative labors. There is much he fails to notice in Kierkegaard, but he feels extremely close to him and is shaken by his fate. His encounter with Kierkegaard is a crucial event for him. Shestov is an existential philosopher. But existential philosophy, i.e., a philosophy that is directed at the subject, not at the object, cannot only be a tale about experienced human misfortunes. Experienced tragedy can be a source of knowledge, but it is not yet philosophy. Philosophical knowledge is an act of understanding performed by a thinker in

---

1. First published in the magazine *Sovremennye zapiski*, 1936, No. 2, as a review of the French edition of Shestov's *Kierkegaard and Existential Philosophy*.—Trans.

relation to the experienced tragedy. Shestov rejects this cognitive act, asserting that it has been suggested by the ancient serpent. But lacking consistency, he nonetheless performs this act, and this saves him as a thinker. The difficulties encountered by Shestov when he tries to express his theme are so great that they could have made his position as a philosopher hopeless. He might even have been compelled to remain silent. But all this is smoothed out in his books, and we get an illusion of clarity. This can be explained by his literary talent: by his constant irony, by his captivating lyricism, and by his extraordinary sensitivity which imparts a particular humaneness to his writings. Only emotional language can convey his meaning, a meaning which can be translated into intellectual language (a language, by the way, that is very natural to him) only with great difficulty. We cannot avoid the impression that Shestov is primarily struggling with himself, with his own rationalism and with his own rationalistic obstacles to faith. And he tries to convince us that everyone encounters the same rationalistic obstacles, that all things are in the power of the serpent's reason. And this might appear convincing because he is dealing almost exclusively with philosophers, with men of knowledge, and struggling against them. He does not address witnesses of faith.

In essence, Shestov's thought is very despotic. His despotism of thought always results from the division of the world and the orientations of thought into two elements. The first element is the dark kingdom: Greek philosophy, Socrates, Aristotle, Spinoza, Kant, Hegel, knowledge, reason and morality, universally obligatory truths, necessity. The second element is the luminous kingdom: the Bible, or rather certain passages of the Bible, Tertullian, Pascal, Luther, Nietzsche, Dostoevsky, Kierkegaard, faith, the unlimited possibilities "beyond good and evil," life, freedom. For the dark kingdom of reason, morality, and knowledge there is, in essence, no salvation; there is almost no salvation for all philosophers, and especially for the greatest of them. When I was reading Shestov's book, a very exciting book, I had the excruciating impression that everything in it was conditional and that the author was not convinced of the reality of his conditional constructions. If God exists, then unlimited possibilities exist and that which had once been done—Socrates' poisoning, Nietzsche's progressive paralysis, Kierkegaard's loss of his bride—could be undone. Victory over the necessity that cripples our life would then be possible; the free life of paradise would be possible. But Shestov's thought has a particularly tragic character because God, for whom all things are possible and who is higher that all necessity and all universally obligatory truths, remains a conditional hypothesis. God is postulated for the sake of salvation from the power of reason and morality, not unlike the way Kant postulated Him in order to save morality. Shestov is strong in his negation, not in his affirmation; in his yearning for faith, not in his faith. His books tend to leave the impression that the last word belongs to reason, to the universally obligatory truths, to morality, to necessity, to the impossibility of Nietzsche and Kierkegaard being liberated from their torments.

For Shestov the main thing is faith. In that respect he resembles Luther. Faith, not virtue, is opposite to sin. Only faith can save; only faith in God, for whom all things are possible and who is not constrained by any necessity, can return his bulls and children to Job, Isaac to Abraham, Regine Olsen to Kierkegaard, and so on. Outside of faith there is no salvation from the power of necessity. But how is faith possible and who has it? Reading Shestov, we get the impression that faith is impossible and nobody has ever had it except Abraham, who raised his knife over his beloved son Isaac. Shestov does not believe that so-called "believers" possess faith. Nor did the great saints possess it. After all, nobody moves mountains. Faith does not depend on man; it is sent by God. God gives faith very rarely. He did not give it to Kierkegaard, or to any of Shestov's tragic heroes. The only path turns out to be closed. According to Shestov's maximalistic notion, faith becomes impossible and nobody has it. But this notion does not accord with the greatest testimonies about faith in the history of the human spirit, including the testimonies of the Apostle Paul, and of all the apostles, saints, prophets, and religious reformers. For Shestov, faith is the end of the human tragedy, the end of the struggle, the end of suffering, and the advent of unlimited possibilities and of the life of paradise. But this is an erroneous conception of faith, and many use it as a pretext to justify the rejection of faith. Faith is not the end, not the life of paradise; it is only the beginning of an arduous path, the beginning of a heroic struggle which Shestov rejects. A man who has faith continues to bear the burden of the world's necessity and helps those without faith carry their burdens. A man who has faith passes through trials, doubts, and ambiguities. Man's nature is active, not passive.

Shestov has such a conception of faith because he links the bliss of paradise with the passiveness of man's nature. Meanwhile, he links the activeness of man's nature with reason, knowledge, and morality. Freedom is acquired only from God; man is irrelevant here: he only uses and enjoys freedom, contemplating the morning star, finding love with the princess, and so on. Nothing repels Shestov as much as heroism. The passiveness of man's nature in relation to God is always a form of quietism. Shestov summons man back to the Bible and revelation in order to liberate him from the power of Socrates and of Greek philosophy, from the power of reason and morality, the power of universally obligatory truths. But Shestov takes from the Bible only what he needs for his theme. He is not a Biblical man; he is a man of the end of the 19th century and the beginning of the 20th century. Nietzsche is closer to him than the Bible and remains the chief influence of his life. He makes a Biblical transcription of Nietzsche's theme, of Nietzsche's battle against Socrates, against reason and morality in the name of "life." For Shestov the Bible is virtually exhausted by the story of the Fall and by the stories of Abraham and Job. He seems to forget that the central figure of the Biblical revelation is not Abraham, but the one who spoke face to face with God—Moses. But the Biblical revelation of God through Moses, which constitutes the foundation of Judaism and of the Christian Old Testament is a revelation of the law, of the Ten Commandments. It is perfectly clear that Shestov has no use for Moses and so he puts Moses in the same line as Socrates. But what could be more Biblical than Moses? For both Kierkegaard and Shestov the Abraham who raises his knife over his beloved son is only a literary image, illustrating their theme of faith as the sphere of unlimited possibilities. The figure of Abraham is astonishing, but it represents the primitive belief that human sacrifices can placate God.

What is Shestov's fundamental idea, if it is permissible to speak of ideas in relation to him? He expresses this idea in his book on Kierkegaard with great talent and brilliance and with great force. Shestov relates his myth of the creation of the world and of the fall of man. Here, he gives us an entire compressed cosmogony. The absolutely free God, who is not constrained by any eternal truths and for whom all things are possible, created the world and man. Beautiful was the life that God gave to the world and to man. This was the life of paradise. The life of paradise was the eating from the tree of life. But out of the abyss of non-being (*néant*) came the serpent, and the voice of the serpent bewitched man, tempting him with the fruit from the tree of the knowledge of good and evil. Through the temptation of knowledge the abyss of non-being was transformed into necessity (the eternal truths of knowledge), necessity was transformed into reason and morality, and reason and morality were transformed into eternity. Shestov is an enemy of eternity, considering it the final transformation of non-being. Eternity comes from the serpent, not from God. Shestov is also an enemy of spirit and of mysticism. Eternity, spirit, mysticism, the other world—these are all fictions invented by reason as a consequence of the loss of the sole reality of this earthly life created by God. Shestov is an enemy of eternity because he understands eternity to mean the eternal truths of reason and the eternal laws of nature, i.e., necessity. But what should one do with the eternal life of concrete living beings, with the eternal life of Job, of Socrates, of the unhappy Nietzsche, of the unhappy Kierkegaard, and of Shestov himself? Enmity towards this eternity would be tantamount to recognizing death as the last word of life. But what life of paradise could there be if death triumphs? The same thing goes for Shestov's enmity towards spirit. He understands spirit to mean reason and the necessity engendered by the latter. But spirit can also be understood to mean freedom and the liberation from the kingdom of necessity; and that is the only true understanding of spirit.

This might appear strange, but one finds in Shestov a very strong element of Manicheism. For him the world is wholly under the domination of the serpent. The world is ruled by necessity, which is a transformation of non-being; in other words, the world is ruled by the serpent through reason with its inexorable truth and good. There is no sign anywhere that God acts in the world. God acts exclusively through faith but, as we have seen, nobody possesses any true faith. There is also no sign of freedom. The pinnacle of the world's life is found in human agony, in the despair of men such as Kierkegaard. No path is revealed to Shestov. Every path belongs to the kingdom of ordinariness.

It would be interesting to explore what Shestov means when he speaks of God. The book on Kierkegaard gives us an extremely clear picture of what he means. God is unlimited possibilities, which are needed for the fulfillment of human desires, for the undoing of the great misfortunes experienced by men. God is the return of Isaac to Abraham, of the bulls and children to Job, of his health to Nietzsche, of Regine Olsen to Kierkegaard, and so on. God is the poor youth dreaming of the princess and winning the princess as well as the Underground Man being able to have his tea.[2] But why is Shestov so certain that an absolutely free God (where God's freedom is practically equated with caprice) would want to return Regine Olsen to Kierkegaard or give the princess to the youth? Perhaps, God does not want that at all, but instead prefers that Kierkegaard remain bereft of his bride and that the poor youth go without his princess. In that case, vain are the hopes that Kierkegaard and Shestov have placed on God. The unlimited possibilities of God include the possibility that He does not want Kierkegaard to have Regine Olsen or the poor youth to have the princess. It is very possible that Regine Olsen was taken away from Kierkegaard not by the serpent, not by necessity, not by reason and knowledge, not by Hegel, but by God. I even dare to think that this might be a good thing. Regine Olsen was probably the most ordinary bourgeois girl, and in the case of a happy family life the pastor Kierkegaard would have delivered virtuous sermons and written banal theological books, but we would not have his works of genius and Shestov would not have the occasion to write a splendid book about him. The "life" that so captivates this enemy of reason and knowledge, of spirit and eternity, this "life" is by no means such a splendid thing. God is not the fulfillment of human desires. God is probably something altogether different. Also, the question of desires is a complicated one. There was a poor youth who dreamt of a princess. Shestov repeats this a thousand times in his book and builds his entire theology on it. But consider another poor youth. He dreams of knowing the mysteries of being or of scientifically discovering the mysteries of nature. It turns

---

2. Dostoevsky's protagonist in *Notes from Underground* muses: "If given a choice between letting the world go to hell or going without my tea, I'd let the world go to hell as long as I could always have my tea."—Trans.

out that God cannot satisfy this youth's desires; only the serpent can satisfy them, for knowledge comes from the serpent, not from God. Shestov does not notice that, with this, he greatly limits God's freedom and possibilities. Everything in Shestov is based on the idealization and apotheosis of life, and in this respect he is an adherent of *Lebensphilosophie*. Klages, who, unlike Shestov, lacks a significant religious problematic, also wants to be nourished exclusively from the tree of life and regards spirit and reason as parasites that suck out the juices of life.[3] But life is all things. Why is knowledge not life? Knowledge, too, is part of life; it is an event in being. The youth dreaming of knowledge is not inferior to the youth dreaming of the princess.

In the book on Kierkegaard we find (perhaps for the first time in Shestov's works) a number of unpleasant passages devoted to Christianity. Christianity is placed in the same line as Socrates, stoicism, and idealism, i.e., in the line of the serpent, in the line of non-being that has been transformed into reason and morality, into eternity. Shestov finds completely alien the mystery of redemption, which he considers an invention of reason. He forgets that the cross was a stumbling block for the Jews and madness for the Greeks. Contra Shestov, it is very easy for reason to view God as an omnipotent being for whom all things are possible and very difficult to view Him as suffering and crucified. Shestov is not impressed by the Divine sacrifice of love and the crucifixion, which he views as limitations of God's freedom and omnipotence. He inherits this from Judaism. Shestov does not accept that God became man. It seems to him that this is acceptable to reason and invented by reason, whereas for reason it is actually an unfathomable mystery and paradox.

May I be forgiven by this warrior against reason, but here I see him as a rationalist. However strange this might appear, Shestov regards religion, especially the Christian religion, as an "opium of the people," as masked reason and morality which reinforce ordinariness by promising an invented eternity, an invented spiritual world. What is hardest to fathom is how Shestov would solve the problem of death, which has always agitated him. Is the existence of concrete beings finite? Does

---

3. Allusion to Ludwig Klages (1872–1956), German psychologist and philosopher.—Trans.

Shestov reject only the eternal truths of reason and morality, or does he also reject eternal life? That is the fundamental question. What would happen with man's infinite strivings? On what could one place one's hopes? On the fact that God is unlimited possibilities? But Kierkegaard died without regaining Regine Olsen; Nietzsche died without being cured of his horrible illness and without truly tasting the fruits from the tree of life; Socrates was poisoned, and there was nothing after that. All of us will die without having fulfilled our infinite desires, without having fully tasted the fruits from the tree of life. There will be no paradise for anyone on this earth, in this time. What's the point of Shestov's appeals to the God for whom all things are possible and who can liberate Kierkegaard from his torments, if this God does not provide resurrection into eternal life? Shestov's battle against reason and ethics turns out to be just as impotent before man's tragic fate as reason and ethics themselves. Let me repeat that I often agree with Shestov's problematic, with his revolt against the power over man's fate of the "general" invented by reason and ethics. But Shestov preaches human passiveness. For Shestov, man is sinful but not responsible, and therefore he is irresponsible and passive. Only God is active, but He does not manifest himself in the world in any way. Knowledge, after all, is one of the manifestations of human activeness. Reason can enslave man, but it can also serve him. The misfortune of man and the world did not come from knowledge; it most certainly did not come from knowledge. Knowledge knows necessity, but does not create it. Necessity is produced by objectification. In my opinion, Shestov's chief philosophical deficiency is that he does not make any distinctions related to the forms and degrees of knowledge. Also, like reason's rationalistic defenders, he believes in the catholicity and homogeneity of reason, whereas reason is mutable and qualitatively variable, reflecting man's qualitative states and the relations of man to man.

9

Theosophy and Anthroposophy in Russia[1]

I

The type of movement I intend to describe can only conditionally be called religious thought. It does not have any outstanding representatives in the Russian literature and cannot be characterized by looking at the thought of any one individual thinker.[2] We will not encounter here a psychology of individual thought, as in the case of Bulgakov and Merezhkovsky; we will try instead to uncover a psychology of thought that is typical and impersonal. The founder of the theosophical society was a remarkable Russian woman, Helena Blavatsky; but the theosophical movement itself is not typical or essential for our Russian thought. And if, nevertheless, I include theosophy when characterizing the types of religious thought in Russia, it is only because it is starting to play a significant role in Russian spiritual life, especially in our cultural stratum, and this role will undoubtedly keep growing. Theosophy and its main variant, i.e., anthroposophy, are being peculiarly refracted in the Russian soul. In his spiritual makeup the Russian theosophist bears little resemblance to the German or English theosophist; one often sees in him an apocalyptic tendency which is completely alien to western theosophy and even contradicts the principles of the theosophical doctrine.

---

1. First published in the magazine *Russkaya mysl'*, November 1916.—Trans.
2. The most independent and talented theosophical writer in Russia is P.D. Ouspensky.—Trans.

When we look at the religious questing of our time, we find another reason why it is not possible to ignore theosophy: for certain strata of our contemporary cultured society, the easiest way to get to religion is by way of theosophy. The theosophical path requires few intellectual sacrifices and renunciations. One need not renounce one's mode of rational thought or one's cultural habits; all kinds of contradictions can be reconciled. Popular theosophy consents to be the natural complement to both positive science and positive culture; it is an extension of naturalism to new planes. Theosophy does not represent a type of creative religious thought and, evidently, it does not pretend to be a creative force. Theosophy fears creative natures and pushes them away from itself. The theosophical literature is nothing more than a popularization of ancient wisdom, handed down through successive teachers. The main tasks of theosophy are pedagogical, not creative. It is difficult to find any creative thinkers among theosophists. The average level of theosophical books is very low. Theosophists are afraid of independent thought and generally are not interested in the multifaceted creative process that is taking place outside their circle. A closed cliquishness is very typical for theosophists and anthroposophists. Nevertheless, it must be said that theosophy fulfills certain deep needs of the contemporary man who is profoundly dissatisfied with official science, official philosophy, and official religion. The widespread propagation of theosophy is a symptom of the crisis of official knowledge, which is grounded not in a concrete mythologeme, but in an abstract philosopheme. Theosophy, on the other hand, popularizes (though often in an arid and boring form) the great myth-making knowledge of past eras. Theosophy is a contemporary gnosticism, which wishes to give to man's soul not religious faith and not abstract scientific knowledge, but wise integral knowledge. Having reached its current stage of development, contemporary man's soul is satisfied neither with science nor with religious faith, but desires wise knowledge. But can one recognize as a higher gnosis our contemporary theosophy as it is represented in the theosophical literature?

If we consider the books of the two principal theosophical writers of our time, Annie Besant and Rudolf Steiner, we will find that the knowledge they teach is a descriptive science, like geography or mineralogy; it is knowledge gained not through personal creative efforts or through personal revelations, but through education. In their style and character, theosophical books have nothing in common with mystical books or with philosophical books; they bear the stamp neither of personal creative inspiration nor of personal creative thought. Theosophical writers seem to make every effort to avoid having their own thoughts and ideas. Their aim is to present a map of the structure of the world in all its planes, to give a pure description of objects and things: here's a river, there's a mountain. All contemporary theosophical books are constructed on this model. It is as if theosophy does not strive to discover the meaning of the world, to decode its riddle, to uncover the final and ultimate things. In this respect, contemporary theosophy resembles contemporary science, though it describes different planes of the cosmos and uncovers deeper layers. Contemporary theosophical books not only do not attempt to solve the problems of the origin of the world and of Divinity and of the meaning of the cosmic process, but they do not even pose them. Theosophy is only a descriptive and externally scientific-like and empirical knowledge of cosmic structure and cosmic evolution. Least of all is it a knowledge of meaning, a method for the creative uncovering of the meaning of being.

The very name "theosophy" turns out to be unjustified, for contemporary theosophical books contain no knowledge of God and even rarely mention the name of God. In this respect, contemporary theosophy is completely dissimilar to the theosophy of Jacob Boehme and other great theosophists of the past who possessed true divine wisdom and knowledge. If it is difficult to find a doctrine of God in contemporary theosophy, it is not less difficult to find a doctrine of man in contemporary anthroposophy. Both theosophy and anthroposophy concern themselves not with God and not with man, but with the cosmos. Theosophy and anthroposophy do not pose the problem of the meaning of cosmic evolution, of its beginning and end, for this problem is already the problem of God and of man, who are not derivable from the cosmos but bring their own light into it. In the final analysis, theosophy is compelled to naturalistically divinize the fact of cosmic evolution, which has neither beginning nor end; and it demands that man obey a process that is meaningless to him. Man's fate is not illuminated by divine knowledge; instead, it is weighed down by the fact of cosmic knowledge. Theosophical knowledge is overly oriented toward the natural sciences and requires nothing more than their extension to other planes of being. Contemporary popular theosophy is very respectful toward science but almost totally ignores philosophy. From the natural sciences it borrows a naive realism. Theosophy does not have its own gnoseology; instead, it uses the gnoseological concepts of naive realism. Contemporary theosophy easily translates the suprasensuous into the language of sensuous perception and it makes the spiritual materialize. And only rarely does it disclose the symbolic nature of the material. The vulgar understanding of theosophy is infected with an uncritical materialism. Popular theosophical knowledge defines itself as uncreative and passively descriptive knowledge, as pure empiricism. It is nothing more than an extended positivism. Theosophy gives us an eclectic synthesis of fragments of the old religious knowledge with fragments of the new scientific knowledge. In essence, theosophy is diametrically opposite to all subjectivism and individualism. In theosophy, contemporary man seeks salvation from psychologism, from self-absorption, from solitary caprice. Theosophy tempts contemporary man with the promise that it will unite him with the ancient cosmic wisdom and insert his soul into the chain of divine cosmic evolution and into the divine cosmic hierarchy. For many people, theosophy is the only bridge by which they can cross into spiritual life, by which they can leave the soulless and meaningless life of the contemporary world. Contemporary theosophy is not a great thing, but it is connected with a great thing and catches the reflected light of the ancient divine wisdom. This cannot fail to be seductive. Great is the spiritual thirst in our epoch and great is man's sense of abandonment. Contemporary man has been torn away from the sources, and theosophy promises to reunite him with them. Theosophy cautiously leads contemporary man to the ancient sources of life, taking into account the habits of his thought and the terror of his soul before the miraculous and catastrophic. The increasing popularity of theosophy is not a superficial and evanescent fashion; it represents a profound process in the spiritual life of our time.

II

In contrast to Bulgakov's reborn Orthodoxy or Merezhkovsky's new Christianity, contemporary theosophy climbs from below upward, from our contemporary consciousness and contemporary science to divine consciousness and spiritual knowledge. Theosophy is very pedagogical; not wishing to frighten him, it employs an evolutionary way of educating contemporary man. Popular theosophy is not intended for people of a high cultural level. It is intended not for creative people, not for thinkers and artists, and not for saints, but for people of average culture who possess spiritual needs. Theosophy is connected with occultism, with the ancient occult traditions. But its esoteric kernel remains hidden; in itself, it is exoteric. A particular exoteric esotericism has evolved in the contemporary theosophical literature. The method of theosophy is always spiritually evolutionary, not spiritually revolutionary or spiritually catastrophic. The path of theosophy is a path without divine grace; not one ray of divine light falls on this path; everything is achieved from below. Nothing in theosophy is a gift of God; everything is achieved through toil and according to justice, nothing through love. Man's soul is condemned to wander through the cosmic corridors, and the fate of this soul is subject to law: it must live under a law that is also divine justice. In contrast to the old Christian and the new Christian consciousness, the theosophical consciousness is a decisive and extreme immanentism and monism. Theosophy identifies the Creator with creation, God with nature. This immanentism and monism is acquired from the ancient religious consciousness of India; it is Aryan and does not accept the Semitic religious inoculation. But the immanentism and monism of contemporary theosophy has an evolutionarily naturalistic character. Theosophy, as a system of spiritual knowledge, transposes the laws of naturalistic evolution into other planes and other worlds, into the life of the spirit. It is not by chance that Steiner allies himself with Haeckel[3] and wants to transpose

---

3. Ernst Haeckel (1834–1919) was a German biologist, naturalist, philosopher, physician, professor, and artist who discovered, described and named thousands of new species, mapped a tree relating all life forms, and coined many terms in biology.—Trans.

Haeckel into other worlds. Steiner's philosophy contains a great deal of naturalistic monism, not the philosophically refined monism of Drews,[4] but the popular natural-scientific monism of Haeckel. Every popular theosophical book contains elements of vulgar naturalistic monism. Theosophy thus seeks a center outside of man and his depths; it objectifies and materializes everything. Man's spirit is placed in slavish dependence on cosmic evolution over vast stretches of time. This theosophically naturalistic evolutionism leads to the rejection of a direct connection between man's spirit and the Absolute. Theosophy rejects the dualism of freedom and necessity, of spirit and nature.

The popular theosophical doctrine of Karma is a doctrine of the naturalistic evolution of the unredeemed soul, of the wanderings of the soul which pulls after itself infinite threads from the past. Karma is the law of nature identified with the law of divine justice; it is the naturalization of divine mysteries. And the eastern doctrine of Karma is the negation of grace-filled love, of creative superabundance. All things occur and all things are given only in proportion to justice. But divine love is not justice; it gives immeasurably more than should be given according to justice. This is the mystery of Christ, the mystery of superabundant grace-filled love which promises the crucified robber that today he will enter the Kingdom of God. According to justice and necessity the robber is not worthy to be with Christ and to see the Kingdom of God, but would have to undergo a thousand agonizing reincarnations. Theosophy does not want to know this mystery of Christ, this miraculous grace-filled liberation from the yoke of the past, from the power of time; it does not want to know this compression of infinite time into a single instant. Everything in theosophy is based on a terrible and inexorable lawfulness, which is introduced into the very depths of divine life. Karmic fate is just and lawful; it does not know forgiveness and mercy, or love and freedom. Christianity, on the other hand, is first and foremost the religion of love and freedom, not of justice and lawfulness. From eastern theosophy, from the doctrine of Kama, the nightmare of the unredeemed past descends upon us and stretches its threads into the infinite future. Man's soul has no way out

---

4. Christian Heinrich Arthur Drews (1865–1935), German philosopher, was one of the most important representatives of German monist thought.—Trans.

of infinite cosmic evolution into absolute divine life. Between me and God there always lies the infinite evolution of an uncountable number of worlds. Man remains in the power of the bad infinity of evolution. There is no grace-filled liberation, no way out into absolute, divine life. The mystery of redemption is not enacted over the soul. The soul must wander eternally and infinitely through dark corridors, enduring its Karma. This is the bad infinity of the natural order translated into divine life. The old Christian consciousness knew an end, a way out, a victory over time, heaven and hell, beyond which there is no natural evolutionary process. Hell was the dear price paid to free oneself from the nightmare of the bad infinity of reincarnations, of infinite evolutions. Even eternal hell is better than this infinite process. An enormous role was played in the religious consciousness of India by the thirst for liberation from the nightmare of infinite reincarnations. Better bliss in divine love or torment in the divine fire, better an end in the divine, than infinity in the natural. Hell itself possesses, as it were, divine absoluteness. This old Christian consciousness possesses a limited field of view but also the great truth of exiting from the natural order into the divine order. As for theosophy, it does not have an eschatology. Its immanentism is naturalistic, not divine. For theosophy, God is even more remote from man than He is for the transcendental dogmatics of the Church. But this is the remoteness of infinite natural evolution. Popular theosophy has by no means solved the problem of time and eternity, the problem of the relative and the absolute. Eternity and absoluteness are naturalized and adapted to this world. The doctrine of reincarnation contains a great truth. Karma is the law of the natural life of the soul. Theosophy penetrates deeper into the structure and evolution of the cosmos than does the traditional metaphysics of the Church. But in Christianity the natural truth of reincarnation is transformed: redeeming grace changes the consequences of the naturalistic evolution of souls; time can be compressed into an instant. The robber who addressed Christ experienced more in a single instant than is experienced in infinite cosmic evolutions. Mysticism always knows this victory over time and over the world, for it is directed at the depths of divine life. Occultism does not know this victory, for it is directed at the infinitude of cosmic life.

III

Having its source in India, in the non-Christian East, theosophy does not recognize what is unique and unrepeatable. It does not know the mystery of the person, of the person of Christ and of every man. For the theosophical consciousness, nothing is unique, everything infinitely repeats itself. There are many Christs; the human person is splintered into a multitude of pieces. Eastern theosophy is not a revelation of "I," of man.[5] It knows only the one, impersonal, non-human spirit. But its impersonal pantheism is united with cosmic multiplicity, with multiple repeatability. Personalistic metaphysics is completely alien to theosophy. In contemporary theosophy the ancient religious and philosophical wisdom of India is popularized and simplified. The Hindu consciousness of God contains something that is inexpressible in our language, something that is untranslatable into our European concepts. Being and non-being mean something wholly different in Hindu wisdom than they do in our European philosophy. But theosophy adapts the wisdom of India to our contemporary language and contemporary concepts, and thus simplifies it. Nevertheless, we have a definite sense that the Christian truth about personhood and about man is alien to the wisdom of India. This wisdom represents the initial stage of the religious revelation of the One. And only in the one and unrepeatable Christ is the uniqueness and unrepeatability of every human person revealed. Eastern theosophy does not know the God-Man. For theosophy, man is only a transitory instrument of cosmic evolution. In the cosmos, man is formed from different shells, from fragments of planetary evolutions. And then man also disintegrates into his constituent parts. Even Christ is formed and disintegrates in this way. There is nothing that does not disintegrate; there is no primordial and divine person, no divine image.

Theosophy does not know the First Adam, the First Man, preceding cosmic evolution and not derivable from it. Boehme's teaching included the First Adam and linked him with the New Adam—Christ.

---

5. To become convinced of the truth of this statement it is sufficient to read Brahman Chatterjee's *Hidden Religious Philosophy of India* or Swami Vivekananda's *Philosophy of Yoga, Raja Yoga*, or *The Voice of Silence*.

His theosophy was a Christian theosophy. Christology and anthropology are indissolubly linked; they are two sides of one and the same truth. Our doctrine of man wholly depends on our doctrine of Christ; they are perfectly similar. And, thus, the incorrect Christology in contemporary theosophy, which represents an enormous step backward compared to Boehme's theosophy, produces an incorrect anthropology. There is no religious anthropology in contemporary theosophical thought. For contemporary theosophy, man and Christ are thrown into cosmic life, into cosmic evolution. But, in cosmic evolution, all things keep forming and disintegrating; there is nothing unique and unrepeatable. The unique and unrepeatable countenance abides in God, not in the world. Christ and man can be seen in God, not in the world. And, truly, man—through Christ, the Absolute Man—abides within the Holy Trinity. Man is primordial and pre-cosmic; he is greater than the world and cosmic evolution, and cannot be their instrument. In cosmic evolution, only the external shells of man are formed and disintegrate, not his unique and unrepeatable countenance, not his image of God. That is the teaching of Christian theosophy, which differs greatly from the theosophy that is taught in contemporary theosophical books. God keeps fleeing and distancing Himself from the theosophical consciousness. He is attainable at the end of cosmic evolution, which does not have an end. The theosophical consciousness, which is wholly directed at cosmic evolution, does not know an end; it does not know divine eternity. Knowledge of the end or of actual infinity is the same knowledge as knowledge of the uniquely individual. Bad infinity and bad repeatability have the same nature. Theosophy is correct when it teaches about man's shells, when it teaches that man has a complex and multi-element constitution and that his fate is connected with cosmic evolution. But the problem is that, for theosophy, the human "I" is the last item at the end of a long evolutionary process; it is appended to the other constituent parts. Theosophical immanentism does not liberate man and it does not bring him close to God. For theosophy, God is not immanent to man; He is not found in man's depths, but is separated from man by cosmic evolution. And a new transcendence appears, transcendent to man—the infinite and remote cosmic evolution.

IV

The contemporary theosophical movement arose in the second half of the 19th century, a period when positivism and materialism were dominant in Europe and when man, torn away from all sacred tradition, had forgotten the ancient religious wisdom. To man in his abandonment it began to seem that only a yawning abyss lay before him, that he had inherited nothing and whatever he acquired could be acquired only by his own painful labor. The most advanced portion of Western mankind no longer considered itself to be Christian. It had to disintegrate and fall away. The empty soul of European man fell into an anguished yearning and felt a profound spiritual hunger, and it then began to await a light from the East. It is as if the sources of spiritual life had dried up in the West, and the gazes of spiritual seekers turned to the ancient cradle of scared wisdom, to India. Painful memories of the past and prejudices of the present made a return to Christianity unacceptable to 19th century Europeans who had lost their faith; they accepted Buddhism or Brahmanism much more readily. It was a very opportune time for Eastern theosophy to enter the spiritual life of Western mankind. The ground had been prepared. Western man who hungered spiritually did not impose on theosophy any conditions connected with Christianity and with the Christian revelation of human personhood. Since he had lost his specifically Christian revelation, he had nothing that could withstand the non-Christian revelation of the East. The Eastern theosophy was immediately able to adapt itself to the scientific consciousness of 19th century European man, to contemporary evolutionism and the contemporary acceptance of scientific law and rejection of miracle. Theosophy proclaimed that Christianity possesses the same truth as all religions and that there is no religion higher than the truth. Theosophy made Christianity acceptable to apostates from Christianity; it defanged Christianity, as it were.

In recent decades, however, radical changes have occurred in the spiritual life of both Western Europe and Russia.[6] We now stand under the sign of religious seekings, of religious rebirth. At the present time

---

6. Berdyaev is referring, among other things, to the "Russian religious renaissance" of the first two decades of the 20th century.—Trans.

neither materialism nor even positivism can be taken seriously.[7] Philosophical thought is becoming more and more metaphysical. Science is undergoing a serious crisis: on the one hand it is expanding and breaking through artificially set boundaries and, on the other hand, it is relegating itself to a more modest and thus more appropriate place. Man is becoming religiously bolder, and he is manifesting his boldness, above all, in the fact that once again he dares to be a Christian and to return to the original spiritual riches of Christianity. Man's spirit is returning to Christian themes, and it can no longer be satisfied by the impersonal revelation of the East.

Theosophy, too, is changing. Blavatsky had a negative attitude toward Christianity. Contemporary theosophists, however, are trying to soften this attitude; they are increasingly introducing Christian themes and concepts into theosophy. Theosophy is moving from the East to the West. And the Christian West is beginning to remember its own forgotten traditions, linking them directly with the wisdom of Greece and Egypt. A western occult tradition is reemerging, which is opposite to the eastern occult tradition. We find evidence of a Christian esotericism, on the basis of which anthroposophy has splintered off from theosophy, leading to Steiner's movement. The dissension between anthroposophy and theosophy, between Steiner's movement and Besant's movement, is not as accidental and trivial as might appear at first glance. This schism is deeply symptomatic and characteristic for the spiritual life of our time, and it is necessary to examine this movement of theosophy in the direction of Christianity and the revelation of the human "I." Christologization and anthropologization are occurring within theosophy itself. And this is felt particularly in Russian recipes of theosophy. But can one find a revelation of man in Steiner and the Steinerians?

In contradistinction to eastern theosophy, Steiner formulates his theosophy as a western and Christian one, placing it under the sign of the "Christ impulse." In recent years Steiner has particularly insisted on the distinctiveness of his path. Eastern theosophy is theosophy that is prior to the cosmic action of the "Christ impulse," prior to the reve-

---

7. This was written before the Russian Revolution, which was accompanied by a new blossoming of materialism.—*A later note.*

lation about "I." It is difficult, however, to distinguish most of Steiner's popular theosophical books from the theosophical books of Annie Besant and other eastern, pre-Christian theosophists. Steiner's books contain little that is his own; instead, they impersonally expound the conventional, traditional theosophical doctrine. They contain the same doctrine of cosmic evolution with an even greater emphasis on naturalism; the same doctrine of planes, of the complex and composite structure of man; the same doctrine of Karma and the transmigration of souls; the same path without grace of the unredeemed soul, perfecting itself every step of the way through arduous toil. One of Steiner's best books, *The Path of Initiation*, is written in a way as if the Christ impulse does not operate in the world. It proposes the usual practice of eastern Yoga. It is only in recent years that we begin to hear other notes, after Steiner's conversion from theosophy to anthroposophy. Christian occultism seems to defeat eastern occultism in him. But in his anthroposophy, which has taken its name from man, man is as difficult to find as he is in theosophy. To be sure, for Steiner our entire solar system and its evolution are under the sign of Man; it is the Great Man. But there is not much joy in this. Man sinks into the infinite process of the past and future; he is a slave to the formative and disintegrating power of time; he does not have his ground in eternity, in God, in anything deeper than the creaturely world. Man is a means of cosmic evolution, a point of intersection of cosmic eddies and currents. For the anthroposophical consciousness, human personhood participates in absolute being only through cosmic evolution, through the chain of karmic reincarnations.

Cosmic evolution itself changes in virtue of the Christ impulse; a new cosmic epoch has begun in which all things progress differently than before Christ. But Christ Himself is only a cosmic agent, only a moment of the cosmic evolution. Steiner sees Christ as a force acting in the cosmos, but he does not see Him in God, in the Divine Trinity. His Christ is naturalistic, a Christ revealed in chemistry. In anthroposophy, Christianity is a cosmic revelation, not a divine one. The anthroposophical doctrine of the immanent action of the Christ impulse in man contains an indisputable and profound truth, but this doctrine does not attain the ultimate reality, the divine proto-source, but remains in the middle of the creaturely cosmic process. The attitude towards Christ in anthroposophy is not religious and not mystical, but exclusively occultistic. But pure occultism is powerless to see the One Countenance of Christ; for occultism this Countenance is fragmented in the world. It is just as powerless when it tries to see the one countenance of man. For both the Countenance of Christ and the countenance of man have their foundation in God, not in the world. That is why the occultistic orientation, when it is asserted apart from the religious and mystical one, denies the creative originality and intrinsic value of personhood and fails to understand human genius and grandeur. Everything is regulated and guided by hidden cosmic agents; there is nothing that is freely creative. Both theosophy and anthroposophy extinguish man's passionate nature, the passionate Dionysian sources of creativity. They deny all that is free, willful, and irrational. Absent is the freedom and independence of man which is grounded in the mystery that limits occult knowledge. This mystery immerses us in the inexpressible depths of divine life, and its denial by occultism throws us into the infinite middle of the cosmic process. The mystery of the divine depths protects man from the atomizing cosmic winds. But it cannot be denied that in recent years the truth about "I" is being increasingly revealed in Steinerism.

V

A great deal of charlatanism and mystification has accumulated around theosophy; the attitude towards this hidden and mysterious sphere of human life has been overly irresponsible. Also, till now this sphere has been treated with insufficient seriousness by the scientific and philosophical circles which regard themselves as the guardians of European culture. Not only does this treatment lack seriousness; it is also foolish, for it is undeniably foolish to treat with mocking rejection that which one does not know, that which one has not experienced and is not prepared to judge. Official scientists and philosophers are full of the most egregious superstitions and prejudices. The world known and recognized by them consists in nothing more that the reality pragmatically created and needed by them. Whole planes of cosmic life have been closed to the ordinary European scientific and philosophical consciousness by virtue of a particular pragmatism of ignorance which can be established alongside a pragmatism of knowledge. For man at a certain stage of his spiritual development, it was not useful and even dangerous to have knowledge of certain cosmic forces and mysteries. He was protected by ignorance until he reached his maturity. It was Christianity that shut off from man the hierarchy of natural spirits and liberated him from the horror of pagan demonology, thereby enabling him to stand spiritually on his feet. In the pre-Christian pagan world, man was enslaved by the demons of nature. The Christian Church locked up the inner life of nature and chased the great Pan into hidden depths, thereby mechanizing nature and making possible the science and technology of the 19th century. Man was separated from the inner life of the cosmos and domiciled on the limited territory of natural and social life. That, in essence, is positivism.

But the world and man are now entering the maturity of their existence, where ignorance becomes dangerous and leaves man defenseless. Man is becoming conscious of himself as a cosmic being, an inhabitant of a great cosmos which is immeasurable in depth and breadth. Man is abandoning the limited provincialism of his existence on the external shell of the earth. And if in the past it was dangerous for man to see and hear too much, lest he be blinded and deafened, in the present day it is dangerous not to see and not to hear, because unknown cosmic energies are surging at man from all directions and demanding wise and seeing activity from him.

The enormous significance of the theosophical and anthroposophical movements consists in the fact that they direct the attention of contemporary man at the mysteries of cosmic life and expand his knowledge to all the planes of the cosmos. The theosophical type of thought poses not the anthropological but the cosmological problem. This problem is treated neither by Bulgakov's Orthodox consciousness nor by Merezhkovsy's Christian consciousness, for they are afraid of gnosticism and are repelled by all secret knowledge. Only occultism can give us the true knowledge that the material, objectified world is only a temporary stage of cosmic evolution, and not something absolutely stable and unchangeable. For realism, as well as for Kantian idealism, this entire closed and law-governed material natural order is equated with nature, with the cosmos, and its limits are absolute and unchangeable: there is no way out into other planes of the cosmos and no energies from other planes can penetrate into this closed world.

Only the theosophical consciousness can sense the mysterious stratification of the cosmos, the spilling of cosmic energies from one plane into another, the transitional character of that synthesis of the natural material world which the scientific consciousness regards as eternal and imperishable and with which even the religious consciousness too closely links itself. Consider for example the Akashic records, this chronicle of the world, this clairvoyant reading of the memory of cosmic history imprinted in the cosmos. The Akashic records remove the artificial boundaries separating the period of the cosmic process when the latter is manifested as the eternal material world from preceding periods in which such physical materiality had not yet existed—the boundaries separating our incarnation of the earth from other incarnations of it.[8] The only problem is that, for example, for Steiner the world is dematerialized as it were in the Akashic records and it is spiritual knowledge that materializes. He tells us not about the spiritual world, of which our material world is a particular phenomenon, but about the external, empirical evolution of this material world, which condenses and liquefies. Steiner's secret knowledge produces the impression not of intuitive knowledge, not of an integral penetration into the mysteries of being, but of an analytical anatomizing of being. This type of clairvoyance must see the corpselike character of the world. All that is organically integral disintegrates. All boundaries are erased and all planes are mixed up. This corresponds to a particular stage of the cosmic process. But this clairvoyant contemplation of this corpselike character, produced by cosmic decomposition and disintegration, by disincarnation and atomization, will infect man with a corpse poison unless he opposes to these processes his own integral image and likeness, which have their source in the depths of divine being. It is necessary to enter onto the path of spiritual knowledge of the cosmos, but it is also necessary to preserve man in these cosmic whirlwinds. Man is called to be an active creator in cosmic life, not a passive instrument of a cosmic process whose meaning is alien and unknown to him.

---

8. See Steiner: *From the Akasha Chronicle*.

VI

The theosophical type of thought is not directed at history and historical tasks. Theosophy and anthroposophy do not pay any attention to social problems. Steiner is very interested in Haeckel's problems, but not at all in Marx's problems. For Steiner the spirit of the 19th century is the spirit of natural science. But it would be even more correct to say that the spirit of the 19th century is the spirit of sociology. One could even say that, in the 19th century, theology was replaced by sociology, that all thought was seen in the light of sociology and the ultimate meaning of life was sought in social phenomena. The overcoming of Marx is not less important than the overcoming of Haeckel. Marx was a man of genius, whereas Haeckel is a mediocre popularizer and his monism is insultingly shallow.

Steiner and the other theosophists have no understanding of the enormous, even religious significance of the social problem for contemporary mankind. The whole meaning of theosophy consists in its approach to the cosmic problem, and from this side too it is possible to illuminate the social problem. The sociological consciousness separated human social life from cosmic life and limited it to the surface of the earth. All social utopias of total earthly bliss are unrealizable and pitiful precisely because they want to organize mankind's social destiny independently of the structure of the vast cosmos, whose forces act upon and enter into social life. Social life is an internally cosmic phenomenon, and it is necessary to understand the connection between social life and the cosmos. It would thus be possible to formulate the problem of cosmic social life, of cosmic communality. But theosophy does not do so, and it remains elementary and naïve in the sphere of social thought. For theosophy the problem of social life is replaced by the problem of the perfecting of souls. Theosophy is characterized by an unpleasant moralizing, which makes the whole theosophical path uncreative. It replaces social and historical creativity with perfectionment and evolution; and to social and historical problems it responds with the truth of Karma and karmic reincarnations.[9]

---

9. More social in nature is French occultism as exemplified by Antoine Fabre d'Olivet, Alexandre Saint-Yves d'Alveydre, and others.

Theosophy and Anthroposophy in Russia

It is difficult to combine creativity with the practice of Yoga as it is preached in theosophy. Those who enter onto the "path" give up all creativity. The theosophical path does not produce any internal transformation or lead to true spiritual freedom. Despite the fact that theosophy rebels against all traditional religious authorities and all exoteric faiths, for itself it maintains the principle of authority and demands blind faith. After all, the basis of the theosophical path is the authority of the teachers and faith in the teachers. A pupil must believe what he does not yet know, and usually he knows very little; only the teacher knows a lot. Clairvoyant reading of the Akashic records in the memory of the world is free knowledge. But an overly reverent reading of Steiner's book *From the Akasha Chronicle*, written in the fear of confusing Saturn with Jupiter, does not produce free knowledge, but rather reminds one of authoritarian faith. The problem is that Steiner's path has little in common with the path of the Steinerians. Steiner's path is the path of gnosis, while the path of the Steinerians is the path of faith. Theosophy and anthroposophy reject the faith of the Church as a childish state, but they themselves demand a faith that is qualitatively inferior to it. It is impossible to demand from men faith in an occultistic teacher that is equal to faith in Christ, the God-Man. An uncritical and reverent attitude toward the teacher is recommended as a method, as the discipline and path to initiation. It is suggested that, initially, the theosophical doctrine be accepted on faith, without criticism and without verification of it by one's own experience; and it is promised that, with time, all these things will be known autonomously and experientially. But in that case why does theosophy look down on the demand that Church doctrine be accepted on faith? Between man and God, between man and the world, there rises a complex hierarchy of teachers. Here we arrive at what is for me the most interesting aspect of my exploration of the role of the theosophical and anthroposophical movement in Russia and of the type of thought and psychology of Russian theosophists and anthroposophists. My goal is not to analyze the theosophical doctrine and all the theosophical schemes, but to explore the fundamental features of theosophical thought and of the theosophical experience of being.

VII

The theosophical society has an international character. Comparisons of theosophy with Volapük do not lack wit. In contemporary theosophy there are no traces of creative national thought or experience. That is one of the reasons for the astonishing dullness of theosophical books; theosophical ideas are bloodless—they have as little bloom of life as the constructed Volapük language. The anthroposophical society is empirically and incidentally connected with Germany, but in essence it is just as international as the theosophical society. Some people associate Steiner with the Germanic spirit, but his theosophy lacks the vital creative inspiration associated with a national spirit, with the juices of a national life. The whole of the theosophical literature is marked by the deadness of international schemes, of geographical maps of being. Popular theosophical books bear a formal resemblance to popular social-democratic books. This is not free creativity, but party-oriented and clique-oriented propaganda. Any free creativity is clearly subservient to the propaganda aims of party or clique. The theosophical literature can contribute nothing to any national spiritual culture or to the growth of any national spirit. Theosophy speaks a lot about races, but these races have little in common with historical races based on blood. Theosophy develops cosmopolitan, international types, wandering from country to country, from city to city in search of enlightenment. And it is easiest for theosophy to catch souls whose lives have endured serious bankruptcy and who have been torn away from their countries and nations. It is difficult for a theosophist to participate actively in the spiritual life of his nation and in its unique historical fate. A theosophist usually remains neutral; he does not make choices; he is forbidden that selective love which is always biased. In this process, man becomes bloodless; his passionate nature is extinguished. The immediate perception of being is increasingly replaced by the perception of schemes of being. All immediacy vanishes, and one is beset by a constant worry: how does one prevent living experience and judgment from diverging from the doctrine, from the teachings of the master?

Especially prone to this kind of thing are Russian theosophists and anthroposophists, who are easily transformed into abstract beings, into bloodless and fleshless shadows. They become too domesticated and obedient, too passive and fearful of any free and spontaneous creativity. In this popularity of theosophical and anthroposophical movements in Russia one senses the femininity of the Russian soul, its search for masculine organizers from the West, especially Germany, and its inability to organize itself by its own powers. The chaotic souls of Russians are particularly drawn to Steinerian discipline. The Russian Logos does not penetrate into the chaos of the Russian soul. The organizing, disciplining, light-bearing principle is experienced by the Russian soul as something transcendent, as occurring somewhere in the distance. The nature of the inner experience of Russian theosophists and anthroposophists is transcendent, not immanent; they seek the center not in their own depths, but outside, in the distance. Among them there are more than a few of the "Russian boys"[10] about whom Dostoevsky spoke, and these are the best of our theosophists. Much lower than this is the semi-cultured sphere consisting mainly of fashionable ladies who are drawn to theosophy for the same lukewarm reasons they are drawn to charitable works, moral teachings, and the small miracles of personal life.

There is great intensity as well as great spiritual depth in the anthroposophical movement. The spreading of popular theosophical and anthroposophical movements in Russia can play a very positive role, raising the average spiritual level. The main attraction for most theosophists is theosophical morality which preaches a special path of moral perfectionment. It is very hard for a man to tolerate abandonment where he is left to his own devices, but theosophy provides initiates and teachers who help people. Theosophy provides discipline to the soul, rescuing it from chaos and disintegration. Many are initiated into spiritual and moral life for the first time because of theosophy. But the widespread propagation of theosophy can be an obstacle to our own national consciousness and our own national creativity. Eastern theosophy is a typical example of Westernization on Russian soil; it is Westernization to the same degree as, for example, Marxism or positivism. But Russia must, finally, find a way out of this period of Westerniza-

---

10. Young men like Ivan Karamazov who are obsessed with metaphysical, moral, or social questions.—Trans.

tion; and in doing so, it must overcome both the Westernizers and the Slavophiles. Theosophy does not awaken immanent spiritual activity in the Russian soul; it does not facilitate religious liberation of the personality. But, in the case of the most creative and independent natures, theosophy's light is refracted in a special manner in the Russian medium. Anthroposophy acquires an apocalyptic character in Russia. This can be observed in the case of Andrey Bely, perhaps the most creatively gifted Russian to become an adherent of anthroposophy. Bely is very Russian, and his path is highly typical for the Russian soul. It is very unlikely that Steinerism can foster artistic creativity. Creativity presupposes the overcoming of Karma, not the eternal undergoing of Karma. Creativity presupposes the dualism of the world of spiritual freedom and the world of natural necessity. But Bely receives creative impulses from anthroposophy, and so his is an exceptional case.

VIII

The positive significance of the theosophical movement in general and in Russia in particular must be seen in the fact that it is directed at gnosis, at the expansion and deepening of knowledge, at spiritual knowledge. Gnosticism must be reborn and enter forever into our life. Contemporary popular theosophy allows us to glimpse the ancient gnostic doctrines in a superficial and diluted form, a form overly adapted to the average consciousness of people of our time. But it is gradually leading to the rediscovery in our time of gnosis, of wise sophianic knowledge. So, anthroposophy in the deep Boehmian sense must be nothing other than the disclosure of Sophia, the Wisdom of God, in man—her immanent revelation in man. We must ally ourselves with Boehme's tradition of theosophy and anthroposophy, with truly Christian theosophy and anthroposophy. And we must ally ourselves even more deeply with the traditions of esoteric Christianity. But our alliance with the great traditions of Boehmian and Christian gnosticism must be creative; it must direct us to the path of a completely new and creatively active knowledge. Our contemporaries who seek God and divine life are greatly fearful of thought and knowledge; the main tendency of their will is often anti-gnostic. They allow the possibility only of passive, abstract knowledge. They cannot accept knowledge as a creative act that brings light into the life of the world; they cannot accept knowledge as being and life.

The magic of knowledge repels and frightens contemporary people, or they regard it as falsehood and charlatanism. But knowledge must be restored in its magical and cosmically sovereign rights. Russians in particular fear any presence of thought in religion and persecute it. This is connected with the dominant emphasis on moral values in Russian thought. Russians who enter onto the religious path are subservient to the power of the cult of holiness; they believe only in the holiness of life and desire only the holiness of life. Solovyov's gnosticism seems non-Russian and repels many Russians. The moral path and the path of holiness are regarded as the only paths to the light. Russian mystical sectarianism also recognizes the ecstatic path. As for knowledge, it is considered to be opposed to being. But true knowledge *is* being. True thought *is* light. Religious thought *is* religious activity. Gnosis is an organic part of religious life. Life is transfigured from the light of knowledge. If it is deprived of the light of knowledge, religious experience can only be elementary and embryonic in character. There is a tendency today to consider spiritual life to be authentic and real only if it is simple and elementary, only if it is unilluminated by the light of knowledge; but this tendency constitutes a creative weakness and self-deception, a negation of the meaning of the cosmogonic and anthropogonic process. All religious thought and knowledge are feared as a rationalization. But this fear itself is a manifestation of extreme rationalism for which thought and knowledge are always rational, always abstract, always inactive and lifeless. The great mystics did not fear knowledge; they saw in gnosis not a rationalization, but divine communion and divine act. Contemporary irrationalism, alogism, adogmatism, the contemporary fear of the light, contempt for thought and hatred of knowledge—all these things are only the reverse side of contemporary rationalism, of the positivism of contemporary knowledge, of the despotic power of contemporary positive science. We must liberate ourselves from these constraints and enter into the freedom of creative thought and creative knowledge, into the world-transfiguring gnostic light. Contemporary theosophy does not yet accomplish this, but it does indirectly prepare the soil for this in the soul of the average semi-cultured man. Representatives of non-Christian religious movements have an especially hostile attitude towards religious knowledge and gnostic thought. They insist that religious experiences are completely irrational and inexpressible. They prefer the simple, moral side of religion. Some of them, confusing spiritual and mystical experience with psychological experience, are ready to affirm a foggy, irrational, unrevealed mysticism, a mysticism that knows no name. To all these movements we must decisively oppose light-filled religious thought, a creative gnosis, the revelation in man of Sophia the Wisdom of God, the magic of knowledge.

10

Darkened Countenances: *Remembrances of A. A. Blok* by Andrey Bely[1]

One reads Andrey Bely's unfinished remembrances of Alexander Blok[2] with great fascination. Though the remembrances are of course centered around Blok, this work is much broader than the title suggests. The theme of these remembrances is a very profound one; it includes the dawns seen at the beginning of the 20th century by the souls of prophetically attuned poets.[3] It also includes Solovyov's, Blok's, and Bely's revelations of Sophia, and the relation of these revelations to presentiments of revolution. Is the Russian revolution the true revelation of Sophia in Russian life? There is a great temptation to equate the yearned-for revelation and revolution of the spirit with the external Russian Revolution of 1917, but we must expose this equation as a corrupting falsehood. Bely is the greatest Russian novelist of the past several decades, the only one with flashes of true genius. Blok is undoubtedly our most remarkable poet since Fet.[4] Bely, as a phenome-

1. Berdyaev's review of Bely's remembrances of Alexander Blok was first published in *Sophia: Problems of Spiritual Culture and Religious Philosophy*, ed. N.A. Berdyaev, Berlin, 1923.—Trans.

2. See Andrey Bely, *Remembrances of A.A. Blok*, *Epopeia*, Nos. 1–2, Berlin, 1922. Berdyaev is reviewing only the first part of Bely's remembrances published in the magazine *Epopeia*. The concluding parts were published in *Epopeia* No. 3 (December 1922) and No. 4 (April 1923).—Trans.

3. Allusion to the early poems of Blok and Bely, especially Blok's *Ante Lucem* and *Verses about the Beautiful Lady*.—Trans.

4. Blok was a much greater poet than Afanasy Fet. It would be more appropriate to call Blok the greatest Russian poet since Pushkin and Lemontov.—Trans.

[163]

non, is larger and more significant than Blok, but Blok is more of a poet. In the years of the Revolution, both of them were in thrall to this temptation and falsehood; lacking the power of spiritual discernment, they were both in the power of countenances of deception. They were both possessed by the demon of Revolution and did not have the strength to rise spiritually above it and overcome it.

The prophetic character of Russian literature is astonishing. In the course of the entire 19th century this literature was full of presentiments of the coming revolution; it was extraordinarily sensitive to subterranean tremors. Pushkin was agitated by the possibility of revolution in Russia, and he foresaw its character. Lermontov wrote the amazing poem "The year will come, Russia's black year, when the tsars' crown will fall."[5] Tyutchev was always troubled by the problem of world revolution. In the 1880s, in a period of the apparent prosperity of the Russian monarchy, Konstantin Leontiev predicted that Russia would infect Europe with communism and lead into Europe a China infected with communism. Finally, Dostoevsky was a true prophet of Russian revolution; he exposed the profound spiritual foundations of revolution and embodied it in artistic images. Dostoevsky fully understood the ongoing revolution of the spirit, uncovered its internal dialectic, and foresaw its inexorable consequences. The revolution of the spirit started primarily with Dostoevsky; he was the herald of a new world epoch, as it were. Even Solovyov was not as great a herald. For Bely and Blok, Solovyov is only a pretext to reveal their own sophianic experiences and presentiments. They are both very remote from the real Solovyov, taken in his wholeness; and he would not have agreed with their version of him. What does Blok have in common with Solovyov as a philosopher, theologian, or political writer; as a Catholic or Orthodox whose goal is the unification of the Churches? Solovyov first believed in Christ, and only then in Sophia; whereas Blok first believed, or wanted to believe, in Sophia, and never believed in Christ. What do Bely and Blok, these optimists in relation to the future, have in common with the great creation of Solovyov's prophetic spirit: "The Tale about the Antichrist"? In this work which

---

5. From Lermontov's poem "Prediction" (1830).—Trans.

Darkened Countenances: Remembrances of A. A. Blok

addresses the coming catastrophe, Solovyov, a pessimist and apocalyptic, exposes the spirit of Antichrist which captivates Blok and Bely. Only a few sophianic poems connect Solovyov with Blok. Solovyov, though very interesting in his themes, is nevertheless a minor poet, much inferior to Blok. Blok and Belyi have heard only one thing in Solovyov:

> But know this: the eternal feminine
> In incorruptible body is now coming to the earth.
> In the unfading light of the new goddess
> Heaven has merged with the watery abyss.[6]

And now we must raise the question of the significance and meaning of sophianic themes in Russian mysticism, Russian religious-philosophical thought, and Russian poetry. Solovyov's sophiology has influenced not only Blok and Bely but also Florensky, Bulgakov, and Ern. The cult of Sophia is very characteristic of Russian spiritual currents. And it is significant that the sophianic attitude toward Russia and toward the Russian people takes two diametrically opposite forms: some see Sophia in the Russian monarchy, whereas others see her in the Russian Revolution. In both cases, the wise feminine element of the people, white or red, is divinized; one awaits truth from the feminine elemental principle in the life of the people, not from the masculine spirit, not from masculine spiritual activity. But Solovyov himself never divinized the elemental principle of the people; he was never a mystical populist. Nevertheless, his intimate cult of Sophia is being used to justify mystical populism.

Solovyov's doctrine of Sophia and his sophianic poetry contained a certain falsehood which muddied our spiritual currents. Solovyov confused Sophia, the Wisdom of God, the Heavenly Virgin, with an earthly goddess, with the eternal feminine. That is why he was able to write the alarming witticisms about his beloved, Sofia Petrovna, where the Third Testament—that of Sophia—was united with the Second Testament—that of Peter; and that is why she was able to send notes to

---

6. From Solovyov's poem *"Das Ewig-Weibliche"* (the Eternal Feminine).—Trans.

him signed "Sophia."[7] That is also why he found so painful his encounter with Anna Schmidt,[8] an image of femininity whose genius exceeded any he had ever met, but whom he found so physically unattractive and repulsive. Sophia was Solovyov's temptation, his romantic agony; she was the eternal longing for encounters with the Unknown Woman[9] and she was eternal disenchantment, the eternal possibility of confusion and deception. For Solovyov Sophia was not the Virgin of his soul, his virginity, his purity and chastity, the way she was in Jacob Boehme's doctrine, the profoundest and purest doctrine of Sophia. Solovyov's Sophia was not a Virgin that a man has lost and must reacquire like his own Virginität; she was a Woman in whom heaven has merged overly much with the watery abyss, with the earthly element.

This cult of Sophia does not strengthen a man, but weakens him; it does not restore the integrity of his androgynous image, but divides him into two. Sophia can therefore appear in various kinds of garb—as the Heavenly Virgin but also as a wayward earthly woman; she can turn into the "reactionary" or "revolutionary" element of the Russian land. On this terrain, one finds the cultivation of irrational mystical movements which are hostile to the Logos. One is astonished by this passiveness of Russian religious mystical seekings. Russians await a new Revelation, the revelation of the Spirit, the coming of Sophia; they feel themselves to be permeated with mystical currents; they answer the calls of the unknown and mysterious Future and bow down before the mystical character of the Russian people and the Russian land. People of the West find this hard to understand. People of the West set active tasks for themselves and make spiritual efforts to fulfill them. Their mysticism guides them to paths of spiritual ascent. Their theosophy teaches them to develop new organs of perception. They cannot understand the state of expectation and passive mystical trepidation

---

7. Allusion to Sofia Petrovna Khitrovo. Her patrynomic means "daughter of Peter."—Trans.

8. A middle-aged woman who came to see Solovyov shortly before his death in 1900 and announced that she was the earthly incarnation of the Divine Sophia. Florensky and Bulgakov considered her to be a mystically gifted writer.—Trans.

9. Allusion to Blok's poem with this title. In this poem the poet encounters a bewitching woman in a bar.—Trans.

Darkened Countenances: Remembrances of A. A. Blok

before the future. They make revolution, or oppose it, but they do not passively offer themselves up to its ineffable mystical meaning. Mystically attuned "Russian boys,"[10] on the other hand, await the revelation of what is to come, directing their gazes at new dawns; they sense themselves enveloped in a mystical element whose meaning is spiritually incomprehensible and inexpressible for them.

Blok's poems are filled with incoherent incantations and conjurations; the Word, Logos, does not lend itself to expressing his presentiments. This signifies the clear dominance of the astral over the spiritual and leads to all manner of confusions and deceiving substitutions. When the revolutionary storm was unleashed, Blok and Bely did not exhibit a masculine activity of the spirit or any power of spiritual discernment; instead, they were overwhelmed by the irrational element of revolution and, pierced by its currents and passively surrendering themselves to them, in the revolution they attempted to see Her with whom they were awaiting encounters. But was this the coming of what they had so long awaited in a passive state, of what they had foreseen when at the beginning of the century they glimpsed new dawns? How tempting and comforting this was! At last something great had happened; the mysterious element of revolution was unleashed and there was no resisting it. This was the profoundly wise element of the eternal feminine, the sophianic element. She seems grotesque only at first sight, only for the rationalistic consciousness. From her we must await the truth and beauty of new life. It is remarkable that the "Russian boys" exhibit a passively feminine relation to this feminine element, not an actively masculine one.

Andrey Bely constantly confuses and equates the "revolution of the spirit" with the external socio-political revolution. Blok does the same thing. But that is the great falsehood and temptation that must be exposed. It is a temptation of the Antichrist. In his remembrances, Bely dares to say the following: "Christ is inscribed in the 'I' of the proletariat: the ideology of the proletariat is the ideology of the unrecognized Christian Paul, an ideology which rose up against the Christianity of Peter as well as against the 'I' of the bourgeois, who had held a monop-

---

10. Dostoevsky's phrase. See note 10 to the essay on "Theosophy and Anthroposophy in Russia."—Trans.

oly in the freedom of Christ." Further, Bely explains that the revolution of the spirit constitutes a transition from the always limited and closed single individual "to the collective individualism and heroic cosmism that is clearly inscribed in the culture of the proletariat."[11] The revolution of the spirit turns out to be a class revolution, and the Christianity of Paul turns out to be a class Christianity. But what is the proletariat? Is it an economic category, signifying the class of factory workers; or is it a spiritual category? Bely grounds his justification of revolution in an ambiguous play on words. Christ can be inscribed in the proletarian "I" only if it overcomes its "proletarianness," just as He can be inscribed in the bourgeois "I" only if it overcomes its "bourgeoisness." "Proletarianness" and "bourgeoisness" are of equal worth: they are opposite sides of the same spiritual degeneration. When the proletariat is in its most proletarian state, it is spiteful, envious, and vengeful; Christ is not within it. But a worker can escape such a proletarian state, and then Christ can live within him. Christ is inscribed only in the human "I," not in the proletarian or bourgeois "I." But the revolution of the spirit awaited by Bely must, it seems, overcome and revoke man, replacing him with a superhuman collective. That is precisely the temptation of the Antichrist. In Christ, man, the human countenance, is saved and preserved for eternal life, whereas in the Antichrist the human countenance perishes and is replaced by the inhuman collective. It is this kind of revolution of the spirit—a revolution that wants to destroys the human countenance and replace it with an inhuman one—that we Christians, faithful to the religion of the God-Man and the Divine Humanity, must oppose. This is a revolution directed at the destruction of the eternal foundations of being; it is anti-ontological.

In Bely's creative works it is not humanism that perishes (and it indeed must be overcome), but man, the image and likeness of God; and Bely consents to this perishing, believing that it will produce new life and new consciousness. He offers man up to destruction by cosmic spirits. In anthroposophy, too, he values the fact that it regards man as a transitory stage of cosmic evolution. Cosmic Sophia, not Divine Sophia, has replaced Christ, and therefore man is no longer seen in

---

11. *Remembrances of A. A. Blok*, pp. 10, 12.—Trans.

God. Instead of the divine image of man, masks have appeared everywhere.[12]

Russian literature of the last quarter century is frequently infected with an ontological decay, corruption, and disintegration, and we find this in the most remarkable examples of this literature. Cosmic whirlwinds have blown apart the image of man, the image of the world, the image of God, the image of all solid being. This is not a moral, but an ontological disintegration. This is fertile ground for pseudo-mysticism. True mysticism is communion with God, the touching of the depths of spiritual life, the touching of what is most real, of what is most laden with being. Contemporary mysticism, associated as it is with contemporary literary currents, revolves in spheres of the crises of man and of culture, spheres of the disintegration of being; it reflects the tragic fate of the soul of contemporary man; it is astral. The terrifying mystical arrogance of our contemporary poets and novelists is an index of our spiritual illness. We live in an epoch of the false transvaluation of the mystical significance of art. Too many poets of our time claim that they have had mystical experiences and visions, and so they look down on the rest of humanity. But, in reality, it is easier for simple mortals to have mystical experience than for our contemporary poets; in people who are simple in heart there are fewer deceptions, less murkiness. Poetic experience and mystical experience differ qualitatively.

Bely and Blok claim to perceive and experience the Revolution spiritually and mystically. However, not only are they poeticizing, but one would have to look very hard to find in them any discernment of the spirits of the Revolution, since they are possessed by its elemental whirlwinds and are thus deprived of freedom of spirit. In Bely's remembrances one senses the spirit of unhealthy literary cliquishness, where one's own little circle is elevated above everything else. The reverse side of this cliquishness is veneration of the "people," of its mysteriousness and "authenticity." This is very common. The religious error and arrogance of Bely and Blok are rooted, first and foremost, in the fact that they do not accept the First and Second Testament, but instead await the revelation of the Third Testament,

---

12. Masks are a favorite theme of Bely's novels.—Trans.

the revelation of Sophia, the revelation of the Spirit. Bely and Blok rip apart time and eternity, the past, the present and the future, and offer themselves up to the false idol of the future. They are pessimists in relation to the past and rosy red optimists in relation to the future. This makes their mysticism fundamentally areligious and antireligious. Religion is connection, the acquisition of kinship and closeness, the overcoming of the rupture between past and future, the inclusion of every separated moment of time into eternity, the revivifying veneration of ancestors. But Bely and Blok want to remain in the revolutionary rupture between past and future. Revolutionism is always antireligious, for it opposes the establishment of connection and kinship in eternity between past and future. Mystical intoxication with revolutions—i.e., with processes in time that rip apart all connections—is always antireligious. Bely does not know the hypostasis of the Father; the experience of religious veneration (which is a significant part of religious experience) seems alien to him. He insists on his spiritually "proletarian" origins, whereas a Christian must insist on his spiritually aristocratic origins, i.e., his connection with the hypostasis of the Father. That is why Bely thinks the revolution of the spirit, the creative birth of new life, can be accomplished through destruction, hatred, and vengeance in relation to all that comes from the Father.

But it would be a true miracle of the transfiguration of our sinful and wicked life if a revolution of love could be accomplished in the world. Only Christians can expect such a revolution. Marx made the discovery that good can be accomplished in the world through evil, that rage and hatred is the path to a higher social harmony; and vast masses of humanity have followed him. Christians cannot accept this path. But Bely and Blok are not Christians; they are only sophians—they worship the cosmic elements, and they find it acceptable to do so. All mystical accepters of revolution think wrongly that they are maximalists. No, they are minimalists; taking the path of least resistance, they adapt themselves to the necessary and fateful processes of history. The name "maximalists" should be given to those who by the power of their spirit oppose the elements, the masses, the inexorable movements; to those who are spiritually faithful to what can fail to be victorious in the future. Faithfulness to a reviled past can be more of a maximalism than reverence for a triumphant future. Exclusive revolutionary striving

Darkened Countenances: Remembrances of A. A. Blok

toward the future is always characterized by an absence of nobility, faithfulness, and religious veneration. Solovyov possessed religious veneration, faithfulness to the holy traditions of the fathers, and a noble resistance to the "spirit of the time." That is why Blok and Bely have little in common with him. They replaced veneration of Sophia as Divine Humanity by veneration of Sophia as a cosmic element that is neither divine nor human.

The Revolution came out of Chernyshevsky's[13] spirit, not out of Solovyov's spirit. Nor can Solovyov be linked with Lavrov,[14] as Bely suggests. The Revolution was engendered by a century-long movement including such radicals as Belinsky, Bakunin, Chernyshevsky, Dobroliubov, Mikhailovsky, Lavrov, Plekhanov, and Lenin, but not including such religious thinkers as Chaadaev, Khomiakov, the Kireevskys, the Aksakovs, Gogol, Tyutchev, Dostoevsky, Solovyov, and Leontiev, all great figures who have been denounced as reactionaries. This is something worth thinking about. Revolutionaries are "Socratics," in the contemptuous, Nietzschean sense in which Bely and Blok use this word. In its essence, revolution is rationalism taken to its extreme. Extreme socialism and extreme anarchism are rationalistic systems taken to the limit. Russian Bolshevism is rationalistic madness taken to the extreme. Revolutionism is always motivated not only by a thirst for destruction, but also by a crazy will to the complete rationalization of society, by a will to perfect order, organized by collective reason. Revolution ignores the organically irrational forces in society, even though it itself is an irrational force. Herein lies the contradictoriness of revolution. Blok and Bely represent the final transformation of Russian populism. But the fundamental falsehood of populism is that it exalts not the spirit but the masses, not quality but quantity. Populism is a product of the consciousness and attitudes of the intelligentsia. For this consciousness and these attitudes the people are a mystery that must be worshipped, a mystery in which the truth and God are concealed. This is a heteronomous consciousness, not an autonomous one. It is based on the powerlessness to consider oneself part of the people

---

13. Nikolay Chernyshevsky (1828–1889), Russian revolutionary writer. He influenced Lenin.—Trans.

14. Pyotr Lavrov (1823–1900), Russian radical thinker.—Trans.

and to uncover God and the truth in one's depths; the unclarity and confusion in one's depths are projected outward, onto the people. For those who are aware of themselves as being part of the people, populism is meaningless. Truth, a new life, and God are revealed in the suprapersonal depths of the people.

Bely's remembrances of Blok are as yet unfinished,[15] and he has not yet brought to light Blok's tragic fate. It is difficult to say how he will accomplish this, if he in fact finishes his remembrances. But Blok's fate is very remarkable and significant. His fate was to experience the tragic downfall of his false sophianic romanticism and to see its inner impotence. His "Beautiful Lady"[16] was not real, not ontological. There is not the remotest presence here of the ontological Sophia. Everything is submerged in a murky atmosphere of doubleness. And he offers no spiritual resistance to this murk and doubleness. *Puppet Show*, Blok's very remarkable play, represents the downfall of the "Beautiful Lady." The irreality, inauthenticity, and non-ontologicity of everything is exposed. The murk in Blok's soul grows darker. But a few years before his death the phantasm of the "Beautiful Lady" appears again to Blok: it is Sophia in a terrible new image, in the image of the Russian Revolution. Here the image of Sophia sinks into the final murk; the image of divinity can no longer be seen. Blok paid with a cruel death for his hallucination, for the strange deception to which he had offered himself up. He writes *The Twelve*—an amazing poem, almost a work of genius, the best thing written about the Revolution. *The Twelve* gives an authentic image of the Revolution with all of its terror and horror, but its doubleness and ambiguity reach the point of blasphemy. Blok allows himself a terrible game with the image of Christ. Blok's romantically dreamy sophianism did not disclose for him a path to the perception of the image and countenance of Christ. It is only through Christ that one can overcome the temptation of doubling thoughts. After this, Blok's life sinks into total darkness. The deceptive image of the "Beautiful Lady" again fades for him, and he is left before a void of emptiness. He dies from a spiritual sickness, from the spiritual darkness and unfaith that enveloped him. Blok is a soul without faith, his entire life longing

---

15. See note 2.—Trans.
16. The sophianic figure of Blok's early poems.—Trans.

Darkened Countenances: Remembrances of A. A. Blok

in anguish for faith. He saw illusory dawns, mirages in the wilderness, but not the true dawn. So, in his tragic fate the falsehood of this entire path is exposed, the falsehood of this entire current in Russian spiritual life. Our literature foresaw the Revolution; the Revolution took place in the literature before it took place in life. But only he deserves the name of prophet who rises spiritually above the object of his prophesy. After his death, Blok was crowned as the greatest Russian poet, and that is just. But a poet is not obligated to be a spiritual teacher and prophet, and those who call him one are worthy of blame.

11
Stylized Orthodoxy: On Father Pavel Florensky[1]

Father Pavel Florensky's book *The Pillar and Ground of the Truth: An Essay in Orthodox Theodicy in Twelve Letters* is unique of its kind, an exciting and enchanting book. There has never been a book so subtle and refined in the Russian theological literature. This is the first manifestation of estheticism in Russian Orthodox theology, a manifestation made possible by the growth of a refined esthetic culture in Russia at the end of the 19th century and the beginning of the 20th century. Father Florensky's every word bears the stamp of a deeply experienced esthetic decadence. It is an autumnal book; one hears in it the rustling of falling leaves. Father Florensky's refined flowers of Orthodoxy became possible only in the same epoch when Huysmans became possible in Catholicism. I'm not happy to say, however, that Father Florensky's estheticism is not always accompanied by good taste. His spiritual rhetoric sometimes becomes tasteless: for example, "I know that I have done no more than light a little candle of yellow wax," "this little flame trembling in my unaccustomed hands," "like fragrant dew on fleece, like heavenly manna, the grace-filled power of God-illuminated souls has descended here," "afire with myriads of myriads ... of looks, glistening, sparkling, playing like the beams of a rainbow or like an infinite number of radiant splashes, the treasures of the Church produce in my poor soul a state of awe and trepidation,"[2] and so on. Though, by his nature, Father Florensky is distant from the "spiritual" world, his manner of writing bears the indelible stamp of "spiritual" eloquence.

---

1. First published in the magazine *Russkaya mysl'*, January 1914.—Trans.

2. Quotations from "To the Reader" section in *The Pillar and Ground of the Truth*.—Trans.

There is no naiveté or directness in Father Florensky. Just consider how naïve and direct the Orthodoxy of the Slavophiles was compared to Father Florensky's. In *The Pillar and Ground of the Truth* there is nothing simple or direct, not a single word that comes straight out of the depths of the soul. Such books cannot have a religious effect. This refined book, so intelligent and learned, is deprived of all inspiration. Father Florensky does not say a single word loudly and powerfully, with inspiration. Very evident here is a self-accounting, a flight from oneself, a fear of oneself. One gets the impression that Father Florensky is a repentant decadent and therefore summons us to simplicity and naturalness, that he is a spiritual aristocrat and therefore summons us to ecclesiastical democratism, and that he is full of sinful tendencies to gnosticism and occultism and therefore fiercely attacks all gnosticism and occultism. One gets the impression that if he lets himself go a little, he'll immediately beget innumerable heresies and all chaos will break loose. Everywhere one looks, there's artificiality and art. Such people shouldn't preach.

Father Pavel Florensky is a brilliant, gifted, subtly intelligent, and subtly learned stylizer of Orthodoxy; there is not a single one of his thoughts or words that has not passed through stylization. His Orthodoxy is not a living, direct, and naive Orthodoxy, but one that is stylized and sentimental (in Schiller's sense). It is an Orthodoxy of complex and refined esthetic reflections, not an Orthodoxy of direct creative life; an Orthodoxy of an epoch of decline, not of blossoming. Father Florensky's book is filled with the spirit of archaism, the spirit of stylized primitivism. The archaic and primitive cannot exist in the 20th century, and this stylization attains high levels of art. Father Florensky is an Alexandrian; in his spirit he is close to the late Hellenistic world, not to archaic Greece. I do not dare doubt the sincerity and profundity of Father Florensky's religious life; I do not think it possible even to speak about this. I do not doubt the authenticity and significance of the religious experiences of the author of *The Pillar and Ground of the Truth*; but the expression of these experiences in the form of an archaic Orthodoxy constitutes a stylization. As a philosopher and theologian, as a writer and preacher, he is a stylizer of archaic Orthodoxy, a decadent. The book's allure and seductiveness consists in this gifted and refined decadence. But a scary deadness emanates from this

Stylized Orthodoxy: On Father Pavel Florensky

stylized simplicity, serenity, and humility. A large and subtle intelligence and a profound and refined learning are combined with creative impotence. Father Florensky plants myriads of dead, artificial flowers, tormenting the reader with this deadening restoration of the style of archaic Orthodoxy. Much too evident is his decadent detachment from—and resulting stylization of—the true life of archaic Orthodoxy. Father Florensky has many smart and subtle things to say about love, but the reader does not feel this love directly. His book is full of the traditional Orthodox aversion to people and to the world, but this aversion is expressed in the form of a stylized, esthetic indignation against heretical life and heretical thought. His words do not express any real, fervent indignation, but only a decadent, esthetic indifference to evil and good. Not a single line of his book seethes with real, fervent indignation against the evil of the world; there is no militant condemnation of evil or resistance to falsehood and injustice. Father Florensky's writings lack all sense of world citizenship (not in the political, but in a much more profound sense). He is metaphysically asocial. Given his kind of stylized serenity and humility, one can expose heresies everywhere and anathematize everything that is not one's "own," but one is unable to passionately condemn evil—one is unable to express indignation against the evil of life and to struggle against it.

Father Florensky is very consistent in disliking the heroic principle; instead, he idealizes ordinary, everyday life as more authentic and pleasing to God. For him, heroism is nothing more than a pose; heroism is not ontological and does not provide a way out from "this world" into a higher, authentic spiritual life. Rejection of the heroic life and esthetic delight in the ordinariness and provincialism of life, in everyday serenity, are part and parcel of his stylized and archaic Orthodoxy. He looks backward, only backward. But no matter how much he tries to stylize himself with respect to simplicity, there is less simplicity in him than in any of the gnostics, than, for example, in Jacob Boehme, who had a great simplicity of heart and a great immediacy. In Father Florensky's humble aspiration to expound not his "own" views and not his "own" system but the views and system of the Church, there are a particular pride and lack of simplicity. "If my work contains any of 'my own' views, that is due only to my ignorance and lack of understanding, to my failure to think things through."[3] Father Florensky has many interesting views on the overcoming of skepticism, on the antinomic character of the truth, on Gehenna, on Sophia. There is much that is original in these views, much that is his "own," and he would express much greater humility by taking pride in these views of his than by regarding them with stylized humility as due only to his "ignorance" and "failure to think things through" or by passing them off as the voice of the Church herself. If he sincerely, and not just for the sake of a humble style, regarded all of his views as due only to his "ignorance and lack of understanding," to his "failure to think things through," then he shouldn't philosophize and theosophize; he shouldn't write an "essay in Orthodox theodicy." All philosophy and theosophy are, in essence, always anthropological, always a revelation of wisdom in and through man. A philosopher is always a heretic in the literal sense of the word, i.e., one who chooses freely. It is dishonest for a man to cast contempt on his own knowledge, thought, and understanding in order to promote his style of humility. Father Florensky offers us his *own* "essay in Orthodox theodicy" which is grounded in an original way and is definitely "thought through," so it is disingenuous of him to speak of his "ignorance and lack of understanding" and of his "failure to think things through." This is an insult to human dignity. One might regard some of his "own" views as verging on genius, if they were not so stylized. A stylization can be very talented but, alas, it can never be a work of genius. All works of genius are direct and simple, even if they might be incomprehensible for the majority of people. Khomiakov's ideas about the Church possess a simplicity of genius, but Father Florensky is very far from these ideas.

He could have been an extraordinary scholar, a mathematician,[4] a philologist, perhaps an investigator of the occult sciences, but he suppressed this side of himself. He is drawn more to the particular than to the universal. He loves fine, artistic, filigree work, detailed analysis, scientific miniatures. He is like a fine jeweler. He is weaker when it comes to creative synthesis. There is depth in him but no flight, no

---

3. See p. 360 of the Russian edition of *The Pillar and Ground of the Truth*.—Trans.
4. Very remarkable is his essay "Symbols of Infinity" in *Novyi Put'*, where he develops a theory of potential and actual infinity.

Stylized Orthodoxy: On Father Pavel Florensky

breadth. He is more of a scientist (in the best sense of the word) and an original artist-stylizer than a thinker and philosopher. He teases us with his jewel-like philological investigations. There is more literature in him than philosophy. Just as a literary manner in painting is unpleasant for one who lovingly seeks the revelations that painting gives, so a literary manner in philosophy is unpleasant for one who lovingly seeks philosophical revelations. Father Florensky is a scholastic, though in a subtle, not seminarian, sense. The freedom and flights of a philosopher are absent in him. His "Orthodox theodicy" is a self-salvation, fetters he imposes on himself and on others; it is not a free search for truth and divine wisdom. There is no freedom on his pathways of knowledge. The most painful and unpleasant thing in Father Florensky's book is his dislike of freedom, his indifference to freedom, his misunderstanding of Christian freedom, of freedom in the Spirit. Indeed, he almost never uses the word "freedom." It is in his relation to freedom that we truly see in Father Florensky "ignorance and lack of understanding" and a "failure to think things through." His religion is not a religion of freedom; the pathos of freedom is alien to him. This puts its stamp on the whole book. *The Pillar and Ground of the Truth* is a suffocating, hothouse kind of book. One can suffocate in the atmosphere of this little subterranean church with low vaults, hot and permeated with the odor of wax candles and incense. When you read this hothouse book, you want to break out into the fresh air, into the expanses, into freedom, into the creativity of the free human spirit.

    Father Florensky bears a certain kinship with Pascal. It is this kinship that makes him an interesting phenomenon. The chapter on doubt is the most brilliant and remarkable one in the book. His powerful gnoseological description of the torments of skepticism, of what he calls "epoche," is very much a description of the torments of hell, of hell on earth. This could have been written only by a man who has himself experienced the hellish torments of epoche and for whom the overcoming of skepticism is the most urgent and vital task. He writes well and powerfully about these torments, and here his stylization is almost absent, for in this chapter he reveals his true skeptical nature, very akin to Pascal's. The gnoseological transcription of the psychological experience of doubt is not as universally obligatory as Father Florensky thinks, for not everyone is as sensitive to the prison of rationality which produces the torments of epoche. Indeed, I don't believe that the torments of doubt are so acute in our time. In our religious questing we are very free of the fetters of rationality and of the epoche they impose.

Father Florensky's analysis of doubt tends to be a brilliant psychology rather than a gnoseology. It is a marvelous study in religious psychology. His psychology becomes a theology, and his theology is chock full of scholasticism. He overcomes the torments of doubt by means of Trinity, the Triune Truth; that is, he overcomes psychology by means of theology. According to Father Florensky, every immanent path of knowledge, whether discursive or intuitive, leads to hell. He condemns to the torments of hell anyone who follows the path of knowledge without having accepted the transcendent Trinity: "It [Trinity] is the last resource. If there is no Triune Truth, then where is one to seek the truth?"[5] He postulates the Triune Truth as the only way out of the torments of hell; he accepts the Triune God out of despair. Father Florensky's method reminds one of Kant's moral postulation of God; this might appear strange because Kant is so foreign to Father Florensky. Father Florensky accepts the hypothesis of the Triune Truth and of the Triune God—a hypothesis transcendental in relation to both knowledge and spiritual experience—in order to save himself from hellish despair. *His goal is not knowledge, but self-salvation.* He postulates the hypothesis of Trinity, and only this transcendental postulation enables him to save himself from the immanent torments of epoche. But the Triune Truth and of the Triune God are not revealed in immanent spiritual life. The Divine Truth is completely transcendental in relation to spiritual experience. As will be seen later, this predetermines Father Florensky's attitude toward mysticism. In his postulation of the dogma of Trinity, this dogma remains external to mystical experience; it is not revealed immanently in this experience as inner light and illumination, but is a transcendental salvific hypothesis. Thus, gnoseologically, he already asserts that divine revelation has an external nature, transcendental in relation to all spiritual, mystical experience. According to his gnoseology, it is impossible to immanently attain the light of the truth: every immanent, inner path of knowledge—even the path of

---

5. See p. 69 of the Russian edition.—Trans.

Stylized Orthodoxy: On Father Pavel Florensky

mystical experience and the higher spiritual life—leads to hell, into the consuming fire of epoche.

If Father Florensky had said that the light of the Truth (not of truths) is attained through sacrifice, self-renunciation, and the crucifixion of rationality, he would have been right with a holy rightness. The ultimate Truth is revealed through the One who said: "I am the Truth." In order to see this Truth, one must surrender everything to Him, lay everything at His feet; in order to receive everything from Him, one must renounce—for the sake of Him who is the Truth—all truths. But this is the immanent path of spiritual, mystical life—the path of the birth of Christ in the soul. Father Florensky affirms something else. He desires not a sacrificial transcensus as a stage of religious experience, as birth into new spiritual life; instead, he desires an absolutely transcendental, external revelation, a transcription of religious experience in terms of transcendental ontology. Mystical life involves passage through voluntary death, through the redemptive sacrifice of Golgotha, but this is an immanent experience that does not involve anything completely external or transcendental. But Father Florensky's Triune Truth and Triune God are completely transcendental and external. This serves to reinforce a selfish psychology of religious immaturity. The method by which Father Florensky tries to show that the Truth is Triunity turns out to be fatally scholastic. His refined religious psychology becomes a scholastic theology; the dogma of Triunity, as transcendental in relation to mystical experience, inevitably turns out to be theological. Theology is always based on the idea of external revelation, as opposed to mysticism, which is based on the idea of inner revelation. Theology is transcendentism, whereas mysticism is immanentism (in the deep sense). Father Florensky is not as free of theological scholasticism as he desires to be and as he should be. Into his writings he surreptitiously introduces a disguised scholasticism. This represents an inevitable punishment for his postulation of dogma before and outside the spiritual life of mystical experience. As a refined man, Father Florensky wants an experiential theology. But experiential theology cannot postulate external dogma and revelation that is transcendental to the human spirit; it sees the birth of God in man; it stops being theology and becomes theosophy. Theology has always been an expression of religious immaturity, authoritarianism, and external transcendence in the religious consciousness. For Father Florensky the dogma of the Triune Truth and Triune God are transcendental both in relation to the experience of knowledge and in relation to the experience of love, since both knowledge and love are possible only after the acceptance of this dogma. But if all authoritarianism in the acceptance of the dogma is removed, the dogma will turn out to be only a transcription of inner religious experience, of the inner path of love and knowledge, of the path of passage through the sacrifice of rationality and the renunciation of self-assertion; it will turn out to be a description of mystical encounters. It must also be pointed out that Father Florensky's gnoseological doctrine that the Truth is Triunity gives rise to major gnoseological difficulties. In reality, epoche is overcome not only by Triunity. In essence, epoche is always overcome by an act of selective and sundering will, by cognitive eros. In the case of many great philosophers this cognitive will to the Truth attained the light without the direct acceptance of Triunity. Here, Father Florensky is doomed to the scholastic imposition of Trinity by means of the experiential way of knowledge. His scholastic gnoseology, though it began with living experience, fatally affected his attitude toward the Church and toward mysticism.

He meticulously stylizes himself according to an Old Testament fanaticism. Church fanaticism has always been a manifestation of the Old Testament spirit in Christianity, of the spirit of separation and self-exaltation: only "we" possess the truth. Father Florensky keeps exposing heresies. But his fanaticism lacks all immediacy and simplicity; he is incapable of passionate indignation and fanatically wars against heresies for the sake of an Orthodox style and a well-ordered system. Father Florensky's attitude toward Catholicism is very unpleasant; it is a leftover Slavophilism. It's embarrassing to keep repeating that everything's great and wonderful in our Orthodox East while in the West there's nothing but corruption. Father Florensky knows perfectly well that in our Orthodox East everything is not wonderful, that our actual Orthodoxy has very little in common with Khomiakov's ideal Orthodoxy. Even Khomiakov knew that, but he possessed a naiveté and a direct simplicity that are foreign to Father Florensky. Indeed, we have experienced much since the good old Slavophile times; entire spiritual revolutions separate us from those times; much has been uncovered and bared. Our falsehood now parades naked along the boulevards. But Father Florensky's style does not wish to know the religious realism of history. In any case, it is impermissible to regard all of Catholic mysticism as a mysticism of the stomach, as opposed to Orthodox mysticism, which is regarded as a mysticism of the heart. The memory of St. Francis' sacred heart rises up against this. Deep down in his soul this cannot be Father Florensky's real opinion of the great saints and mystics of the western world, the world of "sacred miracles."[6] Meanwhile, in his stylization of Orthodox fanaticism he says the most absurd things: "Herein lies a profound distinction between Orthodox mysticism and heretical mysticism, which is always possessed by the spirit of perversion and corruption."[7] If we consider that for Father Florensky non-heretical, ecclesial mysticism can be found only in Orthodox mysticism in the narrow and precise sense, e.g., in St. Symeon the New Theologian or in St. Macarius of Egypt, then such righteous and pure mystics (though without the official stamp of sainthood) as Meister Eckhart and Jacob Boehme must be regarded as possessed by the spirit of perversion and corruption. Even St. Francis and St. Catherine of Siena would have to be accused of perversion and corruption, since their mysticism is heretical, i.e., not Orthodox. Such assertions are foolish and should not be tolerated.

Father Florensky's transcendental gnoseology leads him to an extreme exaggeration of the significance of dogmas in religious life—of dogmas as an external given. Here we come to the fundamental defect of Father Florensky's entire religious philosophy, of his entire conception of the Church. As a refined and modern man, he recognizes, of course, only experiential theology; his attention is directed at spiritual life and he can have only contempt for the scholasticism of the seminaries. But here he is confused. On the one hand, dogmas are revealed in spiritual experience, in spiritual life; on the other hand, they are the criteria of a healthy and correct spiritual experience and spiritual life. On the one hand, dogmas are immanently revealed in spiritual experience; on the other hand, they are transcendentally imposed on spiritual experience. Father Florensky's attitude toward

---

6. Dostoevsky called the West the "land of sacred miracles."—Trans.
7. See p. 342 of the Russian edition.—Trans.

spiritual experience and spiritual life is a suspicious and doubting one; he demands constant testing of the spirit by Church dogmas. What is considered spiritual might actually be psychical in character; what is considered divine might be human arbitrariness and self-assertion.

But I ask: what does Father Florensky regard as the formal attributes of spirituality? How does he know what is authentically spiritual and what is not? Ecclesial, dogmatic consciousness is, in his view, the religious criterion of spirituality, of life in the spirit. But from the very first pages of his book it is evident that, like Khomiakov, he does not recognize any external or formal criteria of ecclesiality. "The indefinability of Orthodox ecclesiality is the best proof that it is vital and living.... What is ecclesiality? New life, life in the Spirit. What is the criterion of the rightness of this life? Beauty."[8] But if ecclesiality is life in the Spirit and if the criterion of the rightness of ecclesial life is Beauty, then why is it thought that Jacob Boehme (for example) did not live in ecclesiality, in the life of the Spirit? According to external and formal criteria of ecclesiality, Boehme was a Lutheran and gnostic-heretic before the court of judgment of the official Catholic and Orthodox consciousness; but according to the criteria of the Spirit and Beauty, he was a true ecclesial Christian. Why must one excommunicate from ecclesiality and regard as heretics many mystics who lived a true and righteous life in the Spirit and in Beauty but who are not acceptable according to formal and official criteria?

In my opinion, Khomiakov's conception of the Church as life in the Spirit, in love and in freedom, has very radical consequences. His conception of the Church does not allow any external authority, any materialization of spiritual life on the physical plane; spiritual life does not need to listen to the voice of the Pope or even to the voice of the Synod and the patriarchs. Khomiakov's conception contains an eternal, imperishable truth which transcends temporal and historical Slavophilism. But Father Florensky is sitting between two chairs: his consciousness is torn apart by a morbid duality, not by an antinomicity, but by a duality and ambiguity. *Ecclesiality does not have any external and formal attributes or criteria; it is life in the Spirit and in Beauty.* That is one thesis of Father Florensky. The other thesis, which he employs throughout

---

8. See p. 7 of the Russian edition.—Trans.

Stylized Orthodoxy: On Father Pavel Florensky

his book, goes as follows: *The only life in the Spirit and in Beauty that is religiously acceptable, right, and justified is that which is ecclesial according to formal and external criteria of ecclesiality. All that is non-Orthodox in the literal, confessional, external and formal sense is suspect and unhealthy—it is spiritual delusion and even perversion.* But here I propose that Father Florensky stop sitting between two chairs and choose between these two theses. As a modernist and refined mystic, he values the first thesis and supplements Khomiakov's conception of ecclesiality with the criterion of Beauty. As a stylizer of archaic Orthodoxy and a defender of the tradition and faith of the fathers, as a man seeking to be saved, he holds to the second thesis. Like all decadents, he is unable to make a heroic choice; nor is he capable of a creative synthesis. He finds a stylistic way out. "The spiritual elders were great discerners of the quality of spiritual life. The Orthodox taste, the Orthodoxy style, is something that is felt; it is not something that is subject to arithmetical determination; Orthodoxy is shown, not proved."[9] (Not only the Orthodox taste but, alas, also Orthodox tastelessness is something that is frequently felt, and I'm sure that Father Florensky feels it too.) He imposes his esthetics on the Orthodoxy that actually exists. And it is a great pity that Father Florensky himself is a "great discerner" and exposer of heresies. Behind every exposure and anathematization of heresies one is likely to find ill will and malice. True gnosis begins only when interest in heresies and orthodoxy wanes. The will to the defense of orthodoxy and the exposure of heresies closes off the path of gnosis for the ecclesial consciousness. We see then the degeneration of orthodoxy into an external and formal criterion which is hostile to every movement of spiritual life. Transcendentism degenerates into formalism, into an external barrier to inner life, into a police measure against immanent spiritual experience—the experience of love and of knowledge in spiritual freedom.

Father Florensky recognizes, of course, that dogmas have an experiential origin. Dogmas are facts; they are mystical encounters. A dogma is not an external revelation, not an external given, but an inner revelation, an illumination immanent to the human spirit. The dogmatic formulas only gave an ontological transcription of religious experience;

---

9. See p. 8 of the Russian edition.—Trans.

they were a democratic affirmation and expression of stable and eternal elements of religious experience. Dogmas contain absolute and imperishable truth. But a dogmatics becomes deadly if its statics opposes its dynamics, if some elements of religious experience nullify other elements of this experience; that is, if the experience stagnates and is statically absolutized. Transcendentism, which erects a barrier between man and God and between the world and God, is an inevitable stage of religious experience, an inevitable passage through dualism, through polar opposition. Only the experiential transcription of transcendentism is true. Every ontological transcription and absolutization of transcendentism contains the danger of static stagnation in religious experience. Absolute transcendentism is the Old Testament. The New Testament is immanentism; the Gospel is the news that God is immanent to the human spirit. Any ontology of pure transcendentism in Christianity is a survival of the Old Testament heritage. Abstract transcendentism is a religious immaturity. The whole transcendental doctrine of the creation of the world and of man, the whole of Christianity's orthodox theology, cosmology, and anthropology comes from the Old Testament, not the New. The antinomy of the transcendent and the immanent is overcome in the mature Christian consciousness, in the new Adam.

The most valuable thing in Father Florensky's book is his doctrine of antinomy. In its essence religious life is antinomic; it contains theses that are incompatible and contradictory for reason, and it mysteriously overcomes these contradictions.[10] The antinomy of the transcendent and the immanent cannot be overcome rationally; it can be overcome only in religious experience. Opposites are harmonized in a higher illumination. Everything that Father Florensky says about antinomy is superb; these are the best parts of his book, sometimes very profound. But he himself is not consistent in applying antinomy; instead, he takes a wholly different path. Thus, the extreme absolutization and dogmatization of transcendentism is a betrayal of the antinomic religious life in which transcendentism and immanentism are mysteriously united. Father Florensky wants to find a traditional and orthodox resolution in

---

10. In my book *The Philosophy of Freedom* I defended the antinomicity of the religious consciousness which is madness for this age.

Stylized Orthodoxy: On Father Pavel Florensky

transcendental ontology and dogmatics to that which can be resolved only in religious experience. The transcendent and the immanent are antinomic moments of religious experience; they are not ontology, metaphysics, or dogmatics. Father Florensky is a Platonist and therefore a dualist. Church Platonism can turn out to be a static and absolutized dualism which restrains and limits spiritual experience. Heavenly and divine reality turns out to be transcendent in relation to earthly and human reality; all movement ceases in spiritual life and religious experience. Everywhere we find chasm and remoteness. Platonism was great and full of light for the pagan world, but it is dangerous and bears bitter fruits for the Christian world; it can engender materialism, which is the reverse side of Platonism. Platonic dualism engenders an apprehensive and suspicious attitude toward spiritual experience. For Father Florensky, spiritual experience is not authentic and healthy unless it bears an official stamp of saintliness. But what are we, poor sinners, to do? Do we have the strength to dare to live by a higher spiritual life?

Father Florensky considers suspect any initiative in spiritual life, any bold attempt to live in the Spirit; he considers it a manifestation of human pride and capriciousness. But saintliness too, which later received the stamp of official recognition and was venerated statically in the iconography of saints' countenances, had been, in its own time, a bold initiative. Father Florensky is led astray by the formal and official criteria of saintliness. As a stylizer of archaic Orthodoxy, he prefers the "humility" of average and ordinary life in sin to the "pride" of spiritual exaltation, to the boldness of distant spiritual voyages. (This is the style of the Russian elders, who instructed people to bear the burden of obedience to the consequences of sin, to humble themselves before the "world"—these elders who were so tolerant of unexceptional, petty bourgeois life.)[11] The doctrine of sin degenerates into hostility to all spiritual movement and ascent. Evidently, we are poor little sinners, and spiritual life is not for us. We need humility, not the exaltation of spiritual life and the revelation of other worlds; we need acceptance of

---

11. Very typical in this respect is Father S. Chetverikov's book on Elder Amvrosy of Optina. We are very unpleasantly struck by how Amvrosy adapted Orthodoxy to petty bourgeois needs.

the burdens of the "world," not liberation from the "world" and the creation of new life. This amounts to the spiritual democratization of Christianity, to hostility to its spiritual aristocratization. It amounts to the adaptation of Christianity to average, petty bourgeois life, to the "world." It amounts to Christian exotericism, which, by his nature, Father Florensky cannot fully accept and which he conjoins with certain hints at Christian esotericism (see p. 418 of the Russian edition). But he goes too far in his stylization of archaic, democratic, petty bourgeois Orthodoxy; he goes farther perhaps than he wants, for he himself is not petty bourgeois, and is pulled toward something else. Father Florensky's dualism is constantly visible: this spiritual aristocrat stylizes himself as a democrat. The degeneration of humility is associated with a great religious and moral peril; it is an obstacle to the fulfillment of Christ's commandment: "Be ye ... perfect, even as your Father which is in heaven is perfect." This false humility retards spiritual growth, leaving one behind in the lower planes of life; it is not the New Testament pathos of the infinite closeness of man and God and of the infinite movement of spiritual life, but the pathos of an infinite distance, of a transcendent chasm between man and God. The final limit of this humility, of this humbling transcendental dualism, is materialism and positivism, the rupture between religion and life.

Father Florensky knows perfectly well that the nature of the Spirit has not been sufficiently revealed in Christianity: "In general ... the personal life of a Christian (with the exception of a few extraordinary ascents) and the everyday life of the Church (with the exception of the chosen ones of Heaven) *know the Holy Spirit as a Person only dimly and darkly*. This is connected with insufficient ... knowledge of the heavenly nature of the creature."[12] "This is not an accident of the history of *theology*, but follows inevitably from the fulfillment of the times and seasons—it is a necessary and inevitable disclosure of the relatively dim revelation of the Spirit as *Hypostasis*; it is an insufficiency of life itself."[13] "It is as if some fabric ... of hyperfine stellar rays is being woven in the cosmic foundations: *Something* is awaited. There is an insufficiency of *something*. The soul, desiring ... to be with Christ,

---

12. See p. 111 of the Russian edition.—Trans.
13. Ibid., p. 118.

Stylized Orthodoxy: On Father Pavel Florensky

yearns for *something*."[14] Father Florensky is a new soul, and there is no doubt that he experiences such yearnings, expectations, and seekings, and that he awaits a new revelation of the Spirit. But he is so afraid of himself and stylizes himself in the archaic Orthodox manner to such a degree that his seekings of the revelation of the Spirit are too timid. He has been too frightened by the helpless failures of the "new religious consciousness."[15] He is afraid of any human initiative in the disclosure of the Spirit, of any human daring in spiritual life. But the Spirit is revealed in man and humanity through man and humanity; the revelation of the Spirit is not a transcendent voice above and outside, but an immanent voice inside, in the depths of the soul. The Spirit cannot be revealed without human activity, without the exertion of man's nature, for life in the Spirit is Divine-human life, the conjoined action of God and man. Because of his fear Father Florensky condemns man to a passive waiting to which no end can be foreseen. Father Florensky consoles himself with the fact that the new revelation of the Spirit has already been initiated by St. Seraphim of Sarov, by Elder Amvrosy, and by other Russian elders; and he, himself, does not desire to take up the burden and responsibility of revealing the Spirit. The saints and elders must act for us, whereas we must wait passively and humble ourselves. But, however we try, we cannot find in Amvrosy and the other elders "the new, hitherto almost unseen, *rosy* rays of the coming Unfading Day."[16] We find this in Father Zosima, in Dostoevsky's creative insights of genius, but we do not find it in the real Amvrosy, who bore the burden of the "world" and was not liberated from drab everydayness. St. Seraphim's countenance is uniquely radiant, but it is hard to connect even him with the new yearnings. One can find no traces in Father Florensky of the authentic new consciousness, of the consciousness that the world is now entering an epoch of anthropological revelation, the initiative of which man must, at his own risk, take upon himself—the consciousness that divine revelation is passing into man and is continuing through him.

14. Ibid., p. 128.
15. See the first essay in the present collection. Berdyaev is probably referring to the "failures" of Merezhkovsky's doctrine.—Trans.
16. A saying of Father Zosima in Dostoevsky's *The Brothers Karamazov*.—Trans.

This means that man is entering into his religious maturity. Father Florensky is holding on to religious immaturity, to ecclesial democratism. He has a panic fear of tearing himself away from ecclesiality as it is manifested on the physical plane of being. He wants to retain and defend the physical corporeality and materiality of religious life; that is, he wants to remain, and make others remain, in the childish period of Christianity. He has deliberately closed his eyes to the profound instability of the physical plane of being, of the physical corporeality of life, of the materiality of everyday human existence. In the cosmic process of development, man has outgrown the relative stability of physical and material life that had seemed absolutely stable. This physical plane of life has turned out to be not being, but shaky everyday existence. The agonizing crisis of the transition of material and physical manifestations and symbols into the manifestation of the higher spiritual life is occurring in all spheres. It is a cosmic crisis.

This crisis is having a painful effect on the life of the Church. Grounded in a dualistic, transcendental, Platonic metaphysics, the authoritarian order of the Church has often supported, on the pathways of the education of mankind, a materialism of everyday human existence. In the present day, the physical and material flesh of the Church is disintegrating; the manifestations of the Church on the physical plane are always historically relative. In the life of the Church we are seeing a mysterious cosmic break that is revealing the Spirit in man and clothing him in spiritual flesh. The inert physical flesh of ecclesiality is warring against the search for a higher spiritual life and keeping man on lower, childish levels. Materialistic ecclesiality has the face of an infant, but one that is wrinkled with old age. But the Church has also always had secret, mystical traditions; and behind the materialistic and democratic face of the Church there has always been concealed an eternal, absolute, and mysterious face against which the gates of hell will not prevail. In this epoch of the instability and disintegration of the physical plane of being, in this epoch of cosmic whirlwinds which are blowing to pieces the material stability of everyday human existence, the spiritual flesh of the Church—her eternal face and hidden essence—must be revealed. But Father Florensky does not want this; he is afraid of it. With astonishing consistency he stylizes himself to keep in accordance with materialistic ecclesiality. He is for the

Stylized Orthodoxy: On Father Pavel Florensky

"world" and "naturalness" against excess spirituality; he is for the petty bourgeois everydayness of the Church against liberation in the Spirit. He is an enemy of the yearning for spiritual liberation from the "world," from physical sexual love, from meat, from the whole burdensomeness of materialistic everydayness. It is good to abstain from sexual life, but it is bad to be spiritually free from the physical life of sex, to overcome the latter by spiritual love; it is good to fast, but bad to be a vegetarian. This idealization of the organic life of the people as opposed to all that comes from the cultured intelligentsia is so typical. But what was natural in the Slavophiles becomes stylized in Father Florensky, because the organically beautiful everyday structure of peasant, merchant, and noble life no longer exists. This is anachronistic romanticism. Everything is disintegrating in our material, traditional life; there is nothing left to protect in it. Everywhere and always Father Florensky defends the law and the commandments with an Old Testament pathos, and what frightens him most is spiritual freedom. He equates law, the law-governed and the finished, with the cosmic. He is so afraid of the old flesh of the world that he remains in the law, in obedience to the consequences of sin.

But no matter how Father Florensky tries to stylize himself as a traditional, conservative Orthodox believer, he cannot avoid accusations of heresy, free thinking, and novelty. The old, external, materialistic ecclesiality cannot accept his doctrines of Gehenna, Sophia, and so on. He is too original, genuinely original. I would even say that, with respect to the whole character of his thought, Father Florensky is an original who sometimes verges on eccentricity. This is always interesting—sometimes attractive, sometimes not attractive. But official ecclesiality cannot tolerate anything original; it is offended by any spiritual independence. Father Florensky's doctrine of Gehenna is positively original, interesting, and probably not Orthodox; it undoubtedly contains elements of the detested Origenism as well as elements of a peculiar gnosticism and a rejection of the torments of hell accepted by the Church. But however brilliant his doctrine of Gehenna might be and however high it might rise above the coarse ideas of the Church's materialism, it nevertheless absolutizes individual moments of religious experience, transforming the religious path into an ontology. The horror of perdition and the thirst for salvation are stages of the religious path, moments of religious experience through which the Christian soul must pass; they are not an absolute and conclusive ontology. A psychology of perdition is possible, but an ontology of perdition is not—just as an ontology of absolute transcendentism is an unsound ontology. The problem of Gehenna is the problem of the soul's pilgrimage. The Church has never formulated an orthodox solution to the problem of the soul's origins and destiny, of the soul's relation to the cosmic process; there is only an empty place here, a yawning abyss at beginning and end. Father Florensky is too intelligent and subtle not to realize this. And he timidly and cautiously speaks of some preexistence of the soul, though he is afraid to use the word "preexistence," which was compromised by Origen. But Father Florensky does not connect the eschatological problem of Gehenna with the problem of the preexistence of the soul, the problem of the origin of the soul. But this is one and the same problem. Father Florensky is an artistic miniaturist in his investigation of particular problems; he does not synthesize. One must say outright that the Church has by no means solved the problem of reincarnation or the problem of the connection of the soul with cosmic development. The only thing that is clear is that the Christian consciousness does not accept the eastern doctrine of Karma, since the law of Karma is the destiny of the unredeemed soul which has not received the free grace of Christ the Redeemer. But the Christian reworking of the doctrine of reincarnation is a task of Christian gnosis. Through Christ's grace the soul is liberated from the law of Karma, and its achievements surpass all natural evolution. The problem of Gehenna must be transposed from the phase of infantile transcendentism to the phase of mature immanentism. But Father Florensky deliberately closes his eyes to this. Even so, he cannot avoid accusations of heresy, for all free and independent expression is "heretical."

The final chapters of *The Pillar and Ground of the Truth* are dedicated to friendship and jealousy. The letters on friendship and jealousy contain the whole pathos of the book. Father Florensky regards friendship as the purely human element of ecclesiality. He has many good and beautiful things to say about friendship, but these things are infinitely far from Orthodox reality, in which one would have to search very hard to find any traces of the pathos of friendship. But this is something

Stylized Orthodoxy: On Father Pavel Florensky

completely idiosyncratic and lyrical on his part, this "Orthodoxization" of antique emotions. But, in reality, the pathos of ill will and condemnation is much stronger in official Orthodoxy than the pathos of friendship and love. And this is not only because man's nature is sinful, but also because the decaying forms of quasi-Orthodox consciousness are accompanied by a destructive ill will toward man and toward all that is human. But this ill will does not further what is divine in life; just the opposite. Only positive goodwill toward man and toward what is human furthers the disclosure of what is divine in man.

It is very significant that Father Florensky ends his book with an apologia of jealousy. There is an element of forced originality in this pathos-filled apologia, but the praise of jealousy is internally necessary if Father Florensky is to carry through to the end the spiritual style of the book. The pathos of jealousy is an Old Testament pathos; in its deepest religious meaning, it has a Old Testament nature. Jealousy is a fanaticism, a sense of possessiveness, a will to separation. In ordinary life, jealousy loves only its own—its own circle, its own home. In religious life, jealousy claims that it is not true that the Spirit "bloweth where it listeth," but that, instead, it "bloweth" only among "us." In the life of the Church, jealousy has been an eternal source of fanaticism, hatred, and malice. It is a survival of the Old Testament spirit in Christianity, rooted in Jehovah's jealousy toward the chosen nation of Israel and in Israel's jealousy toward Jehovah. (In religious jealousy, one always senses a religious immaturity, the same sort of religious immaturity as in the case of religious fear.) But it was something humanity had to pass through. Jealousy should not be confused with the knightly sense of fidelity and the militant defense of one's truth. Father Florensky's spiritual style must sing the praises of jealousy, but he is hostile to the spirit of knighthood. Our church life has too little knightly nobility and too much false jealousy, false fanaticism, and false condemnation. Fanatical jealousy, often conjoined with betrayal of what is sacred, supplants positive religious feelings and positive spiritual life. Jealousy and fanaticism are associated with a false hysterical excitement. As a counterweight to Father Florensky's apologia of jealousy, I would propose an apologia of *nobility*. More than anything else, we need a pathos of nobility. That is because a noble origin obligates a man. One must choose: either the path of perfection like the perfection of our Heavenly Father, the path of spiritual development, the evangelical path, the path of the great mystics, which lessens the distance between man and God; or the path of false humility and obedience, a path which increases the distance between man and God and keeps man from rising. The first path is spiritual; the second path is psychical. Only the first path, the Divine-human one, presupposes man's creative activity and the nobility of the human spirit.

Father Florensky's book is remarkable; one reads it with very great interest. One does not immediately recognize how decadent it is. It is profoundly hostile to new religious life, to the creative spirit. With an enormous spiritual effort Father Florensky has eradicated in himself the sprouts of new life and stifled the new soul in himself. For him the stylization of Orthodoxy is a serious constraint, a serious self-limitation, not an esthetic game. It is a mystery of his individuality why his complex spiritual experience did not find an adequate and direct expression. The only thing we know is that Father Florensky wrote a refined and stylized book, an almost inaccessible and incomprehensible book intended for a very few readers. His stylized Orthodoxy will not satisfy the old Orthodox world, which is drowning in materialism; nor will it even be comprehensible to this non-spiritual "spiritual world." *The Pillar and Ground of the Truth* will probably be the last "essay in Orthodox theodicy" before the birth of a new religious life. For those who seek higher spiritual life in the present time, these artificially stylized and poisonous flowers of "Orthodox theodicy" will only have the value of teaching them what to oppose. Nobody needs Father Florensky's book; it is nothing but the document of a soul fleeing itself. Our religious maturity and spiritual liberation are approaching, but the spirit of freedom is completely alien to Father Florensky. His book, which aims to treat the fundamental problems of the Christian consciousness, completely ignores the religious problem of man, the problem of his creative vocation in the world, the problem of anthropological revelation. Christ is hardly ever mentioned in the book. For Father Florensky, Christianity is not a Divine-human religion; one finds in him the Monophysitic deviation that is characteristic of Orthodoxy. Let us not forget the remarkable chapter on Sophia. Father Florensky is a representative of the sophiological current in theology, a current originated by Father Sergius Bulgakov. In the main,

Stylized Orthodoxy: On Father Pavel Florensky

Father Florensky continues the tradition of Origen and St. Gregory of Nyssa; that is, he battles against the idea of the eternal torments of hell. This could not have pleased official theology, but in this respect Father Florensky is typically Russian. One can only lament that Father Florensky's great natural gifts have yielded so few fruits. One can only lament that a man who has completed such an enormous spiritual labor lacks creativity: he is a victim of the nonreligious pathways of life and in horror attempts to save himself on dead, archaic religious pathways. But he cannot retard spiritual movement. Archeological restoration cannot become authentic life. Orthodoxy contains an eternal and imperishable sacred world. But this sacred world does not need external protections and stylized restorations; it will pass mysteriously into a new, creative religious life.

12
The Rebirth of Orthodoxy: On Father Sergius Bulgakov[1]

I

The spiritual life of Russia over the past fifteen years has been characterized by the emergence and development of new religious-philosophical currents and by the questing after faith and efforts to justify faith. The traditional world-view of positivism and materialism has undergone a serious crisis and become entirely bankrupt in the spiritually advanced stratum of the Russian intelligentsia. Russia entered the 20th century with fervent questionings and with a readiness to devote her spiritual energy to religious-philosophical thought. Meanwhile, broad strata of society continued to be dominated by the traditional world-view of the intelligentsia, and the old positivism had not yet lost its credit. But it is not these quantitative criteria that determine what is most central and essential in our national spiritual life. The creative energy of thought has passed from the old ideologies to the new religious-philosophical currents. Even the enemies of these currents must admit this. But it would be false to assert that the Russian religious thought of the 20th century does not have precursors in the 19th century. Dostoevsky, Tolstoy, and Solovyov predetermined the direction of our advanced religious thought in the 20th century. These very great Russian thinkers formulated the themes which our consciousness is

---

1. First published in the magazine *Russkaya mysl'*, June 1916. Because of a later reworking of this essay, Berdyaev sometimes refers to Bulgakov as "Father Sergius," although Bulgakov was not ordained as a priest until 1918.—Trans.

now processing. We have gone far beyond their doctrines, but we must always remember these great figures when we try to determine what our own origins are. It is they who produced a great shift in the Russian consciousness and directed our thought to new pathways. Russian religious thought revolves around Christianity, and it is essentially characterized by what is connected with Christian themes and questionings. This also defines the goal of my essay. I consider important and necessary only those currents that have some connection with Christianity, even if in a very unorthodox way. Only currents of this kind have a creative future in Russia. Religious thought in Russia has many different shades. But some forms of religious thought have only a transitional significance and are elementary and embryonic for the religious consciousness. Every developed and mature religious consciousness must think deeply about Christianity and concern itself with Christian themes. This is true even for the theosophical currents.

One can discern several fundamental types of world-view in the multiple and diverse manifestations of Russian religious thought.[2] Chief among these is the type of Orthodox religious thought expressed in various attempts to produce a rebirth of Orthodoxy. What interests me most is the psychology of religious thought. The Orthodox current is characterized by a tendency to religious seriousness and historical monumentality: it seeks the roots and age-old foundations of religious consciousness and fears human capriciousness which tries to supplant what is authentically religious with what is contrived and artificial. But this good tendency does not prevent the revivers of historically monumental Orthodoxy from artificially stylizing the past and artificially recreating in themselves the ancient religious emotions; it does not prevent them from falling into decadent estheticism and surrendering themselves to unconscious or half-conscious deceptions and substitutions. This is felt most vividly in the most brilliant and talented representative of our Orthodox thought—Father Pavel Florensky, whose book *The Pillar and Ground of the Truth* must be recognized as the most

---

2. The classification of types used by me is, of course, conditional, and it is significantly determined by the interests of my own religious thought, but I also believe it reflects something objective that produces the divisions in our spiritual life.

The Rebirth of Orthodoxy: On Father Sergius Bulgakov

important event in this current of thought.[3] S. N. Bulgakov, Father Florensky, Prince E. N. Trubetskoy, V. Ern, Alexander Volzhsky, and others may not yet constitute a new Christianity and a new religious consciousness, but in any case they do constitute a new Orthodoxy, a new direction in Orthodoxy.[4] They are not successful in completely stylizing themselves in the manner of archaic historical Orthodoxy: though they see their *point d'honneur* in not being modernists, they remain modernists, but the split in their wills and consciousnesses makes their modernism uncreative. This phenomenon is the reverse of what we see in Catholic modernism, where authentic Catholics are captivated by the contemporary spirit and seek new life and new thought. In Russia, people of the contemporary spirit are captivated by the old religious truth and seek pathways back into the womb of the Church. But the Orthodoxy of these people does not resemble the Orthodoxy of Bishop Feofan the Recluse or of such contemporary defenders of conservative Orthodoxy as M. Novoselov, V. Kozhevnikov, F. Samarin, and others. Even Vyacheslav Ivanov[5] is able to find points of convergence with the new Orthodoxy and to establish mystical-esthetic connections with it.

II

The religious consciousness in which we are interested is characterized by a never-satisfied yearning to flee from the contemporary world and to *return* to the maternal womb of the Church; it is a never-ending process of conversion to Christianity. The creative powers of this current are undermined by a never-ending repentance of thought, by a self-overcoming and a negative reaction against one's past, against the world-view of the nonreligious intelligentsia to which one had belonged. The representatives of this type of religious thought think they are being bold and daring when they abandon their past atheism and return to Orthodox Christianity. They admire themselves for hav-

---

3. See the essay "Stylized Orthodoxy: On Father Pavel Orthodoxy" in the present collection.—Trans.
4. Prince Trubetskoy stands a little to the side and is less typical.
5. The most refined of the Russian modernist poets.—Trans.

ing become Orthodox churchmen; they compete to prove they are more Orthodox than others and rejoice like children in their new position in the world. But within Christianity itself they lack boldness of initiative and creative power. They are modernists not because they enter onto the path of religious creativity, but because they cannot overcome in themselves the dualism that characterizes contemporary people. But their pride is directed at making themselves as orthodox as possible, as faithful as possible to the old traditions. They desire to accept the whole historical edifice, not only the Church herself, but also ecclesiastical authority and the routine of everyday life in the Church; and they try to esthetically frighten themselves and others by the grotesqueness of the new, contemporary world that man is creating. But by the force of necessity they are fated to remain intermediaries between the old Orthodoxy and contemporary culture, which is splintered apart. People of this religious type are fatally deprived of religious wholeness and greedily seek to gain this wholeness by returning to the old orthodoxy, to a past organic state. They are constantly looking back and fleeing from themselves and their own epoch; and they thereby weaken themselves and are not able to find in themselves a solid point of support for creative movement forward. This current possesses a fairly high philosophical culture and is characterized by a high (perhaps too high) degree of consciousness. The return to Orthodox wholeness and Orthodox primitivism in this current is entirely conscious, intentional, philosophical, cultural, and intellectual. It is impossible to find any *naiveté* of experiences or *naiveté* of thought in this current. Only one's own new contemporary creations can be experienced naively and directly. Old things created by others can be experienced only sentimentally, in a reflective consciousness. In a certain epoch of the life of a Christian nation, religious materialism and naïve religious realism are asserted directly, naively, integrally, and in an atmosphere of a national poetic sense of life, but in our contemporary reborn Orthodoxy they are asserted consciously and philosophically, with reflection and stylization that look backward. Conscious *naiveté*, reflective wholeness, and modernized archaicity are the things that characterize the contemporary rebirth of Orthodoxy. But all this conceals an authentic yearning for integral faith.

S. N. Bulgakov is our most typical *public* representative of this type

The Rebirth of Orthodoxy: On Father Sergius Bulgakov

of religious thought. His path is a typical one: he came to Orthodoxy from Marxism through idealism. He is the leader of a certain religious-philosophical current. He can be called a repentant member of the intelligentsia, just as in the past we had repentant noblemen. This is a new phenomenon in Russian life. Father Pavel Florensky is more original, brilliant, and religiously innovative than Bulgakov. A priest and a professor of the Moscow Theological Academy who abides close to elders and to hermitages, Florensky is the inspiration behind the whole contemporary school of Orthodox thought and—by virtue of the religious path he has followed and the position he occupies—he has the authority to issue religious directives. In spite of his youth, he is considered an authority. Many people do not discern the decadence in Father Florensky, his artificial stylization, his Alexandrianism, his endless self-examination and flight from himself, his terrifying skepticism, and the absence in him of a creative spirit. But however one assesses Father Florensky, it is necessary to acknowledge that his significance is generally an individual one and lies outside the historical mainstream of Russian thought. There is an exotic hothouse quality about him. Bulgakov's significance is more general, more historically typical, more broadly public in character. As a thinker and writer, Bulgakov is not intimate; he is afraid of intimacy and does not have the gift of intimacy. In the character of his thought and his manner of writing, he remains a member of the intelligentsia, even though the spirit of the intelligentsia is something he flees from. In the type represented by Bulgakov there is something historically universal and typical for Russian spiritual life and Russian questing. Into his Orthodoxy Bulgakov has introduced his former Marxism, and in his very flight from the camp of the Russian intelligentsia one senses a typical trait of the intelligentsia. He is a characteristic figure in relation to the spiritual crisis of the intelligentsia. In his spiritual type he was and is a dogmatist who is torn apart by reflection and is eternally tempted by what is alien to him and outside of him. V. F. Ern sails in the same religious-philosophical channel as Bulgakov, but Ern has as yet insufficiently expressed himself in literature and is less typical and less connected with the fundamental currents of Russian thought; he is narrower and lacks Bulgakov's agitation. Prince E. N. Trubetskoy stands a bit to the side; he is less extreme, too academic, and insufficiently sensitive to mystical themes. But his book on Vladimir Solovyov is characteristic and interesting for Orthodox thought.[6] In characterizing the type of religious thought which can be called a "rebirth of Orthodoxy," I will primarily have Bulgakov in mind.[7]

III

Bulgakov's world-view and religious philosophy are characterized by a consistent dualism, a transcendental opposition of things.[8] This extreme dualism is evidently the sole mode by which he apprehends life, and he tries to find a religious and philosophical sanction for it. Everything he writes is marked by his constant vacillations between the world of Orthodox holiness (hermitages, elders, asceticism, prayer, Divine transcendence) and the cultural and social life of the world with its life-organizing reason, science, philosophy, and economy and economics, i.e., all the things that are immanent to humanity. This dualism is inherited by Bulgakov from the entire pathway of his life. One always has the sense that he is powerless to experience with religious pathos and immanent illumination the values of culture and social life, the values of his life in the world, and the values of his thought, knowledge, and human activity. He cannot live without cultural and social activity, without thought, knowledge, and social interaction in the world; but he is unable to introduce religious pathos into these things; he is unable to feel the inner presence of God in them. He finds religious pathos only in flight from the world and its values into deserts and hermitages, to elders, to the stable experience of Orthodoxy. Nevertheless, he keeps returning to the world and turning his economic,

---

6. See my essay "On Earthly and Heavenly Utopianism: On Trubetskoy's Book *Vladimir Solovyov's World-view*" in *Russkaya mysl'*, September 1913.

7. Bulgakov's deep religious feeling and the significance of his religious path were confirmed by the fact that, in 1918, he was ordained as a priest.—*A later note*.

8. For characterizing Bulgakov his book *The Philosophy of Economy* is essential. We should also mention his important essays on the philosophy of religion published in the magazine *Voprosy filosofii i psikhologii*, as well as the two-volume collection of essays *Two Cities*. (After the present essay was written, Bulgakov published his book on religious philosophy, *The Unfading Light*. This book does not substantially alter my characterization of Bulgakov.—*A later note*.)

[202]

The Rebirth of Orthodoxy: On Father Sergius Bulgakov

rational, prudent, and organizing aspect toward it. God remains transcendent in relation to man and the world, and man and the world remain transcendent in relation to God. Bulgakov is constantly fleeing man and the world into what is transcendent; he is constantly afraid of man and the world. And he keeps returning to man and to the world, but he does not bring what is transcendent into the life of man and of the world. So, what is transcendent does not become immanent; it does not produce any inner transfiguration and illumination of life. He does not demonstrate any inner religious fire or pathos in his creativity. He has only one mode for justifying life in the world: he justifies the life of the world as obedience, as the bearing of burdens, as the enduring of the consequences of sin. This is the path of the justification of life that Bulgakov takes. His religious pathos is the pathos of distance, of infinite distance between man and God and between the world and God, the pathos of God's transcendence, the pathos of the lowliness and insignificance of the creature before the face of the Creator. Bulgakov seems to regard the experiencing of this transcendent distance as the religious experience par excellence. In experiences of religious immanence, of Divine closeness, he tends to see a deviation toward the unlawful divinization of man and of the world.

This sense of the infinite transcendent distance between God and the world and between God and man is inherited by Bulgakov from his former positivism and Marxism. For positivism and Marxism, God is completely and conclusively transcendent in relation to the world and man; the divine light does not shine from within. In its essence, positivism is the most extreme transcendentism of the Divine consciousness: God is totally removed from the being of man and the world and transposed to a realm where He is unattainable. This atheistic poison has remained in Bulgakov and ceaselessly frightens him. This pathos of transcendence makes him inwardly unfree; it constantly oppresses him and makes him timid. He does not introduce his human experience into his religious consciousness; he does not enrich his religious thought by the path he has taken, for he is in constant terror of his own humanity and constantly flees from it, judging it to be a being deprived of all Divinity. And this prevents him from playing a creative religious role. He is not advancing toward new life but is fated to be a restorer. Bulgakov's path, like the path of many in the contemporary religious movement, consists in flight from man and humanity into Divine transcendence. He seeks the religious center not within himself, not in his own depths, not in that which is deeply immanent in him, but outside, an infinite distance away from him, in that which is totally transcendent in relation to him. And this is so typical for contemporary man, for his weariness caused by a godless human existence; it so clearly exhibits the religious impotence caused by wanderings in the deserts of positivism! The religious yearning of weary and frightened man finds expression in the transcendent religious consciousness.

Bulgakov's transcendent dualism also finds expression in his manner of writing, in his inability to find a single style. He cannot liberate himself from academism, from the old rationalistic manner, from a totally discursive method of treating mystical themes. In the composition of his sentences one senses that he is afraid of approaching religious and mystical problems freely and from within. But this cautious and timorous rationalistic manner alternates with a lyricism that cannot be called successful. This lack of success is determined by his fundamental dualism, by his sense of the Divine not as an inner principle but as an object of aspiration. Bulgakov does not regard his writing as a pathos-filled expression of his inner spiritual energy. He cannot free himself of the duty to prove and justify his truth the way he used to when he was a Marxist and Kantian. He does not like science and lacks the pathos of scientific knowledge; he is afraid of science and considers it a threatening external force. He regards science as something transcendent, i.e., unfree. His language lacks inner religious pathos, for he regards all literature as worldly and totally transcendent in relation to the Divine; he almost regards it as sinful and illegitimate. It is better to pray silently. Bulgakov goes from the world to God; he never goes from God to the world. It is as if he is contemptuous of his own ideas and is afraid of them; it is as if he is always conscious of their sinful impurity. Given such a sense of impurity, it is impossible to think and write with pathos, to develop a style adequate to one's inner spiritual life. Bulgakov constructs a religious philosophy and is contemptuous of it; he is not sure that this form of occupation is righteous and valuable. And he is envious of holiness. He wants to flee from his own thought, from his own writing. The work of the thinker and writer in the world remains unjustified. For the reborn Orthodox consciousness all cultural creativity is poisoned, all the fruits of human creativity are bitter. The only thing left is to lead a dual existence rooted in compromise, to oscillate ceaselessly between two mutually transcendent poles. The most characteristic thing for Bulgakov is that he totally lacks the pathos of power, that he can experience nothing as his own inner potency.

IV

Bulgakov's philosophy attempts to justify this worldly cultural life, a life that remains unjustified by his psychology. Since the Divine has been removed from man and from the world, since God is not immanent and it is impossible to create life with religious pathos, the only thing that remains is to justify all life in the world as obedience, as the bearing of the burdens of the sinful world. Bulgakov's philosophy is highly modernized and equipped with all the advanced philosophical weaponry, but, fundamentally, its spirit is the same as that in the case of Bishop Feofan the Recluse,[9] for whom all life in the world was justified as obedience to the consequences of sin. Feofan's Orthodox theology had an economic theme similar to the one found in Bulgakov's contemporary philosophy. Russian Orthodoxy, in its spiritual quotidianness, contains economy as an element. Bulgakov's contemporary economy, which is connected with his economic materialism, has merged with Feofan's old Orthodox economy.[10] Bulgakov, too, adopts an economic attitude toward life and fearfully rejects the creative attitude toward life. For him the religious experiencing of life in the world means obedience, the bearing of burdens, not creativity; this experiencing is determined not by abundant creative energy, but by the insufficiencies of our sinful nature.

The Philosophy of Economy[11] is Bulgakov's most important and original book. In this book he has succeeded in expressing his world-view

---

9. Prolific 19th-century theologian whose writings defined for many people the meaning of traditional Orthodoxy.—Trans.

10. See Bishop Feofan's very characteristic book *A Sketch of Christian Moral Teaching*.

11. Bulgakov's book *The Unfading Light* is religiously more profound and more interesting in its themes than *The Philosophy of Economy*, but it is less coherent in its ideas and not as well written—*A later note*.

and grounding it philosophically. The title is imprecise and too narrow. In essence, what he presents is not a philosophy of economy but an economic philosophy or even an economic religion. Bulgakov expounds a particular type of religious thought. Economics is not just the object of Bulgakov's thought; it also completely permeates the subject of the thought. Bulgakov is a theologian in economics and an economist in theology. He has remained an economic materialist and transposed his economic materialism to heaven—he has irrigated heaven with the sweat of labor. He has imparted an economic character even to Sophia and sophianicity. He has transformed economy into a whole metaphysics of being, even into an original kind of mysticism. He views the world as an economy and God as the Master. Man is the Master's steward, and the task assigned to him is to cultivate the earth. His task is to oversee, to cultivate, to manage the economy on his Master's earth, but he cannot be a creator, an original artist of life. Bulgakov absolutizes economy and gives it a universal character. He understands man's relation to nature exclusively as an economic relation. And he is forced to define culture as an economy: "Culture is hewn out of nature only by the labor of humanity, and in this sense one can agree with economic materialism that all culture is economy."[12] He rejects the view that culture is creative abundance. And this is so typical of Russian thought. The economic world-view opposes all artistism and aristocratism, all pathos of freedom and creativity. But economic labor as obedience is the fundamental thing for Bulgakov and the sole source of his religious justification of life. He seems to be unaware that the economic relation to nature is always selfish and full of care and that it therefore cannot be a Christian, New Testament type of relation. The Christian, New Testament type of relation to nature and to life must be unselfish and free of care; it must be a contemplation of the divine beauty of the cosmos and the creation of a new cosmic life. The economic relation to nature is an Old Testament type of relation of subordination to the law. It lacks the spiritual freedom of the New Testament, and Bulgakov does not know the pathos of Christian freedom. In his relation to life and in his philosophy one feels the yoke of the subordination to law. His economic religious life is based on the Old Testament sense of life, on Biblical curse

---

12. See *The Philosophy of Economy*, p. 308.

as reworked in economic materialism, on the eternal dependence on natural necessity. Bulgakov's economic religion is a religion of the species, of the accursed natural species.

Sophia herself, who is nearly a figure of cult for him and with whom he links the most intimate aspects of his religious philosophy, is a Sophia of the species, giving birth and taking care of the economy of the earth. Therefore, economy itself turns out to be sophianic in nature. But the Heavenly Virgin, Sophia, is not in charge of economy in the human race; she does not have anything to do with economic cares and the sweat of labor. These planes are completely incommensurable. But, for Bulgakov, the economic turns out to be divine in its own way. In his economic religious philosophy he arrives at a justification of quotidian existence, and he thus finds himself in harmony with old Orthodoxy. Russian elders such as Amvrosy of Optina[13] or Orthodox writers such as Feofan the Recluse religiously justified everyday existence, including economic cares, the natural and traditional management of practical duties. For Amvrosy and Feofan the selling of goods in a store was more justified than philosophical, artistic, or social creativity. Ordinary, everyday existence is justified as a form of obedience. In contrast, human creativity is a manifestation of arrogant boldness and can be a satanical deviation toward the illegitimate divinization of man. For Bulgakov all this is more sophisticated, complex, and modern than it was for Amvrosy and Feofan, who were more naive and primitive. But the result is the same.

V

Bulgakov is very consistent in rejecting man's creative nature and fears creativity as if it were a form of satanism. Concerning this, we find some striking passages in *The Philosophy of Economy*. He tries to find in Platonism a philosophical justification for his religious fear of creativity. First, he denies that knowledge is a form of creativity. The source of his rejection of human creativity lies in the religious pathos of the transcendent distance between creature and Creator. In the depths of

---

13. See Father S. Chetverikov's interesting book *A Description of the Life of the Optina Elder Hieroschemamonk Amvrosy of Blessed Memory*.

the creaturely nature there are no sources of creativity; these sources always lie in that which transcends the creaturely nature. Man is not given the ability to create out of nothing, i.e., out of freedom, out of the depths; he is only given the ability to redistribute the given elements of a closed and finished creaturely nature. For Bulgakov the creature's pretension to autonomous creativity is a form of satanism: Knowledge "is a disclosure of what is metaphysically given. It is therefore *not* creativity *out of nothing*, but only a recreation or reproduction of the given which has become a *task to accomplish*; and this recreation becomes creativity only insofar as it is a free reproduction effected through labor. Therefore, human creativity does not contain anything *metaphysically new*; it only reproduces and recreates out of already existing and created elements and according to newly discovered and recreated, though also already existing, specimens. Creativity in the strict sense, as the creation of what is metaphysically new, is not given to man as a creaturely entity; it belongs exclusively to the Creator.... Human creativity creates not an 'image,' which is given, but a 'likeness,' which is a task to be accomplished; it reproduces in a free historical process through labor that which pre-eternally *exists* as an ideal proto-image. And the revolt of the creature against the Creator, the deviation toward satanism, is metaphysically reducible to the attempt to erase this difference, to become 'as gods,' to have all of one's own from oneself alone."[14]

Thus, Bulgakov proclaims as a deviation toward Satanism any immanent religious consciousness that reveals in man's inner depths a creative divine energy. The transcendent and absolute opposition between creature and Creator is the schema into which he wants to fit orthodox, pious, God-fearing Christianity. Creation is finished and closed; the creative process does not continue in man and through man. Man is a trembling and lowly creature. His only task is to economically cultivate God's estate, created by God. This view of man is permeated with a religious servilism, which treats man as a child. The ultimate and essential thing is obedience to the transcendent, i.e., to the external and remote will of God. This is a heteronomous, not an autonomous, religious consciousness. By thus locating the center out-

---

14. See *The Philosophy of Economy*, pp. 140–141.

The Rebirth of Orthodoxy: On Father Sergius Bulgakov

side of man's depths, one produces the timidity and lowliness of a slave, a timidity that is experienced almost ecstatically. But it would seem that it is Christianity that sets before humanity the great task of becoming "as gods"; it would seem that Christianity is the attainment of the perfect immanence of God to man, raises man to unprecedented heights and, through the God-Man, enables him to participate in the Divine mysteries of the Holy Trinity. But, in his religious ontology, Bulgakov absolutizes just one of the stages of religious experience and of the religious path—the passage through the dualistic split and opposition of the human and the Divine, of creature and Creator. By rationalistically absolutizing this inevitable stage in religious life, he establishes an eternally fixed and static religious ontology. He does this in his own way, though he follows the external Christianity of a certain age of mankind. His Christianity remains in the naturalistic stage; it is a religion of the species. Philosophically and religiously, Bulgakov accepts objective materialism and realism. He is not a symbolist. He believes that the materialization of Christianity on the natural and historical plane is the most ultimate and essential reality. He does not make any distinction between inner, hidden, esoteric Christianity and external, visible, exoteric Christianity. He believes that all the things that are materially visible and embodied in Christianity are not symbols of something other and hidden, but ultimate realities. This nonsymbolic, realistically materialistic view of Christianity leads to a hopeless dependence on the external and always culminates in the enslavement of the spirit. The spirit is liberated only by absorbing all things into itself and apprehending all external things as symbols of the inner and hidden which is being enacted within its depths.

From the transcendentism and materialism of Bulgakov's religious philosophy it follows that, for him, freedom is swallowed up by necessity. He lacks the pathos of religious freedom. He has no place for the irrational mystery of freedom, for bottomless freedom. His freedom is subordinate to law and subject to necessity. He never loses his fear of freedom, and he experiences the divine fatum, divine necessity, with religious pathos. "Freedom . . . must be confined within the solid limits of necessity in order for it to serve the disclosure of a unitary plan. . . . Freedom is the general foundation of the creative process, while necessity determines the frame of this process, thereby predetermining freedom and guiding its path. For individuals as well as for historical humankind, necessity is the law of life."[15] "For God, man with his hidden possibilities and forces of history is perfectly transparent, and this guarantees a resolution of history that accords with the divine plan. Freedom applies only to the progress of the historical process, not to its resolution. Divine Providence, leading man by the pathway of necessity, is therefore the supreme law of history."[16] Then there is Bulgakov's passive conception of the Apocalypse of universal history: Man and mankind are not the active creator of the world's historical destiny. Man passively and with trepidation awaits the enactment over him of apocalyptic destiny. Bulgakov's economism, materialism, naturalism, pathos of labor and obedience, and rejection of creative freedom are all interconnected in his religious philosophy. All these elements flow from one another and support one another.

Outwardly, Bulgakov's doctrine of Sophia is unsuccessful and seems to lack an organic character. But if we look deeper into his world-view, it will become clear that he necessarily had to arrive at sophianicity. His sophianicity is an expression of passively feminine religiosity which obediently accepts the given cosmic order. The highest point of this sophianic religiosity is tenderness and soft gentleness. For a more masculine religious spirit, Sophia is the human being's quest for his lost virginity, for his androgynous image. Sophia is connected with the problem of man. But, in Bulgakov's religious-philosophical consciousness, Sophia is the eternal sanction of matter as divine matter, the sanction of the species as divine hypostasis. Here, one hides from the cold and fire of the religious path of the One who dared to take upon Himself the cross and crucifixion. Sophianicity is the intimately lyrical, joyous aspect of that which is objectively and compulsorily revealed to Bulgakov as economy. This entire Moscow Orthodox current[17] shows almost no sense of intimate closeness to Christ. One has the impression that Sophia has replaced Christ; it as if Christ Himself is feared. It is even more difficult to find Christ in Father Pavel Florensky.

---

15. Ibid., p. 236.
16. Ibid., p. 237.
17. Along with Bulgakov, Berdyaev includes Florensky in this current.—Trans.

The Rebirth of Orthodoxy: On Father Sergius Bulgakov

VI

In order to characterize Bulgakov's type of religious thought, it is essential to examine the chapters he has published from his planned volume of philosophy of religion.[18] It is very characteristic and interesting that in his approach to problems of the philosophy of religion he remains a Kantian, just as in his philosophy of economy he remains an economic materialist. He pretends to be a Kantian; out of fear before scientific philosophy he dresses himself in the clothing of the Kantianism which he detests. Such titles as "The Transcendental Problem of Religion" and "How Is Religion Possible?" seem very strange to us when they come from a Russian Orthodox thinker who has always opposed his ontologism to Kantian transcendentalism. In his method Bulgakov remains a rationalist in the philosophy of religion; he deals primarily with transcendental categories. One senses in him a divided and doubting mind whose dogmatism is never immanent. The object of his faith always remains transcendental in relation to his thought. He is not a gnostic; he is an anti-gnostic. A gnostic is someone who is completely free in the pathways of his religious knowledge, who does not need a transcendental authority and does not accept any values which are heteronomous and external to his inner depths. Bulgakov is completely unfree in the pathways of his religious knowledge; locating the center outside of himself, he inevitably has recourse to a transcendental authority. He is unfree partly because he lacks the pathos of science and never regards science as his own task but is afraid of the science of others, "their" science, and constantly adapts himself to it. Science for him is another authority. He adapts himself to it, meanwhile occupying a defensive, apologetic position. He is clearly troubled by the activity of "their" science in the domain of religion. The transcendental formulation of problems of the philosophy of religion, the translation of prayer and sacrament into gnoseological language, the examination of Christianity as a myth and all myth as a reality and as an *a priori* synthetic religious judgment—all these things are not Bulgakov's immanent gnosis and free knowledge, but a protective

---

18. These chapters were published in the magazine *Voprosy filosofii i psikhologii*. (Later they were incorporated into *The Unfading Light.—A later note.*)

adaptation, a defense measure against enemies that adopts some of the enemies' tactics. In knowledge, obedience is everything for Bulgakov; inspiration is nothing. He likes to use such expressions as "scientific piety," "obedience to science," and so on.

Bulgakov's makes a fundamental objective philosophical error which consists in his completely incorrect formulation of the problem of immanence and transcendence and its incorrect solution. He seems to confuse immanentism with subjectivism, and transcendentism with objectivism. "That which is confined within the limits of a given closed circle of consciousness is immanent; that which is outside this circle is transcendent or does not exist within these limits." But the religious problem of immanence exists beyond the subjective and the objective in the gnoseological or psychological sense of these notions. Religious immanentism does not signify confinement "within the limits of a given closed circle of consciousness." Just the opposite. It signifies unlimited movement of the spirit into the depths, the limitlessness of inner religious experience, the absence of any insuperable limits to religious knowledge. Is it possible to say that such a typical religious immanentist as Meister Eckhart is confined "within the limits of a closed circle of consciousness," that he is limited by subjectivity? In essence, all mystics have been immanentists and immanentism always signifies experiential movement from every periphery and shell into the depths of the divine; it signifies the experience of the divine as deeply inner. But Bulgakov's entire religion consists in *objectification*. His transcendentism is actually an objectification, the spewing outward of that which lies in the depths. In spite of his formal gnoseologism, he does not even attempt to pose an essential question for religious gnoseology: What do the terms "object" and "objective" mean in religious life? It never enters his head to try to overcome "objectification" in religion, something all mystics have aspired to do. In general, is there any separation between subject and object in religious life and religious knowledge? Do religious life and religious knowledge not transpire in the identity of subject and object? Is not every opposition of object to subject a rationalization? Can God be an object? Bulgakov does not even pose any of these questions, and he therefore uses the terms "objective" and "subjective" incorrectly. In the rationalistic aspect, God can appear to be an object. But that is not where we find deep religious life and experience. And, of course, Bulgakov's own deep religious experience lies outside his objectification of the transcendent. "God is the transcendent. . . . He is the sole authentic *Not-I*. . . . Between the world and God there is an absolute distance, insuperable for the world. . . ." "Religion is based on the polarization of consciousness, on an intense sense of the opposition between the transcendent and the immanent, between God-consciousness and world-consciousness." None of these definitions go down to the deepest depths. All of them are secondary, not primary—a rationalization and objectification, an external, exoteric expression of what is deeply inner. Bulgakov wants to pass off the penultimate as the ultimate; he wants to absolutize and eternalize the stage of objectification on the spiritual path. He is pursued everywhere by the phantasm of illegitimate human divinization; this phantasm is the main terror of this life and his fear of it prevents him from recognizing the immanence of the divine in man, the deeply inner action of divine reason and divine energies in man. He also approaches this central theme of his from the direction of negative theology.

VII

Bulgakov has interesting things to say about negative theology, but here too one always feels his apprehensiveness and lack of freedom. It is as if everything for him is external and distant, not inner and near. He objectifies his lack of freedom in his transcendental consciousness. The most valuable thing for Bulgakov is the antinomic character of the religious consciousness. "Antinomy is a clear sign of the permanent transcendence of the object of thought for thought and also of the collapse of rational, gnoseological immanentism. Antinomic thought possesses its object and makes it immanent to itself only partly or up to a certain limit, which is disclosed in antinomy." Thus, Bulgakov makes antinomy a guard that prevents movement on the immanent paths of knowledge and spiritual life. But Bulgakov has an incorrect understanding of the nature of religious autonomy. Antinomy does not exist in order to reject immanentism and affirm transcendentism. A completely different conception of antinomy is possible. Antinomy is always directed toward the "world" and toward the "reason of this world." For the world the mysteries of divine life are hidden behind antinomy, and rational thought cannot penetrate this antinomy. Antinomy is the hiddenness of the divine fullness for which no rationalistically limiting either/or exists, e.g., either the One God or the Trine God. But, always correlative with this "world" and with its "reason," this antinomy is removed within religious experience, in the experiencing of the mysteries of divine life and divine knowledge. Religious experience and religious knowledge are always immanent, not transcendent. The transcendent exists only for the life of "this" world and in order to know the reason of the world. Antinomy is the guard that prevents the "world" and the "reason of the world" from approaching the mysteries of divine life without sacrifice and renunciation. But the human spirit is immanent to divine life, and divine life is immanent to the human spirit. The human spirit knows divinity not only in the aspect of its protective antinomy which is directed at "this world."

Perhaps, Bulgakov's fundamental error is that he regards man as always immanent to this world and as transcendent in relation to God, whereas man's depths are immanent to God and transcend the world. Antinomy is directed against rationalism, not against deep and authentic immanentism. Bulgakov's fundamental thesis is that there is a *discontinuity*, an insuperable chasm of transcendence between the Absolute and the relative, the Creator and creation, God and man, but this thesis can be directed only against popular pantheism and vulgar monism which equate God with the world and with nature. But it is necessary to consider more complex and subtle forms of God-consciousness. Bulgakov stylizes too simplistically the type of God-consciousness which he dislikes, and he thereby gains too easy a victory. Smooth rationalism and monism reject all discontinuity and antinomy in thought and in experience; instead, they affirm evolutionary continuity. But Bulgakov seems to think that every gnostic, even the greatest of mystics like Boehme, is this type of smooth rationalist and monist and that the same arguments are applicable to him. But authentically mystical gnosis takes a different path; it penetrates down to depths that antinomy does not know; it is immanent to the divine, not the worldly; divine reason operates in it, not the reason of this world. The immanent continuity of divine thought and life is open for mystical gnosis; the chasm has been miraculously and mysteriously overcome. But Bulgakov does not believe in gnosis; he fears it and does not want it. Maintaining the distance and "holy ignorance" are what he values most. He views gnosis as a form of pride and as a threat to the very existence of religion. But every penetration into the depths of divine life and the divine mystery threatens existence, and from this point of view one should always keep man and God apart! Such is the paradox of religious life: too deep a penetration into religious life abolishes religion, which was created for those remote and fallen away from God. Bulgakov seems to prefer to remain on the periphery, as long as he has religion. He puts a higher value on religion than on divine life.

For Bulgakov, all mysticism and all mystical gnosis are forms of rationalism, and Eckhart and Boehme are rationalists. For him, only the transcendental dogmatics of the Church is not a rationalism; it is an overcoming of rationalism. The doctors of the Church are not rationalists. Basil the Great is not a rationalist and the lesser doctors of the Church are not rationalists, for they recognize transcendental discontinuity, holy agnosticism. In essence, Bulgakov must reject all the mystics known to history. External, exoteric Christianity is higher for him than inner, esoteric Christianity. To remain on the periphery is to overcome rationalism; to penetrate into the depths is to be a rationalist. Everything is turned upside down; terminology is misused. It is true that most of the doctors of the Church were the most commonplace rationalists. Isaac the Syrian, Maximus the Confessor, and Symeon the New Theologian with their mystical depths were rare pearls in the patristic literature, whereas official theology, which is entirely based on the principle of transcendental discontinuity, contains nothing but deadening scholasticism and superficial rationalistic apologetics. Bulgakov's fundamental schema—discontinuity with its transcensus and chasm and continuity with its immanent knowledge of divine mysteries—is useless if it is applied to making judgments about mysticism, though it is completely orthodox from the point of view of the Church. In essence, Bulgakov repeats, in a more refined and profound form, the usual arguments of the dogmatic authorities of the Church against mysticism and gnosticism. At a certain stage of her development, the Church prohibited gnosticism, strengthening agnosticism. The consciousness of the authorities cannot tolerate the autonomy of mystical gnosis.

As for negative theology, Bulgakov tries to interpret it too as a transcendental theology, leading all knowledge to a transcendental discontinuity. But negative theology, which originated in the works of Pseudo-Dionysius the Areopagite, is a mystical, seraphic theology. Like all mystical God-knowledge, it is based on immanent mystical experience and attains immanent God-knowledge through degrees of detachment. Negation here is only a special, inner method of mystical knowledge, not a limit imposed from outside. The Church's orthodox transcendental theology has always had an awkward relation to mystical negative theology, always suspecting it of a deviation toward pantheism, of borrowings from the Neoplatonists, that is, of religious immanentism. For negative theology the dogma of the transcendent God is an objectification, not the ultimate mystery, not the ultimate depth. For mystical theology, revelation is an immanent, not a transcendental act. The revelation of God and of divine life is accomplished in our depths and with us. Therefore, all religious experience and religious knowledge are immanent, inner, in the depths; they are the most intimate things in us. The negative path of mystical theology leads to the transcendent as the Ineffable Mystery, the Abyss, the primordial Nothing. But this is not the transcendence that Bulgakov wants. Divinity is both closer and more immanent to us and more mysterious and farther from us than the transcendental consciousness asserts. The mysteries of divine life do not end where transcendental theology sees an end; they keep moving down into deeper depths. Transcendental theology remains in some sort of middle, in something intermediary; it regards Divinity as something distant and external and as something well known and not mysterious at all. Such intermediateness is the fate of all objectification, of all outward expulsion. For immanent God-consciousness and God-knowledge, Divinity is Mystery and Abyss; no categories of this objectified and materialized world are applicable to Divinity but, at the same time, infinite immanent progress in spiritual knowledge is possible—the path into the depths of divine life is open. All mystics teach that Divinity opens and closes. Bulgakov's analysis of the Divine Nothing is interesting and might appear convincing, but it is based on external, peripheral, and (in the end) illusory oppositions. He is wrong when he asserts that all immanentism must reject creation and accept some form of emanational doctrine. If God is the Creator and created the world, this does not mean that creation is extra-divine, that it exists not in God. Creation is a revelation of God, a disclosure of God, a tragic process in Him.

VIII

Bulgakov has recently become greatly interested in Jacob Boehme and devoted a great deal of attention to him in his philosophy of religion. Boehme troubles Bulgakov; he seduces and repels him. In his attitude toward Boehme one senses a lack of freedom, a constant looking-over-one's-shoulder, an effort to conform with apologetic goals. Bulgakov desperately desires to squeeze Boehme into his scheme and make Boehme into his opponent. Bulgakov's characterization of Boehme is permeated with our contemporary struggle, with a contemporary settling of religious-philosophical accounts. Bulgakov does not feel Boehme's uniqueness and unrepeatability, the exceptional expression of his countenance. For Bulgakov, Boehme can be placed in the same series as Eckhart and belongs to that same general type of German mysticism, which with apologetic aims must be exposed and refuted. Boehme turns out to be a rationalist, a monist, an acosmist, an immanentist, an evolutionist, and an emanationist; that is, he is afflicted with all the ailments and sins of heretical mysticism in general and of German mysticism in particular. Boehme is already inhabited by Hegel, by Hartmann, and even by Steiner. "In Boehme's God—from His first movement toward revelation to the most distant corner of the universe, from the angel down to the vilest bedbug—all things are *understandable*, explained, and rationalized. Here, there is no place for antinomy with its logical discontinuity; nor is there a place for Mystery: unalloyed rationalism is the reverse side of that omniscience or 'gnosis' which Hegel believed he possessed on certain grounds and which Boehme believed he possessed on different grounds—which is why he turns out to be so kindred to our contemporary 'theosophism,' occultism, and mystical rationalism." Here, Boehme is clearly a victim of apologetic zeal and schematism. Boehme had to turn out to be a rationalist, for Bulgakov pigeonholed him in advance as an adherent of the type of gnosticism that is based on the law of the "continuity of thought."

It turns out that, for the greatest of mystics, who would constantly interrupt his expositions with the exclamation "This is a great mystery" and for whom everything was a Mystery—it turns out that, for Boehme, there was no place for Mystery. Bulgakov is wrong when he asserts that gnosis excludes Mystery; gnosis guides us to Mystery; it opens and closes. The Mystery of mystical gnosis lies deeper and farther away than the Mystery of orthodox theology and dogmatics. Though Bulgakov appears to have read deeply in Boehme, he has assimilated him only externally and for apologetic purposes. Nor has Bulgakov seen the ultimate depths of Boehme, the most mysterious of the mystics and the greatest theosophist of all time, a man who had authentic revelations, who saw flashes of lightning in the darkness. Boehme, who was permeated with the revelations of the cosmos and dedicated most of his works to nature-philosophy, turns out to be an acosmist in Bulgakov's scheme. According to Bulgakov, German mysticism always had to be acosmic. This was predetermined by Eckhart and by the kinship of the German spirit with the spirit of India as well as with Neoplatonism. Boehme turned out to be guilty of impersonalism too, even though his entire mysticism is concrete, not abstract, and is permeated with the revelation of cosmic multiplicity. For Boehme, the person of Christ is at the center. In contrast to the mysticism of Eckhart, Plotinus, and India, Boehme's mysticism is not a mysticism of the One, not a mysticism that views man as a product of the fall and of sin. Boehme had great insights about man as a positive revelation; he was one of the first to confront the anthropological problem. It is wrong to characterize as a rationalist a seer who saw the Abyss that is deeper and farther than God and for whom the primordial furious elements in the cosmos were revealed. Also, in Bulgakov's scheme, Boehme is disgusted by the flesh and repelled by marriage. It is as if there is no difference between him and the Hindus, Eckhart, and Plotinus.

Bulgakov has ignored Boehme's great revelations about Sophia and about the androgyne, revelations with which the problem of man was connected for him. Boehme's Sophia is totally unlike Bulgakov's Sophia. Boehme's mysticism is highly complex and enigmatic; it completely lacks the smoothness of monism. His mysticism is not of the purely Hindu type; it contains a Judaic admixture of the Kabbalah, something which is lacking in the bland mysticism of the One. If one is to understand Boehme, one must study this profound mystic with great intensity and attention.[19] He does not belong to any traditional and easily discernible type; he is highly complex and extraordinarily rich. Only one side of him had any influence on such German thinkers as Hegel and Hartmann. But Boehme had other sides too. Many thinkers are nourished by him. Our own Vladimir Solovyov and all of Christian theosophy were half-consciously nourished by him. In the present time we often get our divine wisdom second hand, not realizing that Boehme's wisdom is its source. Outside of him, there is no path for Christian theosophy.

> The time has come: the face of the Mysteries
> Will be revealed. Into the temple of miracles
> By this Book the doors are opened
> And the day is visible through the fabric of the curtains...
>
> The ages have arrived at the
> Millennial Testament.
> You will be filled with rivers of light
> And Jacob Boehme will be yours forever.[20]

Boehme cannot and should not become a victim of our resistance to the German spirit.[21] Bulgakov clearly has personal reasons for his polemic against Boehme. This polemic is very characteristic for understanding Bulgakov himself. In essence, Bulgakov should have stated openly that he is an enemy of mysticism, that he considers all mysticism to be heretical. But he does not want to express himself fully. He is attracted and lured by mysticism. He rejects mystical gnosis, which is entirely based on concrete mythologemes, and recognizes religious metaphysics, which is based on abstract philosophemes. This is very typical. The majority of the doctors of the Church had the same atti-

---

19. Boehme is a special interest of mine and I plan to write a book about him. That is why I am devoting particular attention to the relation between him and Bulgakov.
20. From a poem by Novalis in a translation by Vyacheslav Ivanov.
21. Berdyaev was writing this in the period of anti-German feelings during the world war.—Trans.

tude in their philosophizing. They often regarded frightened agnosticism as an overcoming of rationalism. But, in reality, Irenaeus was much more of a rationalist than the profound Gnostic Valentinus. Gnosis is drunken, ecstatic knowledge, and it should not be called rationalism. For Bulgakov, thought and knowledge are obedience, not creativity; and he rejects the ecstasies of knowledge as a temptation. Creatively ecstatic knowledge of Boehme's kind carries us miraculously over the chasm, and only an outside observer could think that the gnostic's thought is continuous. Bulgakov seems to want to equate mystical immanentism with positivistic immanentism. But this is nothing more than a purely external coincidence of terms. The equating of gnosticism with rationalism is just as external. We are not convinced by the method of negative qualifications, whereby terms with different meanings coincide. With his qualifications Bulgakov characterizes himself, not Boehme, who slips away from all definitions and is antinomic for all categories. In the final analysis, even pure theism is a rationalism and just as smooth as pantheism. Boehme's theosophy is neither a theism nor a pantheism; it is more mysterious, antinomic, and mystical than these smoothed paths to God-knowledge. Bulgakov's theism, too, is overly rational and smoothed, just like the theism of the Church Fathers. Bulgakov sees monism in the style of Drews[22] everywhere, and he wants to find it in Boehme too. But Boehme's depths are much deeper than that. Our Russian religious consciousness would gain much if it were injected with Boehme's mysticism.

IX

Bulgakov's religious philosophy has certain fatal and unavoidable practical consequences. The impossibility of the immanent or inner sanctification of life and of creativity in the world leads to passive acceptance of the world, to submission to the existing world-order, to sanctification of authoritarian rule. Such a relation to life cuts off our wings and deprives us of creative energy. We encounter an interesting paradox of religious thought. The transcendental rupture between God and the world and the denial of the divinity of the world lead, in

---

22. See note 4 on p. 146 in present edition.—Trans.

practice, to a submissive acceptance of the world as it is, which even includes submission to evil. In contrast, the immanent perception that the world is an inner moment of divine life leads us, in practice, to reject the world as it is and to direct our creative energy at the transfiguration of the world. Bulgakov weakens himself religiously and cannot direct his energy at the revolutionary reform and transfiguration of the world. The path of creative approach to the world is closed to him. The world is extra-divine for him, but he is compelled to accept it as a burden and a torment sent down to us for our sins and to submit to the world-order in the name of the religious virtue of obedience. This leads to an acceptance of the world in its traditional and quotidian aspect. This world-view begins with an extreme rejection of the divinity of the world and ends with an affirmation of the divinity of the quotidian aspect of life, the divinity of the life of family and clan, the divinity of economy in the world, the divinity of the matter of life. Bulgakov is a consistent enemy of the heroic, Promethean principle, which he always regards as illegitimate human divinization and Satanism. To heroism he opposes humility and asceticism.[23] The heroic conception of life recognizes Christ to be not an external, transcendent Redeemer, but an inner, immanent path of the spirit, passing through the crucifixion and the voluntary Golgotha. The conception of life that rejects all heroism and views all the mysteries of religious life in a transcendent opposition, this conception objectifies and materializes the Christian mystery, imposing a cross on Christ and humility on people.

Bulgakov is afraid (and according to his religious premises he must necessarily be afraid) to assert the will to new life. Everywhere he sees illegitimate human divinization, the hidden Antichrist principle. He senses the presence of evil in every human movement of liberation. His conception of evil is wholly transcendental, not immanent. He is afraid of every free disclosure of man's nature, viewing it as the continuing fall of Adam. He views humanism in modern history as a second fall of Adam. He does not understand the inevitability of the experiment of

---

23. Of interest in this connection is his essay in the *Landmarks* collection. [This famous collection, published in 1909, comprises a critique of the positivistic and revolutionary attitudes of the Russian intelligentsia by seven thinkers including Bulgakov, who contributed the essay "Heroism and Asceticism."—Trans.]

humanism and does not want to regard it as a stage in the revelation of man's nature. Bulgakov has never shown any understanding of the immanent pathways of the human spirit, of its trials, of the inevitability of schism and dualism. For Bulgakov, religious truth is static, not dynamic; it is given as a transcendental norm, not as living and moving experience. This is also reflected in his attitude toward social and political life, which he experiences statically, not dynamically.

Bulgakov's path has been very significant and interesting. He began by linking Christianity with progressive political activity, with Christian politics and Christian socialism. But, in essence, his progressive politics and socialism did not flow organically from his immature (at that time) Christianity; they were inherited from his former Marxism and the secular world-view of his youth. As his Christianity became deeper and when he truly converted to Orthodoxy, he fled from his secular past, from what was human, all too human. His entire path is a flight from man to God, and this flight is internally motivated by fear of the human, by failure to believe that the human is divine. Out of this ground a religiously significant drama grew. One must say straight out that as Bulgakov became more "reactionary," he became religiously more significant and authentic. A secular political activist dwells in him, not a religiously justified, immanently sanctified political activist. And that is his tragedy. Secular political activity remains a temptation for him. In the sphere of thought he attempts to derive a "Realpolitik" from his religious philosophy, and sometimes this is very forced. It is very obvious that his dualism is not only a conscious religious principle but also reflects the duality of his nature, his dualistic existence. For that reason the solutions he offers to the fundamental problems of social life are uninspired. As an economist and the author of a philosophy of economy, he regards the whole sphere of social life as a heavy duty and a burden, not as a sphere of inspiration and creativity. He is immersed in economics, but he lacks a true pathos of economy. In a dualistic compromise, he conjoins asceticism and the cult of holy foolishness with the will to economy and enrichment. It is highly characteristic and significant that Bulgakov, who is primarily a social philosopher, has done nothing to formulate and solve the social problem from the religious point of view. He solves many fundamental social problems in the same manner as the most ordinary "bourgeois" ideologues. In his *Philosophy*

The Rebirth of Orthodoxy: On Father Sergius Bulgakov

of Economy he does not utter a single word about the fate of the laboring people, the worker question, or social injustice. He tends, in essence, to justify the "bourgeois" order, giving it a religious foundation in clear contradiction with his asceticism and populism. He tries to derive the capitalistic accumulation of wealth from the religious cast of individuality.[24] He seems not to see the profound opposition between Christianity and all cares related to labor and accumulation, all worries about tomorrow. Bulgakov strives to accept everything that is traditional, everything that is hallowed by the ages, everything that possesses historical continuity.

Because of his religious pathos of humility and obedience he is a conservative, but he is an inconsistent conservative who has assimilated much that is progressive, liberal, and democratic and is incapable of freeing himself from it. From the clerical class he has inherited a mixture of conservatism and democratism. As we have seen, his initial religious point of view was not autonomous, and it led him to a transcendentally sanctified authoritarian politics, not to an immanently sanctified politics. His political stance remains dualistic. He is a liberal reactionary, a democratically oriented bourgeois, and a romantic realpolitician. He cannot free himself from the romanticism of sanctified politics, of the holy state. For him it remains a transcendent dream which he is powerless to actualize. He cannot be ignorant of the monstrous falsehood that is contained in the old, holy, theocratic state. But nor can he openly and decisively justify the path of free and secular politics and the free and secular state. He does not see that the secularization of politics and culture, the liberation of them from all transcendental religious sanctions has a profound religious meaning as a path to the immanent religious sanctification of politics and culture. In order to see this, it is necessary to take as one's starting point the autonomous religious consciousness. We will become religiously free only when we stop looking for holiness in the external world, in the natural and historical order, and when we acquire it in our own depths and begin to create it from out of our depths.

---

24. See Bulgakov's highly characteristic and interesting essay "The Economy of the People and Religious Individuality" in vol. I of his collection *Two Cities*.

X

Bulgakov's religious naturalism and materialism, his faith in primordial organic wholeness and the primordial natural synthesis, is connected with his religious populism (an element which is so characteristic of Russian religious thought). He believes in natural and historical holy matter, in the natural economy of the spirit, established forever by the Creator for His creation. The whole process of the development of culture beginning with the Renaissance is evil for Bulgakov, just as the process of the development of capitalism in Russia is evil for the Russian populists. The secularization of culture and of life is regarded by him as man's falling away from God, as the destruction of the divine cosmic order. He regards all differentiation and splintering as an evil that leads to the corruption of holy matter, and he has a conservative desire to stop the disintegration of the old organic wholeness, to remain in the compulsory wholeness. This faith in the divinely established bond of spirit with organic matter, with the natural life of the species, this absolutization of the relative material order is what can be characterized as religious populism. Religious populism is the enslavement of the spirit by the matter of the species. It abolishes freedom and instills the never-ending fear that the organic wholeness, the old bond of spirit with matter will disintegrate, will be splintered into pieces. But this fear and the striving toward conservation are connected with a particular kind of utilitarianism. Bulgakov's religious populism is inconsistent; it stops half way. He has unconsciously assimilated a great deal from the process of secularization and cultural disintegration. Being a modern man, he vacillates between the divinization of the old organicity and the needs of a new culture. He does not have a strong faith in the possibility of conserving this old organicity, and his attitude is therefore pessimistic. The process of the world's life is going in the opposite direction. This splintering apart of spirit and matter, this disintegration of the organic synthesis of life, this secularization of what seemed forever holy is viewed apocalyptically, as the beginning of the end. But, in reality, it would be more correct to view it as a crisis of the world, as the beginning of a new era of the world. But Bulgakov is frightened by the sacrifice of the old haven and security of organic life, of holy flesh: it as if he does not want to go through death to resurrection, does not want the old Russia to die in order to be resurrected into new life. Like many other Christian thinkers, Bulgakov does not clarify the notion of "flesh"; it remains ambiguous and can mean many things. Spiritual flesh, subtle and transfigured, is confused with material, natural-historical flesh, the flesh of everyday life. This too is characteristic for religious populism. But religious materialism can only be a naive state, a state of religious half-wakefulness; the philosophical and conscious assertion of materialism in religion is impossible. It will always be only an archaic stylization, a form of primitivism, not an authentic life of the spirit. In the present time, religious populism, too, can only be a stylization, not authentic life. We can no longer have living faith in holy organic matter, in the old holy politics. Bulgakov does not have this living faith either; he has only excruciating dualism.

XI

Like many other Russian religious thinkers in the Orthodox camp, Bulgakov has not solved, or even posed, the religious problem of man. The weakness of his religious anthropological consciousness is the source of all his weaknesses. For the reborn Orthodoxy, as well as for the old Orthodoxy, man's nature must be reduced to a state of obedience and humility; it must cede its place to the divine nature. Humility is understood not methodologically, as a path of the purification and strengthening of man, as his liberation from the lower elements, but ontologically, as the ultimate truth about man. The Christian life-path is impossible without the stage of humility. That is the method of liberation. But love, not humility, is ontological in Christianity. The ontology of humility is the ontology of the slaves of God, not of the sons of God. Bulgakov wants to be faithful to the patristic consciousness. He learned the ontology of humility from the holy fathers. But a positive anthropology was not revealed to the patristic consciousness. The anthropology of the doctors of the Church consists only in fragments of pagan anthropology. The entire spiritual energy of the fathers and doctors of the Church was directed at overcoming man's pagan nature, the old Adam. The new Adam was revealed to them at the moment of the redemption of man's sinful nature, in the mystery of humility, unknown to the pagans. But patristic Christianity is not the complete and definitive Christianity; it is only a stage of the Christian path of humanity, revealing only one aspect of Christ's truth. At the higher levels of Christian consciousness it must be revealed to man through his inner creative activity that God Himself awaits the positive revelation of man's nature, that He awaits the birth in His divine nature of man as His enrichment.

The problem of Man is the divine problem par excellence, the problem of God Himself, while the problem of God is the human problem par excellence. The mystery of Christ is the union of two mysteries: the mystery of the birth of God in man and the mystery of the birth of man in God. This is the Divine-human mystery.[25] This was felt by great Christian mystics like Jacob Boehme and Angelus Silesius. But Bulgakov does not even have a presentiment that the hour of the religious revelation about man is at hand—the hour of the disclosure of the human nature awaited by God Himself. Bulgakov's Christian path consists in the desire to liberate himself from the human; it consists in fear of humanism, of human capriciousness and audacity. He is wearied and frightened by his own positivistic humanism and he lacks the strength to lift up the burden of the revelation of the Divine nature of man, this second hypostasis of the Divine nature. The ontology of humility is easier than the ontology of creativity, which presupposes an exclusive spiritual courage, activity, and bold self-sacrifice. Bulgakov and his fellow theologians have replaced the human principle with the angelic principle.

Bulgakov would like to entrust the fate of the world to the angelic principle, not the human principle. This is the usual path of passive feminine religiosity, of the soul that longs to submit and dissolve. The angelic principle is not creative; it only glorifies God and forms around God a transmissive mediumistic environment. In the Church the angelic principle is represented by the priesthood, in which there is nothing human. In the domain of government, the angelic principle can be seen in authority that is totally independent of man's nature, in the royal priesthood. *Papocaesarism* and Caesaropapism, the theocracy of

---

25. See my recent book *The Meaning of the Creative Act: An Essay in the Justification of Man.*

the Pope and the theocracy of the Tsar, are cases of the substitution of the human by the angelic. In practice, this is always a denial of the Divine-human path. It is the coercive domination of the human by the angelic. And this angelic principle often appears in the guise of a beast. Only by entrusting the fate of history and of the world to man and mankind is it possible to defeat the beastly element, over which the angelic principle has no power. In contrast to the angelic principle, the human principle is a masculine principle, active and creative, not femininely receptive and transmissive. The angelic principle cannot wield power in the world; power belongs to man. The work of God's creation, the transfiguration of the world, continues through man, not through angels. Not the human principle, but the priesthood, in the capacity of the angelic principle, must be contained and limited. That is why the theocratic polity is a falsehood and temptation. All polities must be human; they can be divine only through man, through his divinity, by virtue of his immanent depths. The transcendental religious consciousness always has the tendency to subordinate the human to the angelic, the royal and prophetic ministries to the priestly ministry. This closes off the path to anthropological revelation and even to the formulation of the religious problem of man. The rebirth of Orthodoxy, as it is expressed in Bulgakov, does not lead to religious creativity and rebirth. The new apocalyptic notes that can be heard in his writings and distinguish him from the old Slavophiles do not change anything with respect to man and human revelation. Bulgakov's apocalypticism is passive and receptive; it is a permeatedness with mystical currents, not an actively creative disclosure of a new aspect of Christ, of the Coming Christ, a disclosure presupposing an extraordinary inner, immanent exertion of man's nature and the appearance of a new man. Bulgakov does not like man, and nothing is revealed to him in man.

XII

Bulgakov is a Jew, not a Greek. As in the case of the ancient Jews, the vision of God strikes him like lightning and burns him with fire. God is distant and terrifying; anyone who sees Him is in danger of dying. God does not give man wings, does not raise him upward, does not augment his creative energy. Instead, He fills him with the sense of creaturely lowliness, weakness, and sinfulness; He crushes and shatters him with His distant magnificence. The wounds caused by God can be healed only by Sophia. Only divine femininity, Sophia, can be intimately close, gently caressing us and giving us joy. She is the reverse side of Bulgakov's religious nature; she moderates his ancient Judaic religious fear. It is as if Sophia is a defense against God's terrible lightning and fire. Bulgakov remains once-born. His religion has not passed through a second spiritual birth. I am speaking of Bulgakov's religion as it is externally manifested. His inner religious experience is, of course, much more complex and cannot be fully known. But in his religion to the extent we know it there are no signs of a new, twice-born, internally free spirit which apprehends external things as a symbolization of what is internal and achieves independence from the material life of the race. But it is this internally free spirit that must give rise to a religious rebirth, to a new religious life. The religion of the spirit is not a negation of the symbols of the flesh. But a religion of the natural and historical holy flesh is impossible. In outward objectification, in nature and history, one finds only what is relative, not what is absolute; only what is symbolic, not what is real. Bulgakov's type of religiosity produces religious nationalism, the absolutization of national and historical flesh. Extreme religious nationalism is always Judaism on Christian ground and it degenerates easily into Old Testament fanaticism. Bulgakov's temperament is soft, not furious; his religious nationalism tends to be lyrical in nature, not warlike. His dualism prevents him from being a warrior. He is dominated by a desire to dissolve in mother-earth. His religious national messianism is characterized more by a fidelity to the maternal womb than by a creative, masculine call to the future, to the active fulfillment of the national mission in the world. Bulgakov's attitude toward Russia does not know the necessity of the disclosure and development of the human principle in Russia; it does not know the religious revelation of personhood. He would have the Russian people remain in their natural collectivism, which he equates with religious sobornost, though this collectivism is only a precursor to the religious consciousness of personhood.

I am very critical of Bulgakov's type of religious thought and am in religious opposition to it. But Bulgakov's path and quest have great

The Rebirth of Orthodoxy: On Father Sergius Bulgakov

significance and must be valued highly. He is serious and sincere. He is very Russian, and the religious crisis he experienced has significance for the fate of the Russian consciousness. In Bulgakov the Russian intelligentsia breaks with its atheistic and materialistic past and moves toward religious consciousness and Christianity. This process signifies a great deepening. In Bulgakov's religion there is nothing new and creative; but he himself, as a phenomenon of life, is new and agitated in a new way. We put a high value on the agitation of his thought, on its nimbleness, on its ability to ceaselessly enrich itself and expand. All the same, the impression remains that this agitation, this nimbleness and richness of thought, and these questionings do not mean a new birth of the soul. His religiosity is an ancient one, a religiosity of age-old horror. He has returned to the traditional blood-religiosity of his fathers and forefathers.

When we think of Bulgakov, we think of the impossibility of reviving what is ancient in Orthodoxy in such a way that it would have meaning for the fate of Russia and of the world, and not just for the fate of the individual soul. The primary goal of both Bulgakov and of Father Pavel Florensky is to find personal salvation, and all their thought and knowledge is marked by this desire for self-salvation. They seek the truth under the pressure of the panic horror of perdition, and this cannot fail to affect the character of the truth they find: it bears the stamp of slaves of the divine fatum. Neither Bulgakov nor Father Florensky are free. But V.F. Ern, another representative of Orthodox religious thought, *is* free. He affirms his exclusive Orthodoxy out of himself, out of his own freedom, paying attention to nothing and no one else on earth. Behind Ern's religious-philosophical thought one senses not so much an original and independent mind as an original and independent character. There is something non-Russian about him, something clear and serene, something doctrinaire, something that resembles Protestant pietism. Ern is less interesting and significant for Russian religious thought than are Bulgakov and Father Florensky, though, doctrinally, he is one of the most extreme of the Slavophiles. Prince E.N. Trubetskoy, too, is free compared with Bulgakov and Father Florensky. But his path is too clear and lacks complexity; one does not sense in him the agitated trepidation of religious questionings and doubts. Prince Trubetskoy's Christianity is too smooth, too rational, too lacking in antinomies, perhaps too liberal.²⁶ As for Vyacheslav Ivanov, his convergence to some degree with the Moscow Orthodox thinkers, their religious influence on him and his esthetic influence on them, is not reason enough to consider his type of thought a form of Orthodox religious thought. He remains, first and foremost, a significant poet with religious, mystical, and philosophical interests—not a teacher of life, but a teacher of art who does not fully accept any religious faith or any philosophical doctrine. In him we find elements of free mysticism and undisciplined occultism that are incompletely illuminated, though at certain moments he can appear in an Orthodox guise. The most organic thing in Ivanov is his Dionysianism and his pagan-Dionysian interpretation of Christianity. His "Russianism" bears the stamp of a refined Western-type culturedness and of an artistic stylization alien to the Russian soul. Meanwhile, Bulgakov remains the central figure.

XIII

On its mystical peaks, the Orthodox rebirth encounters "imiaslavie,"²⁷ which has produced so much agitation in our ecclesial life. Through imiaslavie, which is being revived and confessed in monasteries and deserts, our contemporary Orthodox thinkers are attempting to reunite themselves with the ancient Orthodox mysticism that goes back to Gregory Palamas and Symeon the New Theologian. A few years ago the leading lights of Russian Orthodoxy placed great hopes in the imiaslavie movement and even entered into conflict with the Synod.²⁸ But their hopes went unjustified: no real religious movement arose and the wave began

---

26. Prince Trubetskoy is more consistent than Bulgakov in asserting the completely extra-divine character of the world, the extreme dualism of God and the world. Even the idea of sophianicity frightens him as a form of pantheism.

27. Also referred to as onomatodoxy, "imiaslavie" (literally: "glorification of the name") is a controversial dogmatic movement within the Russian Orthodox Church which asserts that the Name of God is God Himself. The specific question addressed was whether the name Jesus Christ pronounced in the Prayer of Jesus is God Himself. The movement was particularly strong in Russia around the time Berdyaev wrote this essay. Bulgakov and Florensky were staunch supporters of imiaslavie.—Trans.

28. The governing body of the Russian Orthodox Church in Tsarist Russia.—Trans.

The Rebirth of Orthodoxy: On Father Sergius Bulgakov

to ebb. Imiaslavie did not produce a mystical rebirth of Orthodoxy. The question of the real presence of Divinity Itself in the name Jesus Christ pronounced in the Prayer of Jesus is a highly subtle and deeply inner question of religious-mystical experience. It does not really lend itself to exoteric discussion. No externally expressed, historical movement in the Church can arise on the basis of it. We encounter here a primary mystical experience, a mystical meditation that has a broader significance than an Orthodox Christian interpretation of this experience. But in any case we can say that imiaslavie does not give us anything new and that we should not expect any new religious revelations from it. Imiaslavie has very little connection with problems of religious anthropology. It is just a deeper layer of traditional Orthodoxy. All the expectations of our new Orthodox theologians that there will soon occur a new revelation within the depths of the Church arising from the elders produce an impression of hopeless religious impotence and timidity. These theologians passively await the breath of the Spirit, of the new Spirit, from the depths of the Church and they expect that it will be something transcendental in relation to them, something enacted over them; they themselves take no initiative and discover nothing in their own depths. But all religious movement begins with immanent experience, with immanent creative initiative. The Spirit "bloweth where it listeth," and the breath of the Spirit is something I must first sense within myself, in my own depths, not outside, from some external center. Such transcendentalization of religious experience is a sign of religious decline; it is a diminution and extinction of the Spirit. All religious movement and religious rebirth begin with me myself, and I cannot shift onto the shoulders of others the burden and labor of initiative. My depths are the same thing as the depths of the Church. Religious reform will become possible in Russia only after this deeply inner change, after this new birth in the Spirit. Those who like schematic oppositions might say that this path is a form of Protestantism and is therefore already old. But Protestantism has never posed the religious problem of man, the problem of human revelation. Protestantism is even less anthropological than Catholicism. We shall see what the experience of the new religious consciousness, of the new Christianity, will bring us: a new birth, a shift of the center of gravity into the depths of man; or a continuing dependence of man on what is external to him and enacted over him.

www.ingramcontent.com/pod-product-compliance
Lightning Source LLC
Chambersburg PA
CBHW030106170426
43198CB00009B/510